AQA Advanced

DRAMA & THEATRE STUDIES

Philip Allan Updates, an imprint of Hodder Education, part of Hachette Livre UK, Market Place, Deddington, Oxfordshire OX15 0SE

Orders

Bookpoint Ltd, 130 Milton Park, Abingdon, Oxfordshire OX14 4SB
tel: 01235 827720
fax: 01235 400454
e-mail: uk.orders@bookpoint.co.uk

Lines are open 9.00 a.m.–5.00 p.m., Monday to Saturday, with a 24-hour message answering service. You can also order through the Philip Allan Updates website: www.philipallan.co.uk

© Philip Allan Updates 2008
ISBN 978-1-84489-447-5
0214170 1

Impression number   5   4   3   2   1
Year   2012   2011   2010   2009   2008

The front cover photograph shows a student production of *The Revenger's Tragedy* at Aberystwyth University and is reproduced by permission of Keith Morris/Alamy Images.

Printed in Italy

Hachette Livre UK's policy is to use papers that are natural, renewable and recyclable products and made from wood grown in sustainable forests. The logging and manufacturing processes are expected to conform to the environmental regulations of the country of origin.

P01291

Contents

Unit 3 A2: Written responses to drama

Section A: Pre-twentieth century play

Section B: Twentieth century or contemporary drama

Unit 4 A2: Practical presentation of devised drama

Preface

This building is an example of abandoned magnificence. At one time, not so long ago, it was part of the city's pride, its towering pillars boasting its pre-eminence in both architectural achievement and in the artistic wonders it once housed. Now it stands like an obstinate and embarrassed ghost of another era, a monument to a gaudy and indulgent past. On the wall, a poster peeling and faded that no one thought to remove still hangs limply, advertising a display of ballroom gyrations from more than a year ago. If you manage to break in through the heavy wooden doors you will find a world of decaying splendour, where the dust hangs heavier than the memories of bygone triumphs and the smell of neglect is palpable. This is a building that has outlasted its usefulness — forgotten but not gone. It is an uneconomic anachronism in a world of streamlined efficiency — too large and too expensive to maintain, and far too impractical.

Through the thick walls and shuttered windows, you can still hear the sound of the capital city's gridlocked traffic imposing the noise of the present on the remainders of the past. Can it be that less than a century ago the greatest actor in the world, the first actor to receive the honour of a knighthood, displayed his virtuoso skills to the enthralled multitudes in this same building? A man who in 1870 — the same year he joined the management of the theatre in which you are standing — created such a sensation with his performance of Mathias in Leopold Lewis's *The Bells* that he was declared London's most celebrated actor overnight? Can it be that for all the triumph of past times, this once famous shrine to dramatic art became a Mecca Ballroom in 1950 and is now an abandoned shell?

You are standing in the foyer of the Lyceum Theatre in The Strand in 1986. During the late nineteenth century, this theatre was managed by the legendary Sir Henry Irving, the first world-famous actor and the man credited with revitalising a cynical public's interest in the works of William Shakespeare. And yet a mere 80 years after his death, his spiritual home does not even provide a reminder of those glory days. Less than 50 years after his death, as film and television proceeded with their inexorable rise, it became a ballroom. Only the pub of the same name, next door, carries a plaque dedicated to the great man's life and achievements. Even in the heart of London's West End, it seems there can be no purpose for a place like this. The Lyceum Theatre in 1986 is dead, and its continued existence is an uncomfortable reminder of a prevailing feature in our society: theatre is a spent force.

By 1982, 85% of theatres that were in service in 1914 had been demolished. Of the ones that remained, many were 'dark' (unused). While some were replaced with more modern theatres, many more were not. Going to the theatre as a cultural pastime declined throughout the twentieth century as television audiences increased. Even cinema audiences, which had declined during the 1970s, started to enjoy a renaissance during the 1980s as multi-screens replaced the old Art Deco picture houses of the 1930s. The president of the Frank Matcham Society — a society founded to celebrate one of the most prolific theatre architects of all time — bemoaned the statistic that of the estimated 150 theatres built by his hero between 1880 and 1915, only 28 remained, and only 25 of them as working theatres.

Surely these statistics indicate that theatre has had its day — that whatever it may have been in our society, as a social or cultural force it is now dead? Even the crudest and most basic of surveys reveal that most people do not go to the theatre — at least, not on a regular basis. And even where it thrives — in parts of London's West End, for example — it does so on adaptations from movies and on revivals of old plays. We have to face an unpalatable but unrelenting fact: theatre has had its heyday and we citizens of the twenty-first century are witnessing its inevitable wind down to extinction. In a few years it will be no more.

The A-level course on which you are embarking will be synonymous with the study of antiques: looking at where we have come from in mild curiosity, and perhaps with some bewilderment, that we, as a species, were ever tempted to leave the warmth of our homes and sit in draughty temples like the Lyceum, gazing at other living people on a stage like a set of collective Peeping Toms. There will be no live drama because there will be no need for it. Our dramatic entertainment will be piped to our small and large screens via computer-generated sets and performed by beautiful actors (some of whom, presumably, will also be computer generated). This is the inevitable future of theatre. Isn't it?

*

The mood of the crowd is angry — teetering on the brink of violence. These people have been protesting outside the theatre for several days, and with each passing day the crowd's impatience grows along with its numbers. At the start of the week, it made the local news, but now the event is much more high profile and well-known reporters are on hand to carry the story. Community leaders have held talks with theatre directors but have not secured the changes to the play they sought. The directors claim that talks with the Sikh community were held out of courtesy and that changing the work of a playwright was never on the agenda. As the mood of the crowd turns uglier, missiles are thrown and the theatre's plate-glass windows are shattered. Four hundred protestors attempt to storm the building as 85 police officers — 30 of them in riot gear — struggle to contain them. Leaders of the community are quick to disassociate themselves from any violent action, attributing it to the hot-headed behaviour of some of their more militant supporters. The police, attempting to avoid any further outbreaks of violence, persuade Birmingham Repertory Theatre to close the production of *Behzti*. The playwright Gurpreet Kaur Bhatti goes into hiding as she becomes the subject of threats of violence. Her play, which depicts rape and murder in a Sikh temple, has enraged the local Sikh community. In her programme note, she praises Sikhism but then adds the following statement:

> Clearly the fallibility of human nature means that the simple Sikh principles of equality, compassion and modesty are sometimes discarded in favour of outward appearance, wealth and the quest for power. I believe that drama should be provocative and relevant. I wrote *Behzti* because I passionately oppose injustice and hypocrisy.

The play's performance on 18 December is called off and further performances are suspended. Since then, the play has never been revived and Bhatti has so far not permitted any other theatre to stage it.

If theatre is dead, if it is truly a thing of the past — an extinct art form that has made way for the more advanced technology and mass appeal of film and television — how could a play arouse such passionate feelings in Birmingham as recently as December 2004? Why would members of a community mobilise, besiege a theatre and force a play to close if theatre is without potency or influence? Dominic Dromgoole, Artistic Director of the Oxford Stage Company, writing in the *Guardian* 2 days after the closure of *Behzti*, observed of the incident that it was something:

> ...to shut the pundits up. Every tired old ageing punk who drones on at self-defeating length about the death of theatre — its marginalisation and irrelevance to the modern world — can put this in their pipe and smoke it.

Rather provocatively, he adds later in the article that: 'Theatre asks for this trouble. It has to. Nonconformity is as natural to theatre as conformity is to religion.' He passionately expresses the view that theatre must rigorously challenge the 'various blind yeses' that are part of religious fundamentalism. He sees in theatre the most potent of all media in dealing with and challenging the issues of our time. If Dromgoole is right, not only is theatre not dead, it is more alive than ever before, and possibly more alive than its rivals of television and cinema. What took place outside the Birmingham Repertory Theatre towards the end of 2004 was a remarkable event in the modern era of theatre but by no means unique.

In 1996, a performance of Mark Ravenhill's play *Shopping and Fucking* was interrupted by a group of Christians who, 10 minutes into the first act, stood up in the stalls and started singing hymns as a protest at the play's graphic and, as they perceived it, blasphemous content. Urged on perhaps by the success of members of the Sikh community in cancelling *Behzti*, the BBC was beset by thousands of protestors objecting to the screening of the National Theatre's triumphant production of *Jerry Springer: The Opera*. The protestors gathered outside Broadcasting House, burning their television licences in anger. Although they were objecting to a proposed television event, it was a televising of a theatrical production that was at the root of their complaint.

Although the violent events in Birmingham are hardly cause for celebration, they prove that theatre — as Dromgoole says — is not an 'irrelevance to the modern world'. Birmingham Repertory Theatre has continued to promote plays that raise the profile of black and Asian issues. Ayab Khan-Din's *East is East* is perhaps the most famous example, given its premiere in 1996 and later made into a highly successful film. During 2005, it staged Jess Walter's *Low Dat* about sexual relationships among young black teenagers. The play was toured in schools before enjoying a successful run in the Birmingham Repertory Theatre's studio, 'The Door'. If the experience of *Behzti* has made the theatre directors wary of controversial material, they are doing little to show it.

However, it would be wrong to assume that there is a universally shared set of aims in theatre. The aims of Birmingham Repertory Theatre — reflected by Dromgoole's statement quoted earlier — need not necessarily be those of other practitioners. Just because theatre *can* cause controversy, does not mean that it always does or always should. Gurpreet Kaur Bhatti's aims in writing *Behzti* are different, say, from Ben Elton's aims in creating the 'Queen' tribute show, *We Will Rock You*. It is inevitable that theatre containing technical wizardry, seductive songs and breathtaking scenery, and which unashamedly promotes the 'feel-good factor', is going to be more commercially successful than theatre that aims to challenge and even disturb its audience. Many people view theatre as the means by which they can escape issues of controversy and, as they might see it, heartrending misery — and it is not the purpose of this book to say that they should not.

However, a serious study of the theatre must involve students examining work which has in some way changed the world, or at least made a serious analysis of it, rather than merely celebrated it. Nonetheless, even if some elements of theatre are groundbreaking, controversial and hard hitting, if they are only experienced by a tiny minority can theatre truly be said to be relevant? After all, whatever storms of protest and counter-protest may have occurred outside a theatre in Birmingham just before Christmas 2004, the truth, surely, is that most of the population of this country will remain unaffected by them. In fact, those events will have repercussions for all who make or watch entertainment. Producers of theatre and television will always consider the likely response to pieces of work by an audience before commissioning it, basing the prediction of that response on previous experiences. Will the BBC shy away from aggravating the anger of religious groups in the future by choosing less controversial work to screen than *Jerry Springer: The Opera*? Only time will tell.

*

Although it is true that there are far fewer theatres than there once were, that is an inevitable consequence of the expansion of entertainment media. The power of theatre is not determined by the number of theatres to be found but by the significance of the events that take place in them and our ability to be stirred by such events. Theatres thrived to the extent they did during the early part of the twentieth century because there was no equivalent entertainment medium to compete with them. It would not be unusual, therefore, for a small town to have four or five theatres in the early part of the last century. Although that is no longer the case, it does not mean that theatre has ceased to be important. A happy epilogue to the gloomy description of the disused Lyceum Theatre of 1986 is that it is now thriving once again, has been completely refitted and for the last few years has been home to one of the biggest hits of the West End, *The Lion King*. In January 2005, a joint submission by the Society of London Theatre and the Theatrical Management Association reported an attendance in London theatres of around 12 million in 2004 — 'one of the best years on record'. And as for Frank Matcham's legacy, his supporters may glory in the knowledge that all save one of his surviving theatres are listed buildings, the vast majority of them full-time working theatres. Theatre in the first decade of the twenty-first century, whether controversial or not, seems to be enjoying greater popularity than for some time.

Richard Vergette

Introduction

Notes for the teacher

As we move towards the second decade of the twenty-first century, the curriculum is, yet again, subject to substantial revision. Increasingly, the knowledge-dominated National Curriculum introduced 20 years ago is a thing of the past, and a greater emphasis is being placed on skills. This is made evident in the 14–19 initiatives and, in particular, the government's aims for the newly created diplomas. There is an expectation that learning will equip students with the transferable skills needed to adapt to a changing and challenging world, dictated by the vagaries of a global economy. Whatever the vices or virtues of such a society, issues of how our young people learn and how they develop their curiosities about the world have never been more important.

The new specification for AQA Drama and Theatre Studies places a greater responsibility on the student to explore and understand how theatre has developed over time. The wide variety of set texts — in terms of era, style and content — means that drama students must be prepared to undertake research enthusiastically. This applies not only to the set text itself, but also to the historical, social and cultural context from which it originated. Students are expected to be able to work independently to explore the impact that these texts — both modern and ancient — can have when produced for the theatre today. However, there is also an emphasis on the student's ability to work as part of a team — either leading the decision-making process, or supporting or challenging it as the case may be. While Drama and Theatre Studies is not, in itself, an applied or vocational qualification, this course cannot be delivered successfully without the student developing an understanding and appreciation of the working, functioning modern theatre.

The AQA Drama and Theatre Studies specification enables you to choose from a considerable number of texts. Some of those texts are explored in this book as examples. You may prefer to look at other texts, and the texts included here should not be seen as 'better' than others or as part of a correct route of study. The aim of the section on set texts is to unearth the essence of the plays and explore how they might be realised in production — a process that students must be prepared to embark upon.

This book should be seen as a companion piece to the AQA specification, offering insights into the various areas of study without the specificity of a study guide.

Specification coverage

- AS Unit 1 — Written responses to drama. Sections A and B cover responding to live theatre and a number of AS set texts.
- AS Unit 2 — Practical presentation of a play extract. This section is also relevant to Unit 4 of the specification.
- A2 Unit 3 — Written responses to drama. This contains examples of responses to set texts from both twentieth-century and pre-twentieth-century drama.
- A2 Unit 4 — Practical presentation of devised drama. This covers all aspects of devising a piece of drama, and preparing supporting notes on the piece.

Notes for the student

As a student of drama and theatre studies, you are part of a growing population. The number of students taking the subject at A-level has been rising steadily over the last 5 years, reflecting a nationally increased interest in the power of live theatre both to challenge and to entertain its audience.

The AQA Drama and Theatre Studies specification gives you the freedom to choose the form and content of your presentation work (for scripted work in Unit 2 and devised work in Unit 4) while also studying set texts for written examinations. All these activities are aimed at cultivating in you a sustained interest in and enjoyment of theatre. It is important, therefore, even at the outset of your A-level course, that you are able to define the purpose of theatre for *you*. In attempting to define that purpose, you might consider the following questions:

- Should theatre change the world or celebrate it?
- Is your interest in theatre as a performer, a member of an audience, a writer or a designer?
- Would you rather charm members of an audience with your performance than shock them, or do you think it is possible to achieve both effects?

As you ask yourself what the purpose of theatre is and what your purpose is in studying it, you should realise that your responses to these questions may well change over the 2 years of the course as your knowledge and experience develop.

You are about to undertake a course of study that will make considerable demands on your ability to research and organise information and to express your opinions clearly and persuasively, both on and off stage.

The structure of this book

Unit 1

Section A covers the points involved in responding to a piece of live theatre. Responding to theatre can often be impulsive and subjective and, therefore, a process needs to be established for you to make sense of your responses. Remember that when you respond to a piece of theatre you are doing so as an informed student who is developing a specialist knowledge of theatre — not just as another member of the audience.

Section B deals with the study of your set texts. It is vital that you envisage how you might interpret aspects of the text from the viewpoints of actors, directors and designers. This section takes a number of those texts and explores production possibilities. Even if you are not using these texts, this section is still useful for identifying the interpretative processes you need to master.

Unit 2

This section focuses on the work of influential practitioners who have helped to shape — and in some cases continue to shape — the work we see on stage today. It considers the work of the directors and designers who take the words of the playwright and interpret them for the stage, thus delivering the play to the audience.

When preparing work for either Units 2 or 4, you need to consider the work of contemporary directors and designers. You should study both the style of productions created by influential practitioners and also the processes they develop in rehearsal. Chapter 11 therefore examines the work of practitioners in terms of both their processes and their products, and should be particularly useful to you in the development of your practical work.

Unit 3

This section explores a number of the set texts that could be studied for A2. You should be aware that the detail expected at A2 is greater than at AS. You could use this section to investigate the processes of realising and interpreting a text, even if the texts you study are different from the ones explored here.

Unit 4

This section deals with devising drama and addresses the processes you could undertake in order to achieve a successful piece of devised drama.

A series of guidelines is also offered, detailing some of the common problems inherent in the devising process as well as solutions to these problems. Part of this section is also given over to a discussion of dramatic styles, which might be useful if your group is looking for a specific theatrical genre in which to work.

Unit 1

AS: Written responses to drama

Introduction to Unit 1

There are two areas of focus in Unit 1:

- Section A: responding to and making informed judgements about a piece of live theatre in writing
- Section B: studying a set text with the purpose of making decisions about it that will enable you to respond in writing from the perspective of an actor, a director or a designer

Section A

You should ensure that you see as much live theatre as possible during your AS course. Take in a wide range of styles of theatre, including both amateur and professional productions of set texts, physical theatre, theatre in education, and pantomime.

It is advisable, where appropriate, to carry out some background research into the plays you see and, where there is a published text, to have read it thoroughly before or after seeing the performance. You are preparing to write about a performance in terms of the effectiveness of its theatrical elements and how they contributed to the success, or lack of success, of the production. You should be able to refer to particular moments in this production and to demonstrate that you have thought about and understand:

- the aims of the production
- the creative contribution of the director, designers, actors and production team
- the audience experience and response

In the examination, you answer one question (from a selection of four) on a live production that you have seen. You are allowed access to annotated texts and to brief personal notes on the productions you have seen. You should there-fore make sure that you keep good notes on all the performances you see, paying particular attention to those in which you are most interested.

Section B

For Section B you are required to choose one play from the six set texts and answer one question from a choice of two on that play.

The six set texts are:

- *Antigone* (c. 440s BC)   Sophocles
- *The Taming of the Shrew* (c. 1594)   Shakespeare
- *A Doll's House* (1879)   Henrik Ibsen
- *The Shadow of a Gunman* (1923)   Sean O'Casey
- *Oh! What a Lovely War* (1963)   Joan Littlewood and Theatre Workshop
- *Playhouse Creatures* (1993)   April de Angelis

You can use any edition of these plays except for *Oh! What a Lovely War* and *Playhouse Creatures*, for which the editions are specified. Your teacher will advise you.

You are expected to study your chosen play in terms of its possible interpretation and how it could be performed effectively. You need to be aware of its original historical, social and cultural context, its period and genre, and its potential effectiveness for an audience.

In the examination, you must discuss your interpretation of the play in terms of the practical realisation of its themes and issues. You need to show your understanding of how style, form, dramatic structure and characterisation can be interpreted and realised in a performance to create a specific impression on the audience. In doing this, you could adopt the viewpoint of actor, director or designer.

Chapters 2–4 of this book give a detailed description of three of the set texts of Unit 1 Section B, together with some hints to aid interpretation and sample questions for you to attempt. This should enable you to form a good idea of the kind of understanding you should aim for when studying your chosen play.

Chapter 1

Section A: Live theatre production

Responding to live theatre

In this chapter we will discuss the crucial questions you need to ask in order to form a coherent and meaningful response to the theatre you watch. The questions are generic and therefore appropriate to any theatrical experience in any theatre.

What are your expectations of the visit?

It is almost inconceivable that you will not have expectations prior to a theatre visit. The state of mind and attitude with which you approach the production you are about to see will affect your response to it. It is therefore important to be honest about your preconceptions. If you are familiar with the play you are about to see, what do you anticipate about the performance? Did you enjoy reading the play in class or was it a disappointment? Perhaps you have seen the play on video or DVD, or a film adaptation. If so, how has this experience informed you? Are you approaching the prospect of seeing the play positively or negatively?

If the piece is by a writer of whom you have heard or whose work you have seen, it is likely you will be influenced by that knowledge. Perhaps it is a new play by a famous theatre company, such as Kneehigh or Shared Experience, and you have seen, or heard about, its previous work. You may have heard about one of the actors in the play.

It is unusual for an audience member to approach a play completely objectively. This is a factor you need to take into consideration when assessing the merits of a production.

What sort of place is the venue?

A theatre building can enhance or diminish the experience of watching a dramatic performance. Some pieces of theatre are created for specific venues. For example, John Godber writes plays exclusively for the Hull Truck Theatre — an intimate, virtually studio-sized space. Alan Ayckbourn, writing for the Stephen Joseph Theatre, knows that a cast has to perform to an audience seated on all four sides of a large auditorium.

Most plays, however, need to be adaptable to a variety of different spaces and audience seating arrangements, especially if they are written for a touring company. An intimate, intense piece of theatre, perhaps featuring a small cast, will inevitably work better in a smaller space. This will enable an audience to see the actors at close quarters, and the actors themselves will not need to project their voices above conversation level to be heard. In contrast, a Shakespearean play may be performed in a much larger venue (the Courtyard Theatre in Stratford-upon-Avon or the National Theatre, for example) in order to accommodate a sizable cast or to stage elaborate scenes. Even in these cases, there are intimate or intense moments to convey (for example, Hamlet's soliloquies or the balcony scene in *Romeo and Juliet, c.* 1595–96).

You must bear in mind that most theatres were built for entirely different genres of work than those shown today. It is important to be aware of the different types of theatre design and their particular merits.

The large proscenium arch theatres that dominate London's West End were, in most cases, built in the era of melodrama and music hall. Such theatres sometimes have an orchestra pit separating the stage area from the auditorium. The seating is usually arranged in stalls and a circle, and sometimes an upper circle or gallery. While many of these theatres have undergone radical improvements in line with

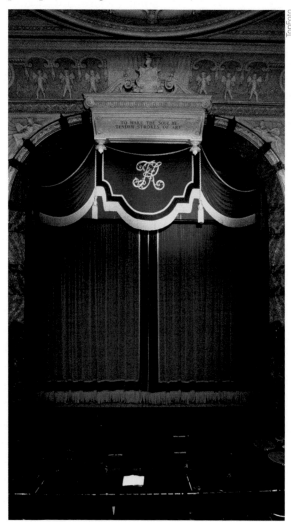

Richmond Theatre has a proscenium arch and orchestra pit

TopFoto

technological developments, it is something of a luxury when a play finds itself staged in an ideal venue.

More modern theatres often make use of a thrust stage, where the stage space extends into the middle of the auditorium. This is reminiscent of the ancient Greek theatre design: an arena stage rather than a raised stage, with seating rising up around it. You can see an example of this design in the Sheffield Crucible; its stage is the floor area with tiered seating around it. The West Yorkshire Playhouse is of a similar design.

Where are you sitting in the theatre?

Some theatres are so large as to afford entirely different perspectives on the action for different members of the audience, depending on the location of their seats. For example, being seated in the upper circle of a theatre places an audience member a long way away from, and a long way above, the action. At such a distance, it may be difficult to absorb the instensity and emotion of a play. This is not the fault of the actors, directors or designers. Consequently, it is critical to objectify the perspective you have on a play, considering carefully the effects of your seating position.

What information do you have about the production?

It is unlikely that you will go to see a play without having some information about it beforehand. Quite apart from the press releases that herald a major production, the theatre itself will usually provide a good deal of information through publicity material and its website. Much depends on the nature of the production — whether a premiere or a revival — but any professional theatre will want to generate as much interest and curiosity as possible about its current and forthcoming productions.

Programmes and education packs

As students often make up a significant proportion of an audience, a production will usually be accompanied by a detailed programme or a well-researched education pack. This may contain interviews with key members of the production team (for example, the director and designer) and commentary from the actors, as well as academic essays on the play and its themes written by a learned associate of the theatre or a specialist in the playwright or dramatic genre being presented.

It is important to use as much of this information as possible. Watching a play with knowledge of the director's concept or the designer's ruling idea enables you to identify the production team's philosophy in action. You can see a director's or designer's ideas unfold before you and make decisions about how successfully they are communicated, how fully they are realised and how they serve the play.

Reviews

Often, reviews of previous productions can alert you to the potential problems or most challenging moments of a play. For example, if you are going to see a production of *Hamlet* (*c.* 1600), most reviewers agree that the title role is one of the most challenging any actor can face. However, it is important not to be too influenced or diverted by a review, no matter how cleverly it is written. It is often the case that a production will receive a variety of reviews. It is best to approach your theatre visit with an open mind.

The theatrical style and genre of production

Although we often discuss theatre in terms of genres and styles, productions frequently do not fall easily into one specific category. There may be elements of a production that could be described, for example, as 'physical theatre', although the production as a whole may not fit that classification.

However, when you are asked to comment on or criticise a production, it is useful to have a good understanding of genres and styles. Sometimes a genre or style may evolve around the work of a particular playwright or theatre company — for example Total Theatre and Stephen Berkoff, or Harold Pinter, whose work inspired the term 'Pinteresque', and the works of other playwrights who emulated Pinter's style. Some theatrical genres are more simply described than others — the best-known genres are tragedy and comedy. Other theatre genres are discussed at length in Unit 2 as part of an assessment of the work of a number of famous practitioners.

Using the terms 'tragedy' and 'comedy'

'Tragedy' does not simply describe a sad occurrence. In theatre, it is used as a technical term to denote certain key features such as the inevitability of fate. The definition of tragedy, and its ancient and modern forms, is discussed in detail in Chapters 2, 12 and 13.

As a student of drama and theatre, you need to consider not just the literary qualifications of a play that define its genre but also its production features. If you are watching a production of Shakespeare's *Macbeth* (*c*. 1606) — universally accepted as a tragedy — you need to consider what qualities the actor playing Macbeth brings to the role that makes the audience appreciate the character's fate as a tragic one. Alternatively, you may find that Macbeth's demise fails to make an impact on an audience. In such cases, think about why this was the case. Was there any inappropriate laughter? Why was this provoked?

The same need to consider genre alongside production features is true for comedy. In Unit 1, you have the option to study Shakespeare's *The Taming of the Shrew*, which is discussed in some detail in Chapter 3. In this play, you need to recognise which features of the text provide the elements of comedy, but also think about how those features are treated in production to make the audience laugh.

The words 'tragedy' or 'comedy', therefore, are useful to categorise a play, but employing such terms on their own rarely amounts to a good description of a particular production. You must develop the habit of rigorously analysing how the people involved in a production make a scene comic or tragic. You need to be able to explain why an unsuccessful production of a comedy was not funny, or why a tragedy left an audience unmoved.

To take a specific example of a tragedy, *Macbeth* was directed and designed by Damian Cruden for York Theatre Royal in 2005. This production used a variety of styles of theatre:

- The production owed much to the devices and techniques of Japanese Kabuki theatre. The play was set in feudal Japan and the actors resembled Samurai warriors. They wore different coloured robes to indicate which family they belonged to.
- The witches were grotesque, nightmarish puppets. One reviewer observed that:

Japanese theatre techniques obviously inspired the use of black-clad puppeteers, who manipulate the three witches (grotesque creatures with the skeletal arms and bloated stomachs of famine victims) and Macbeth's visions.

(J. D. Atkinson, *British Theatre Guide*, March 2005)

- Movement — particularly fight sequences — was carefully choreographed. While *Macbeth* would not traditionally be referred to as a piece of physical theatre, there were striking moments of highly skilled movement that would allow this production to be described as such. The reviewer quoted above commented on Banquo's death scene:

> Banquo's murder, so often staged in the most perfunctory manner, is a wonderfully balletic scene in which the victim's blood is represented by scarlet ribbons unfurled from his costume by 'invisible' attendants.

Simply referring to this production of *Macbeth* as a 'tragedy' would not give a sufficiently accurate analysis of the performance. You would be expected to comment on the distinctive features of the production, particularly where the director makes use of specific styles and genres of theatre. For example, showing the witches as puppets is an unusual production choice — possibly even a controversial one — so it is crucial that, in noting this stylistic feature, you also comment on its effectiveness. Does this choice make the tragedy more or less successful? In terms of the production overall, its reviewers felt that the features used were very effective but overwhelmed the actors' ability to portray their characters. The concluding comment of the reviewer from the *York Evening Press* was:

> However, in turning Japanese, Cruden's *Macbeth* is a series of cinematic set pieces more than a rounded play, submerging [Terence] Maynard's Macbeth in the process.
>
> (*York Evening Press*, 3 March 2005)

J. D. Atkinson also observed:

> As for the performances, the breakneck speed of the production gives the Macbeths (Terence Maynard and Barbara Marten) few opportunities to convey the intense emotional and erotic bonds between them.

The judgement here, then, is that the dynamic and distinctive styles of theatre that Cruden employed in his production, while being visually striking, had a detrimental impact on the actors' ability to convey the tragedy.

Analysing your response

When you are commenting on the style of a production or the genres of theatre employed, follow this process:
- First, identify the genre of the play — e.g. tragedy or comedy.
- Next, try to identify the styles of theatre the director or designer has employed.
- Finally, analyse the impact that the style or genre of production has had on your overall understanding and appreciation of the play.

What kind of acting is called for?

Whatever the genre and subject matter of a play, the acting is likely to be the most dominant aspect of any production. That said, it is important to understand the relationship between acting and directing. An actor's interpretation of a role may combine his or her perceptions with the director's vision for how the role fits within the overall philosophy of the production.

In a traditional theatrical production, the quality of the acting probably affects an audience's enjoyment of a piece more than any other factor, especially where the play is a revival of a classic. Poor acting in a musical or in opera is not as problematic, since the quality of singing and choreography may more than compensate.

Recognising the elements of acting

In order to judge an actor's performance effectively, you need to identify the elements of acting being presented. Depending on the genre or history of a play, specific demands are made on actors in terms of physical representation and vocal dexterity. For example, the complexity of language in a Restoration comedy requires adept verbal skills to reflect the intricate semantics and elaborate structures. Such a piece may also require comic timing and physical agility. These would not be so important for a production of Shakespeare's *Othello* (1604), where it is crucial that the actors convey the sense of tragedy in the verse and impress on the audience the eponymous character's inevitable journey into jealousy, rage and madness.

Appraising the effectiveness of acting

In a long and complex play, an actor's performance may have particular high points. If you are watching a production of *Strife* (1909) by John Galsworthy, the actor playing the part of Roberts — the leader of the strike — faces many challenges. In playing a charismatic political leader, he must show Roberts's great powers of oratory when he persuades the workers to stay out on strike, and yet in the same scene he must show an emotional vulnerability when the news is brought to him that his wife has died of starvation and cold as a result of the poverty forced on her by the strike. In such a production, an actor is required to explore an intense emotional depth to the character while simultaneously showing the technical skills of oratory and projection. As the role of

Roberts is central, if the performance falls short of what is required, the entire production will falter.

Writing about an actor's performance

Distinguishing between character and actor choices

When making judgements about an actor's performance, you must distinguish between the choices made by the actor in his or her interpretation and the choices made by the character. Thus, the actor playing Romeo does not choose to kiss Juliet, the character of Romeo does, as governed by the script. How that kiss is approached, however, is decided by the actor. If you were writing a review, you should not state:

> Romeo showed his nervousness about his feelings for Juliet in the way he hesitated before kissing her.

This is inaccurate. Instead, you must appraise the actor's performance:

> [Name of actor] showed Romeo's nervousness about his feelings for Juliet in the way he approached the kiss. He created a sense of anticipation by hesitating before kissing her.

Not making the important distinction between the separate entities of actor and character is a common mistake, leading to confused descriptions of actors' performances.

Analysing your response

To describe a performance merely as 'good' or 'convincing' is not sufficient. You must gauge the demands a role makes on an actor and appraise the theatrical choices the actor makes in meeting those demands. Your initial response to a performance might be emotional and spontaneous. The skill required of you is to analyse what it is about the performance that is making you respond in the way you do.

Design interpretation

The work of some key designers is discussed in chapter 11, together with the work of some of the more influential directors. However, in this unit, too, it is important for you to reflect on the impact that a designer's interpretation of the director's vision can have.

In Ian Brown's 2002 production of *Hamlet* at the West Yorkshire Playhouse, the mood was one of brooding oppression. Hamlet was played with anger and intensity by Christopher Eccleston. The costumes were almost all dark (Hamlet wore only black) and the courtiers and soldiers were dressed in a military-style uniform similar to those worn by soldiers from Nazi Germany and Fascist Italy. The formality of the court was emphasised in the staging. For example, in Act I scene 2, the king, Claudius, addresses the court while wearing a military uniform, with his courtiers assembled in neat rows. Colour was kept to a minimum, and furniture and other props were sparse.

In this scene, Eccleston's Hamlet stood apart from the rest of the company, and he looked isolated and out of place. It seemed that a ruling idea for the production was to demonstrate the tyrannical and oppressive nature of Claudius's regime — and to make clear that Hamlet could not fit into such a society. This idea was enhanced by the set design, which used imposing walls towering over the sides of the acting area. Lyn Gardner of the *Guardian* started her review of the production with the following observation:

> Searchlights sweep the audience and then settle on the stage — a large, empty, wood-panelled space that is accessed by many doors with small glass peepholes. They are a bit worrying, those doors; they make you think of a prison. Those in the space never know when they are being observed and can be easily surprised by the sudden appearance of others through any of the many entrances. This is not a place to have secrets, although in the Danish court there are many skeletons in cupboards.
>
> (*Guardian*, 8 November 2002)

In this case, the set was such a crucial element in establishing an atmosphere of fear and oppression that the critic mentioned it in the opening lines of her review. Of course, other factors contributed to this atmosphere, but the designer's interpretation ensured that the cheerless and paranoid mood demanded by the production was established by having an enormous walled set and contrasting small peepholes and doors.

In some productions, the design is intended to be the most memorable feature. Many people who have been to see Andrew Lloyd Webber's musical *The Phantom of the Opera* (1986) say that the point when the chandelier comes crashing down is the one that leaves the most lasting impression. Similarly, people who have seen Schönberg and Boublil's *Miss Saigon* (1989) rarely fail to mention the helicopter scene. A more recent example is *Chitty Chitty Bang Bang* (2002) with its flying car. These examples all indicate how far the designer's art can influence the audience's enjoyment of a production.

TopFoto

Sometimes the design of a play is the most memorable aspect, for example the helicopter arriving in *Miss Saigon*

Analysing your response

When watching and responding to live theatre, consider the impact that the set has on you, as Gardner did in her review. Consider how the director's interpretation works with the designer's, and how together they aim to deliver to the audience the 'ruling ideas' or principal themes of the production.

Writing about the design

After a performance, it is important to recall and record the particulars of the design, but these observations should only be made within the context of appreciation and understanding of the whole production; there is no need to list every minute detail. Sometimes a design feature can enhance — or indeed diminish — a moment in the production, so you should always ensure that your observations are analytical as well as descriptive.

If you are reasonably skilled in drawing, you could sketch memorable elements of the set that are important to your analysis. However, you must always ensure that you refer to your sketch in your essay.

Finally, it is always important, but especially so in the area of design, to use appropriate and accurate vocabulary. Examples of design vocabulary include:

- **apron staging** — the stage extends forwards in front of the proscenium arch
- **auditorium** — the area in a theatre where the audience is located in order to hear and watch a performance
- **cyclorama** — a large curtain or wall, often concave, positioned at the back of the stage area
- **'end on' staging** — similar audience layout to a proscenium theatre, but without the arch; the audience is positioned in rows facing the stage
- **off stage** — anywhere the actors cannot be seen by the audience
- **on stage** — anywhere the actors can be seen by the audience
- **promenade staging** — the audience moves and the actors perform among them on a variety of stages
- **proscenium staging** — the audience is positioned in front of the stage, and the stage can be looked upon like a picture frame; the 'frame' itself is called the proscenium arch
- **stage directions** (e.g. 'down stage right', DSR) — directions in the script about how the playwright intends actions or arrangements to be carried out
- **theatre-in-the-round/arena staging** — the audience is seated all around the stage on four sides
- **thrust staging** — the audience is on three sides of the stage, as if the stage has been 'thrust' forward; this can be similar to a catwalk or more like an extended apron stage
- **traverse staging** — the audience members are seated on either side of the stage, facing each other
- **wings** — the unseen backstage area on either side of the stage of a proscenium theatre

Directorial interpretation

A director is responsible for making decisions about artistic concepts, interpretation of text and staging, often working closely with the playwright, actors and creative team. As the primary visionary, he or she is the person most responsible for the overall impact of the production on the audience.

Sometimes — as in the case of Cruden's *Macbeth* — it is clear what the director's vision and input have been. Particular moments of staging or interaction between actors can be unmistakably the work of a specific director.

It is more challenging to discern the impact of a director on a production that has been staged very simply. For example, Kathy Burke's production of Joe Penhall's award-winning play *Blue/Orange* at the Sheffield Crucible in 2004 seemed — and indeed in many ways was — a straightforward production. However, the focus on the development of character and dialogue rather than on technical paraphernalia does not suggest a lack of directorial input. The production of *Blue/Orange* was highly successful and polished. The play is set in an office in the psychiatric wing of a modern hospital and never moves location. It centres around two doctors discussing the fate of a patient, who is also present for much of the action. As they interact with each other and the patient, the dialogue is intense and detailed, with clinical terminology and medical references. The shaping and pace of the dialogue, together with the blocking or movement around the stage, are vital to the play's success. There may be no demand for special effects or even special moments of choreography, but to achieve overall coherence and hold an audience's attention requires strong direction. There is no doubt that Burke's production received that level of attention and was highly acclaimed as a consequence.

A director's interpretation can also radically alter an audience's preconceived ideas about a play. *An Inspector Calls* (1944) by J. B. Priestley (which is referred to more extensively in Chapter 6) was a staple favourite of British theatre for many years and was made into a successful film in 1954. It might, therefore, have been regarded as a dated if worthy classic towards the end of the twentieth century. However, Stephen Daldry's production in 1992 altered perceptions of the play by taking a far more experimental approach. By staging the production in a collapsible dolls-house type of structure, and by combining the historical setting of the play (between 1912 when it was originally set and 1944 when it was written), he challenged the traditional naturalistic treatment the play usually receives.

Directorial interpretation can mean the difference between a triumphant and a disastrous production. For example, if you look at the critical responses to Trevor Nunn's 1976 production of *Macbeth* starring Ian McKellan and Judy

Dench, and contrast them with Bryan Forbes's 1980 production starring Peter O'Toole, you may find it hard to believe that they are about the same play. Nunn's production was pronounced a triumph and Forbes's a disaster (although commercially it was a success because the critical panning it received encouraged audiences to turn out just to see how bad it was). This was not due to any lack of talent on the actors' part. Quite simply, the decisions made by one director resulted in a universally acclaimed production, while the decisions made by the other director resulted in disaster.

The importance of staging choices

The task of staging is obviously a major part of directing, but this is also significantly dependent on the contribution of the actors and their interpretations of the roles.

The staging choices involved in a scene will affect how the audience assimilates, understands and appreciates that scene. It can also affect how an audience might develop a relationship with a character. In a 2001 production of *King Lear* (1605), staged at The Globe and directed by Barrie Kyle, the audience's expectations of Edmund — the principal villain of the play who is traditionally a dark and brooding presence — were subverted as the actor made his first entrance onto stage from the audience and then delivered his opening speech almost as a comic turn while swinging playfully from a post. He was very close to the audience — almost among them — and at one point leant over and took a drink from one of the people standing in the front row. (At The Globe, many of the audience members stand in the main body of the theatre, as they would have done in the time of Shakespeare.)

This moment of staging created an informality in the relationship between Edmund and the audience. He was almost part of the crowd and his future villainy was seen in that context. Although Edmund goes on to commit atrocities and be part of a regime of terror, the audience was initially encouraged to be sympathetic to his plight, and even to like him for his playful antics.

Staging decisions can also affect the relationships that characters develop with each other. In the Sheffield Crucible's 2006 production of Harold Pinter's *The Caretaker*, a large space was used, even though this play is usually seen as a chamber piece (i.e. more suitable for a small studio setting). The entire stage area was used to depict Aston's room to which he invites the tramp Davis. Later in the play, Aston's brother, Mick, arrives and behaves aggressively towards Davis because he suspects him of taking advantage of his rather naïve brother. In this production, Mick was a kind of omnipresence during many of the scenes, observing Davis from a distance and then advancing on him when he wanted to threaten him. The effect of this was to increase the sense of menace in the relationship between the two characters.

As a result of the space being used in this way, the audience was given the impression that Mick was a sinister observer, noting the behaviour and the interaction of the other two before emerging from the shadows and imposing himself on the action. Within such a large space, it was possible for characters to isolate themselves or be isolated from the others. The space between the characters helped to define the state of the relationships between them at any point in the play. This is a particularly significant feature in any play that shares some of Pinter's values and performance principles. Pinter is famous for his economical use of language, and there are many moments of prolonged silence in *The Caretaker* where the looks that pass between characters — sometimes threatening (Mick to Davis), sometimes affectionate (Mick to Aston) — take on an added significance.

Analysing your response

When watching a production, try to discern the balance between the actors' achievements and the director's. This is not always obvious, but the pacing of dialogue and the intensity achieved between actors is usually a combination of their work and the director's.

How is sound used?

When judging the quality of sound in a production, you should consider a number of issues. Sound is not just about sound 'effects' generated by complex recording equipment. Do not overlook the fact that many sound effects can be created by a single human voice or a combination of human voices. Moreover, music used in theatre does not have to be recorded or played on electronic instruments. A rare production of Alfred Tennyson's *The Promise of May* (1882), staged by Numb Compass in April 2008, used a single violin to create musical interludes and accompaniments. The playing of traditional folk airs and ballads helped to establish the era of the nineteenth century, and also contributed to the portrayal of the rural community that is essential to understand and appreciate the play.

Singing was also used in the production to underpin the traditions and customs of the rural community being depicted. *The Promise of May* is concerned with the devastating consequences for a young woman when a worldly and sophisticated socialite preys on her, uses her for sexual gratification and then abandons her. Much of the singing was *a cappella* (without any instrumental accompaniment), which conveyed a sense of the innocence and lack of sophistication of this woman. Remember, therefore, always to respond to the human features of sound as well as to electronic 'effects'.

Sometimes the staging demands of a particular play mean that technical sound effects should be used to enhance the overall impact of the production. In his book *So You Want to be a Theatre Director?*, Stephen Unwin identifies some of the specific challenges for a sound designer presented by Anton Chekhov's *The Cherry Orchard* (1904). He begins by quoting a stage direction and the subsequent dialogue from the second act of the play:

Suddenly a far off noise is heard, as if in the heavens — like the sound of a breaking string, dying away sadly:
Ranevskayar: What's that?
Lophakhin: I don't know. Possibly a coal tub broken loose somewhere, down the mines. A long way from here, anyway.
Gaev: Could be some sort of bird, like a heron.
Trofimov: Or an owl, perhaps…
Ranevskayar *(shudders)*: It's horrible, whatever it is.

> Try to imagine a sound that can satisfy Chekhov's stage directions, allow for both Lopakhin and Gaev's comments, and not make Trofimov seem ridiculous or Ranevskaya hysterical and you'll see just how difficult Chekhov has made it.
>
> (Unwin, S. (2004) *So You Want to Be A Theatre Director?*,
> Nick Hern Books, pp. 213–14)

Jonathan Miller directed *The Cherry Orchard* for the West Yorkshire Playhouse in 2007. In this production, the sound used was quite loud and resounding; it was not obvious what might have made such a sound, and it provided an enigmatic and moving moment in the middle of the play. The characters delivered their lines in a rather detached manner, almost as if they had each heard different sounds. The sound required here is difficult to determine since this is a deliberately mysterious moment. In this production, Miller's interpretation of the sound enhanced rather than solved the mystery.

At the end of the play, the stage direction tells us that the sound of the cherry orchard being chopped down can be heard. Again, this is an important moment — not just because it is the final moment of the play but because it is symbolic of the end of the old order. The owners have had to leave, no longer able to afford to live on the estate, and the trees are to be cut down to make room for new development. In Miller's production, the sound was quite loud and obvious, yet an echo effect provided a dream-like quality. The sound was reminiscent of that heard earlier in the production. It was almost as if the earlier sound had been a rather eerie premonition of the fate of the cherry orchard.

Therefore, when commenting on the use of sound in a production, it is important to consider the challenges presented by the piece and to evaluate the success of the sound — not simply as a technical achievement, but in terms of how and what the sound contributes to the overall production.

How is lighting used?

Technical developments in theatre lighting have been significant in recent years. While you do not need to be an expert on lighting systems, you should be aware of how lighting impacts on an audience.

Like set design, lighting design can greatly influence the audience's enjoyment of a production. At its most basic, it illuminates the action or creates the effects of night or day or warmth or cold, but it can also serve to emphasise ambiance and emotion. The lighting design in Ian Brown's production of *Hamlet* at the West Yorkshire Playhouse in 2002 worked extremely well with the set. Light was focused on the great walls to reveal the small doorways as the action progressed, keeping most of the set in shadow and near-darkness. This lighting design augmented the sense of secrecy and paranoia that defined elements of the production.

In *The Wonderful World of Dissocia* by Anthony Neilson, staged at York Theatre Royal in 2007, the bright lights of the hospital room in the second half of the play — in contrast to the vibrant colours in the first half — made it almost painful to watch. However, that contrast was crucial in reflecting the state of mind of the central character as she moved from the colourful and lurid world of her fantasies into the harsh clinical world of her recovery. In other words, the lighting effects could not be judged as moments in themselves (apart from the perspective of technical merit); they were intrinsically relative to each other and to the experiences of the central character.

Writing about the lighting

While you should make mention of the relevant technical information, it is more important to make sense of how technical features influence the overall impact of the play on the audience.

When you are writing about lighting, it is essential to use correct terminology for the equipment. Examples of lighting terminology include:

- **floodlight** — a lantern that gives a wide-spreading, unfocused beam of light
- **follow spot** — a type of profile spotlight used to follow a performer around the stage in a beam of light of exactly the right size

* **fresnel** — a spotlight that employs a Fresnel lens (a lens with concentric ridged rings) to wash light over an area of the stage; the lens produces a wide, soft-edged beam of light, which is commonly used for back light and top light
* **gel** — a filter placed over the front of a lantern to change the colour of the light
* **gobo** — a piece of metal or glass, which fits into the gate of a profile spotlight and projects a pattern onto the set
* **par can** — a type of lantern that projects a near parallel beam of light
* **profile** — a type of spotlight that produces a narrow, hard-edged beam of light
* **spot** — a type of lantern whose beam is focused through a lens or series of lenses to make it more controllable

How are mood and atmosphere created?

It is important not to overlook what may seem to be the less obvious features of a production. You can comment on a set because it is physically in front of you, and the same is true of sound, lighting and costume. It is also possible to comment on the qualities of individual performances. However, it is equally important to pay attention to how these ingredients work together. For example, the pacing of a scene cannot be dictated by one actor alone; it is created by the way in which the actors respond to each other. There is a link, therefore, between pace and mood.

The speed of responses between the actors can make the pace of a scene frantic, excitable and almost hysterical. Burke's production of *Blue/Orange* discussed on page 15 built tension between the characters through the use of swift, angry exchanges. By contrast, the ponderous pace of the production of *The Caretaker* discussed on pages 16–17 also helped to develop tension — in this case, the prolonged moments of silence allowed the audience to reflect on the characters as they watched and interacted with each other.

As well as pace, the mood or atmosphere of a play can be affected by the design features. For example, *A Moon for the Misbegotten* (1947) by Eugene O'Neill was staged at The Old Vic in 2006. The play is set on a farm in Connecticut; it takes place over the course of a day and centres on the relationships of the three major characters. The production was dominated by three outstanding performances (Colm Meaney, Eve Best and Kevin Spacey), but the actors were not solely responsible for its success. Paule Constable, the lighting designer, successfully conveyed a sense of the summer day drifting into evening and night by using subtle changes of shading and then making the eponymous moon appear. A feat of technical excellence was thus harnessed to create a dramatically appropriate atmosphere.

Who is the audience?

When you make assertions about the impact of a play on an audience, you must give some attention to who that audience is.

When John Godber took over the directorship of the Hull Truck Theatre in 1984, he wrote a play which he knew would attract an audience: *Up 'n' Under*. The play is about Rugby League, and Hull, at the time, had two world-class Rugby League teams. The play proved to be enormously popular, receiving in its audiences people who had seldom, if ever, been to the theatre before. Godber has long been credited with creating the kind of material that encourages otherwise reluctant members of the public to come to the theatre.

Similarly, in 2003 the playwright Mick Martin wrote a play called *Once Upon A Time in Wigan* — about the history of the northern soul scene at the Wigan Casino. Again, people came to see the play not because they were traditional theatre lovers but because they themselves had been involved in the all-night events at the Wigan Casino and other northern venues and therefore were interested in its subject.

The audience at a performance in 2000 of Shakespeare's *The Tempest*, Globe Theatre, London

Photostage

Every production has a target audience. In arriving at repertoire for the season, an artistic director has to argue the value of each production and its relevance to a stipulated target audience. It could be that the target audience is you: students. It could be people from older age groups or interest groups, or it could be less definite than that. It is, however, an important consideration, because the impact of a piece of theatre on a group of school students will invariably be different to its impact on a group of pensioners. While it is unlikely that the audience will be exclusively one group or the other (unless of course it is a performance in a group-specific venue, such as a school), it may well be dominated by one group.

Summary

Responding to a piece of theatre requires:

- recognition of previous theatregoing experiences, or experiences as a drama and theatre student, that may be relevant to the event
- accessing as much information about the production as possible from a variety of sources
- acknowledgement that the theatre environment will affect the experience of a production
- awareness of the director's intentions in staging the play and identification of the target audience
- analysis of technical contributions to the production

Discussion questions

Make thorough notes on the points that arise from your consideration of the following questions, either from discussion or your own observations.

1 Assess the productions you have seen recently. What were the distinguishing features that made them memorable? You should take into account all areas of the production.

2 Explain how elements of the design of one production you have seen helped to convey an appropriate atmosphere.

Essay questions

1 Analyse how sound was used effectively in a specific scene in one production you have seen.

2 Comment on a particularly effective performance from an actor in one production you have seen. Analyse the actor's vocal and physical contribution.

3 Discuss how effective a director's contribution was in one production you have seen. Give specific examples of the director's work in the production.

Chapter 2

Section B: Prescribed plays

Antigone

by Sophocles

Background

Antigone, written around 440–445 BC, is the third play of a trilogy by the Greek playwright Sophocles (*c.* 496–406 BC). These three plays are often referred to as the 'Theban plays'. With the possible exception of the Oresteian trilogy by Aeschylus (*c.* 525–456 BC), who is sometimes referred to as the father of Greek tragedy, Sophocles' Theban plays form the most famous group of plays from the ancient Greek era.

Antigone charts the fates of Oedipus's children. Following Oedipus's death, it was agreed that the city of Thebes would be ruled over by each of his sons in turn — first Eteocles and then Polynices. However, Eteocles refused to relinquish the throne and, as a result, Polynices and his followers waged war against the forces of Thebes. At the height of the battle, both brothers killed each other. Creon, brother of their mother Jocasta (and thus Eteocles' and Polynices' uncle), ordered that Eteocles's body should be given a proper religious burial but that Polynices' body should be left to rot since he attacked his own city and people.

The Theban plays

Sophocles wrote the Theban plays over a period of 36 years. They were not written in chronological order: *Antigone*, the third play in the trilogy, was the first to be written. The middle play, *Oedipus at Colonus*, was the last to be written. The first play, *Oedipus Rex*, is the most famous of the three because of the fate of its hero. The Theban plays follow the tragic downfall of the mythical King Oedipus of Thebes and his descendants.

The background to the story of the Theban plays is that, as a young man, Oedipus heard a rumour that he was adopted and asked the Delphic oracle about his true parentage. Rather than answer him directly, the oracle advised that he was destined to 'Mate with your own mother, and shed with your own hands the blood of your own sire'. Not understanding this cryptic response, and distressed at the thought of killing his own father, Oedipus travelled to Thebes. During his journey, he met a man at a crossroads and they argued about which wagon had the right of way. Oedipus's pride led him to kill the man, ignorant of the fact that he was actually King Laius, his biological father. Oedipus then went on to free the kingdom of Thebes from the Sphinx's curse by solving a riddle, the reward for which was kingship and the hand of the queen, Jocasta, who was in fact his biological mother, although both parties were ignorant of this.

Oedipus Rex begins years after Oedipus is given the throne of Thebes. The citizens of Thebes ask Oedipus for salvation from a terrible plague. He declares his intention to find the cause of the affliction, not realising that he himself has angered the gods by murdering his father and marrying his mother.

Oedipus's quest eventually reveals the truth — that he has fulfilled the terrible prediction of the Delphic oracle. The plague can therefore only be lifted with his banishment from Thebes. The play ends with Oedipus entrusting his children to Creon, his mother's brother, and declaring his intention to live in exile.

In *Oedipus at Colonus*, Oedipus reaches the end of his life but accepts that he is only partly responsible for his crimes as he committed them in ignorance. His daughters Antigone and Ismene return to Thebes.

Characteristics of Greek tragedy

The word 'tragedy' in a theatrical context defines a specific type of dramatic event. In its modern usage, 'tragedy' is often used in association with sudden loss of life or fatal accidents. However, while the events of a 'tragedy' do involve loss of life, this is not its only distinguishing feature.

The term 'tragedy' has its roots in the earliest surviving form of theatre — Greek tragedy. Perhaps the most famous of all the Greek tragedies is *Oedipus Rex* (Sophocles *c.* 430 BC). *Oedipus Rex* provides us with a useful model for tragedy, and its influence can be seen in the tragedies of Shakespeare and many plays up to the present day (e.g. those of Arthur Miller).

Greek playwrights tried to make sense of the world. They took events that could not be explained by reason or cause and effect — such as the plague — and attempted to create some kind of order around the chaos. As a civilisation, the Greeks tried to understand the workings of the universe through astronomy and the workings of the world through mathematics, but it was through poetry and drama that they sought explanations for the inexplicable.

The 'tragic hero' and the 'fatal flaw'

The central character in a tragedy is the tragic hero. Aristotle identified the main qualities of the tragic hero as:

> …that of a man who is not eminently good and just, yet whose misfortune is brought about not by vice or depravity, but by some error or frailty.
>
> (*The Poetics*, section 13, trans. S. H. Butler)

In Greek theatre, the tragic hero's 'fatal flaw' (error or frailty) has usually been committed or manifested before the action of the play begins. For example, at the beginning of *Oedipus Rex*, the citizens of Thebes are suffering the ravages of the plague because of crimes already committed years before by Oedipus.

Aristotle (384–322 BC)

The ideas of the Greek philosopher Aristotle have influenced many aspects of modern life, from religion to science, and from politics to philosophy. Although some of his work has been lost over the centuries, much of it is still studied today. In theatrical terms, his greatest contribution was *The Poetics* (*c.* 333 BC), a piece of work in which he explores the nature of poetry and drama, specifically tragedy.

The 'reversal of situation'

'Reversal of situation' is a dramatic device for tragedy referred to by Aristotle in *The Poetics*. Reversal of situation occurs in *Antigone* when Creon, having remained steadfastly opposed to any advice or counsel, changes his mind at the last moment regarding Antigone's fate and the correctness of his own actions. However, his change of heart occurs too late to save his niece and his son.

The three unities

Aristotle also defined the idea of the 'three unities'. According to Aristotle, the plot of a tragedy should:

- take place over a 24-hour period (unity of time)
- be continuous (unity of action)
- be set in one area (unity of place)

The 'high-ranking protagonist'

Tragedy, as presented by the Greek playwrights and those in the sixteenth and seventeenth centuries, always dealt with the lives of high-ranking protagonists of noble birth.

Staging conditions in ancient Greek theatre

TopFoto

Ruins of an
amphitheatre in
Delphi, Greece

The physical environment

The size of the surviving amphitheatres (particularly at Epidaurus, one of the oldest surviving theatre sites in Greece) gives us some idea of the scale of ancient Greek performances. The Greek amphitheatre was a huge, open-air construction that took advantage of sloping hillsides to form semi-circular terraced seating known as the *theatron* (literally 'seeing place'). The seating was not segregated (as in Elizabethan, Georgian and Victorian theatres), and there was no division between the 'circle', 'stalls' and 'upper gallery'. While this arrangement reflected the democratic ideals of Greek society, it did not mean that people from all walks of life attended the theatre (unlike the theatre of Shakespeare). Women and slaves — a significant proportion of the population — were not included in the ancient idea of democracy and therefore did not attend the theatre.

The *orchestra* and the *skene*

The audience would look down on the circular stage, called the *orchestra*. Behind this was a backdrop or scenic wall called the *skene*, which formed the changing area for the actors. The action of the plays would therefore take place on the *orchestra*, in front of the *skene*. The death of a character was always heard '*ob skene*' ('behind the *skene*'), as it was deemed inappropriate to show a killing before an audience. (This is where the word 'obscene' comes from.)

It would be all too easy to assume that the theatres of ancient Greece were crude or rudimentary. However, thousands of people could be seated in these auditoria, and plays up to 6 hours long could be performed in them without the aid of any artificial amplification system. Mathematics played an important role in the construction of these theatres, in creating acoustics that allowed the actors' voices to be heard throughout the structure.

The actors

Greek performers were professionals paid by the state. Acting was initially a respected profession — partly because of the high status of the religious festival in which actors were key participants. However, as the acting profession moved further away from the influence of religion, society's respect for actors decreased.

To gain attention in the huge theatre space, the actor would wear high-soled shoes or boots (called *cothurni*) to elevate him to a commanding height — often over 7 feet tall. He wore padding and his costume was colour-coded; for example, purple denoted royalty and black indicated mourning.

The actor would also wear a mask with exaggerated features — partly because he was expected to play many different roles, but also (it is supposed) because the shape of the mask helped the actor to make himself heard in the auditorium. The main requirement of the actor in Greek theatre — apart from audibility — was versatility. A large number of characters are present in plays of considerable length and complexity. However, if you examine the plays of Aeschylus and Sophocles, you will see that there are rarely more than two or three individual performers on stage at any one time. One actor would therefore be required to play many roles, often changing gender. The obvious change indicated by a mask allowed the audience's attention to remain focused.

Outline of the plot of Antigone
Lines 1–499

Antigone is the daughter of Oedipus and Jocasta (Oedipus's mother/wife). At the opening of the play she is talking to her sister, Ismene. Creon, Jocasta's brother, has issued his decree that the body of Polynices should not be given a burial. Antigone is incensed by this.

Antigone: What! Has not Creon to the tomb preferred
One of our brothers, and with contumely
Withheld it from the other?

(from *Antigone*, translated by Sir George Young,
Dover Thrift Editions, first published in 1993, p. 2, ll. 24–26)

Antigone is not content to follow the decree and asks for Ismene's help in defying it. She wants to give her brother Polynices a respectful burial rather than leave his corpse out to rot in the open air. Ismene, however, advises Antigone to obey their uncle, thus demonstrating that her nature is rather less formidable than her sister's. She reminds Antigone of the disgrace of their father, the deaths of their two brothers, and the fact that they are now quite alone and vulnerable:

Ismene: […] We now left alone —
Do but consider how most miserably
We too shall perish, if despite of law
We traverse the behest or power of kings.
We must remember we are women born,
Unapt to cope with men;   (p. 3, ll. 68–73)

Antigone does not share her sister's fear. She leaves Ismene, instructing her to reveal to everyone the nature of her intentions. As she leaves, the chorus of Theban senators arrive.

The Greek chorus

The chorus played an important role in classical Greek drama, especially in tragedy. Its function seems to have been varied:

- to give important background information to help the audience follow the performance
- to comment on and underline the main themes of the play
- to influence how the audience responds to the play
- to provide a spectacle suited to open-air theatre with no sound amplification
- to mark scene changes for the audience and to give the principal actors a break
- to represent the powerless nature of ordinary people; members of the chorus are often affected by the activities of the major characters but are largely powerless to influence them

The chorus was used to rejoice in the triumph of good and to mourn over tragedy. It entered into the fortunes and misfortunes of the protagonists, yet stood apart from them. The chorus seldom took an 'individual' stance. It was the voice of the human being amid the judgements and battles of the gods.

The chorus survived beyond classical times: in Elizabethan drama the feelings and comments of 'Everyman' are often represented by nameless individuals, such as 'First gentleman' or 'First lord', who express emotions and opinions similar to those articulated by the Greek chorus.

The chorus in *Antigone*, Old Vic Theatre, London, 1999; written and directed by Declan Donnellan

The chorus tells the story of the battle that has been fought — of Polynices' attempted invasion and of the way the Thebans were able to repel it. There is a mood of celebration and relief.

At the end of the chorus's speech Creon, the new king of Thebes, enters to address his people. He has summoned the chorus of senators to him as they are wise counsellors and he professes to need their advice. He delivers a powerful and authoritative statement in which he affirms that the city is now in safe hands. His first proclamation is as Ismene has already revealed: Eteocles, as the heroic defender of Thebes, is to be given a full funeral while Polynices, the invader, is to be left out to rot.

While the chorus acknowledges Creon's authority in making such an order, the first senator (the chorus leader) does not voice any endorsement of the act:

First senator: Creon Menoeceus' son, we hear your pleasure
Both on this city's friend, and on her foe;
It is your sovereignty's prerogative
To pass with absolute freedom on the dead,
And us, who have survived them.
Creon: Please to see
What has been said performed.   (p. 5, ll. 253–59)

A guard enters and addresses Creon. He informs Creon that someone has buried the corpse of Polynices and carried out due burial rites; he and his fellow guards feel that the king should be told about this. The chorus leader dares to ask the king:

My lord, my heart misgave me from the first
This must be something more than natural.   (p. 11, ll. 334–35)

Creon's response is immediate and uncompromising:

Truce to your speech, before I choke with rage,
Lest you be found at once grey-beard and fool!   (p. 11, ll. 336–37)

Creon is revealed here to be insulting and intemperate. He addresses a senior member of the city of Thebes with contempt and accuses the guard of having been bribed to carry out this treasonous act. He then tells the guard that if he does not find the person responsible, he will pay for the act with his life. Creon leaves, followed by the guard.

The chorus now speaks of the wonder of humankind, its learning, skills and relationship with the earth. It describes man's understanding and resourcefulness but comments that his inventiveness leads him to make choices — some good and some evil. The chorus concludes:

Now bends he to the good, now to the ill,
With craft of ant, subtle past reach of sight;
Wresting his country's laws to his own will,
Spurning the sanctions of celestial right;
High in the city, he is made city-less,
Whoso is corrupt, for his impiety;
He that will work the works of wickedness,
Let him not house, let him not hold, with me!   (pp. 14–15 ll.2, ll. 423–30)

This dire warning could be issued both to whoever has flouted Creon's laws and to Creon himself — a man who is 'Spurning the sanctions of celestial right'.

Perhaps the chorus, even at this early stage of the play, can see that Creon is headed for disaster.

The guard returns with Antigone. The chorus exclaims its surprise at the sight of Antigone. Creon re-enters. With some relief, the guard explains that he caught Antigone attempting to bury the body of Polynices.

Antigone's response to Creon is in complete contrast to that of the guard, who talks at great length in an attempt to exonerate himself. When Creon accuses her of burying the body of Polynices, Antigone simply says:

I say I did it. I deny it not.   (p. 17, l. 487)

Lines 500–983

When Creon asks how Antigone dared to break the law, her reply is unequivocal. She explains that the law of the gods — which demands formal burial and funeral rights — cannot be countermanded by any human. She knows that as a consequence of her actions she will die, but is pleased to do so. She asks why she should not be pleased to die before her time when she is surrounded by so much evil. She ends with a blatant challenge to Creon, delivered plainly and with no respect:

And if my present action seems to you
Foolish — 'tis like I am found guilty of folly
At a fool's mouth!   (p. 18, ll. 515–17)

Renée Faure as
Antigone,
Comédie-
Française, Paris,
October 1959

Creon accuses Antigone of arrogance, of breaking the law and being proud of it. He makes it clear that she will receive no preferential treatment even though she is his blood relative (the child of his sister, the dead queen Jocasta). He goes on to accuse his other niece, Ismene, of collusion, suggesting that her anxiety and distress (which he has just witnessed) reveals her guilty conscience.

Antigone urges Creon to kill her now. Creon is incredulous at this and attempts to justify his decision about Polynices, stating that an evil man cannot expect the same burial rites as a good one. Her brother, as the invader, was an enemy of the country and therefore an evil man. He asks her how he, the king, can be seen to be giving equal treatment to the invader. Antigone maintains that she was simply obeying the law and paying her respects to a beloved brother. The argument is summarised in the final exchange between the two:

Creon: The enemy,
Can never be friend, even in death.
Antigone: Well, I was made for fellowship in love,
Not fellowship in hate. (p. 20, ll. 588–91)

Both positions are resolute and immoveable. However, Creon's final comment indicates that his judgements are based on an assessment of his own authority as a man and a leader, rather than on any moral judgement:

Creon: Then get you down
Thither, and love, if you must love, the dead!
No woman, while I live, shall order me. (p. 20, ll. 592–94)

Ismene's entrance reveals Creon's state of mind still further. He refers to her as a 'viper' and accuses her of collaboration with Antigone. Instead of defending herself, Ismene prefers to be blamed alongside her sister and admits complicity in the plan to bury Polynices. Antigone is outraged and feels insulted that Ismene should now try to claim partial responsibility for actions and ideas that she previously rejected.

Distraught at having to face life alone without Antigone, Ismene asks how she is expected to live without her. She then appeals to Creon:

What, will you put to death your own son's bride? (p. 22, l. 648)

This is the first indication of the fact that Antigone is betrothed to Creon's son. He answers Ismene with seeming callousness:

He may go further afield — (p. 22, l. 649)

Antigone and Ismene are taken into the palace to await their fates and the chorus, left alone with Creon, speaks of the history of the troubled family and how:

For a light of late had spread
O'er the last surviving root
In the house of Oedipus;
Now, the sickle murderous
Of the Rulers of the dead,
And wild words beyond control,
And the frenzy of her own soul,
Again mow down the shoot. (p.23, l. 2, ll. 683–90)

They go on to observe:

If evil good appear,
That soul to his ruin is divinely led —   (p. 24, ll. 2, ll. 767–68)

The chorus is therefore suggesting that Creon's actions — while undertaken in the name of good — could in fact be evil.

Following this commentary, Creon's son, Haemon, arrives. Haemon offers his father support and declares that he will stay true to Creon's leadership. Creon comments that Haemon's actions are appropriate and that he (Creon) must offer strong leadership and never allow his law to be broken or his will contradicted. While Haemon makes his loyalty clear, he also acquaints his father with the unease the city feels at Antigone's fate and tells him that her plight has aroused some sympathy. He goes on to say that, although he is a wise ruler, Creon surely cannot think himself infallible and that it is good to learn from others.

The argument between father and son intensifies and Haemon becomes increasingly frustrated at his father's unwillingness to question his own actions and his inflexible attitude towards Antigone. Creon orders Antigone to be brought out so that she can be executed in front of her fiancé, but Haemon refuses to allow him to do this. Haemon runs into the palace declaring that his father will never see him again.

Creon reveals that he plans to execute Antigone by burying her alive in a cave with provisions to allow her to live for long enough to say her prayers and prepare for death. He also states that he will only execute Antigone and not Ismene. Antigone is then brought out of the palace before making her final journey to the cave. For the first time she displays a sense of regret at her life being cut short, and says that she feels friendless and unloved. Creon dismisses her without pity, saying to the chorus that she should:

[…] leave her alone, apart,
To perish, if she will; or if she live,
To make her tomb her tenement. For us,
We will be guiltless of this maiden's blood;
But here on earth she shall abide no more.   (p. 33, ll. 977–83)

Lines 984–1,508

Antigone makes her final laments and is led away. The blind prophet, Tiresias, is led on and reminds Creon that he has always accepted his judgement in the past. Creon agrees but is alarmed when Tiresias advises him that 'thou dost walk on fortune's razor-edge' (p. 37, l. 1,106).

He tells Creon that the gods will not accept his sacrifices, as the unburied corpse of Polynices is offensive to them. Their altars have been defiled by dogs bringing pieces of decaying flesh from the body. This defilement is a direct result of Creon's policies and his edict regarding the body of Polynices. Tiresias urges Creon to think again and warns him that:

Conceit of will savours of emptiness.

(p. 38, l. 1,140)

However, Creon shows no sign of changing his mind. He accuses Tiresias of using insulting behaviour to promote his craft of prophecy and using it merely as a means of making money.

Tiresias is outraged and further prophesises that Creon's actions will bring about the death of one of his own children. After saying this, he leaves. The chorus tells Creon that it has never known Tiresias to deliver a false prophecy. Creon agrees and, for the first time, shows uncertainty about his decision. The chorus eventually persuades Creon to give way, to release Antigone and to bury the corpse of Polynices. As he accepts the chorus's advice Creon departs for Antigone's tomb so that he can release her in person.

Blindness in classical drama

Blindness is often used in a dramatically ironic way in classical drama. In *Oedipus Rex*, Tiresias, despite being blind, has the gift of insight. Dramatists in later times used the same image. For example, the Earl of Gloucester in Shakespeare's *King Lear* has his eyes pulled out seconds before realising that he has been duped by his treacherous son.

Photostage

At the end of the chorus's prayers a messenger appears and reveals that Haemon has killed himself. Before the messenger can continue, Creon's queen, Eurydice, appears. She has heard of terrible events but is not aware of the fate of her family. The messenger is forced to reveal the news to her and to the chorus.

He tells the story of accompanying Creon and his men to the cave: they pay due rites to the remains of Polynices' corpse but before they can enter the tomb they hear a cry from within. On entering, they see the body of Antigone hanging by the neck, with Haemon holding the corpse. As Creon tries to persuade his son to leave the tomb, Haemon takes his sword and stabs himself.

Richard Evans as Tiresias in an adaptation by Seamus Heaney of *Antigone* entitled *The Burial at Thebes*, Nottingham Playhouse, 2007

On hearing the fate of her son, Eurydice walks silently back into the palace. Creon re-enters holding the corpse of his son and admonishing himself for his death. Creon's wife then takes her own life. At the end of the play, Creon is left to reflect on the fact that his behaviour has brought about the destruction of his household.

Considerations for the director

Why should a play written more than 2,000 years ago still have relevance and meaning for an audience today? Is it possible for *Antigone* to move or shock an audience in the way that it would have done when it was first performed? To answer these questions, a director must consider how to define his or her own interpretation of the play. In particular, the following issues should be addressed.

Religious and cultural context

It is important for a director to acknowledge that he or she is working in both a different era and a different culture from the one in which the play was first performed. Today, we live in a largely secular society — one that is not defined or motivated predominantly by religion. The seriousness of Creon's blasphemy in forbidding the burial of his nephew is not generally apparent to a modern audience.

However, it would be inaccurate to claim that our own society is unaffected by religion and, in particular, religious differences. We are constantly evaluating our relationship with a variety of religions — including Christianity and Islam. This is not to suggest that a director should try to force a link between the actions of Antigone and those of an individual with inflexible religious beliefs; such a comparison could be quite crass and contrived. Nevertheless, attitudes towards religion and people of faith are recognisable themes in our society and strong themes in the play.

Characters and relationships

A director is also concerned with the characters in the play and the relationships between them. The most important characters are Antigone and Creon. They are firmly opposed to each other throughout the play, and neither concedes any ground. This relationship could, for instance, be portrayed as that of the tyrant and the freedom fighter; one involving an implacable ruler who refuses to alter his direction and kills members of his family to prove his strength.

Casting choice can have a considerable impact on the audience's perception of the characters and, therefore, the play as a whole. Creon, for example, could be portrayed as a short figure who is excitable, unpredictable and vicious. Alternatively, he might be played by a taller actor who delivers his lines calmly with only a hint of exasperation. This latter interpretation might lead an audience to believe that Creon's extreme and tyrannical behaviour is out of character, which would be consistent with the shock and outrage that Haemon and Tiresias express. The director will also need to decide whether or not Creon and Antigone previously had a warm relationship. This and similar considerations require thorough exploration and interpretation by the director and actors.

Political stance

Antigone can be interpreted as a political commentary as well as a human play. This can be seen most obviously in the adaptation written by French playwright Jean Anouilh towards the end of the Second World War. France had been occupied by the Nazis for most of the war, and Anouilh's version is very much concerned with the themes of tyranny and human rights.

Creon — representing the might of the state — demonstrates the consequences of the actions of a tyrannical ruler who will not listen to advice and regards any suggestion that he may be wrong as treason and disloyalty, even when it comes from members of his own family (Haemon), from advisers whose counsel he had previously respected (chorus), or from prophets who are always right and who selflessly offer their skills for the good of the state (Tiresias).

Mixing political and human themes

A director can choose to present both political and human themes. A production that emphasises the tragic consequences of a tyrannical approach to government does not necessarily forfeit its interest in human qualities and relationships. For example, Arthur Miller's play *Death of a Salesman* (1949) depicts the final days in the life of an ageing and luckless salesman, Willy Loman. His attempts to earn a living never succeed and at the end of the play he takes his own life, hoping to leave his family with his life insurance money. The play (described by Miller as a tragedy) explodes the myth of the 'American Dream' — the ideal that anyone can aspire to great personal and/or political success simply by working hard.

Death of a Salesman is unquestionably a political play, but it is also a deeply human one. However, because of its naturalistic style it cannot be set in anything other than its own context: the USA in 1949. By contrast, the poetic, non-naturalistic style of *Antigone* allows for a range of interpretations and settings. Rather like the plays of Shakespeare, it is perfectly possible to set *Antigone* in a different era and culture. However, doing this will always have a profound influence on the way the audience perceives its themes and characters.

The director's task

In summary, the director must make a number of key choices that will influence how an audience responds to a production of *Antigone*. He or she must ensure that the audience can respond to a play that is more than 2,000 years old. Furthermore, the director must ensure that the relationships between the characters are carefully thought through and clearly communicated. Weak direction will result in an unclear interpretation and a production that means little to its audience.

Discussion questions

Make thorough notes on the points that arise from your consideration of the following questions, either from discussion or your own observations. You may use these notes to annotate your text.

1 How could a director use the audience's awareness of religious issues to inform a production of *Antigone*?

2 Should a production of *Antigone* be used to reflect some of the religious attitudes that challenge our society today? If so, how?

Essay questions

1 How is *Antigone* a political play? What could a director do in terms of staging and giving advice to actors to give the production a strong political focus?

2 What might the impact be on an audience if the director chose to stage *Antigone* in a more modern setting?

Considerations for the designer

The role of the designer is strongly linked with that of the director. It is impossible for the director to set the play convincingly in a different era if the designer is unable to realise this vision.

Set design

Clearly, the choice of theatre space will have an impact on all set design considerations. As discussed in Chapter 1, the theatre environment — and where you are placed in it — can have a significant impact on how effectively the performance is communicated to you. The designer must therefore reflect on the potential of the space available and the way in which it is seen by different sections of the audience.

Designing a set is not merely the creation of the physical environment where the action takes place; it is also about the creation of the world of the play. It must, therefore, underpin the themes of the play as identified by the director.

We know that the play is set outdoors — outside the palace in Thebes. Royal characters enter and exit from the palace and Eurydice goes to her death there. As a result, the palace will probably be the focus of a stage designer's efforts and will provide the significant 'backdrop' to the events of the play. Since the scene never changes and there is no break in the action, it is important that the impact of the set is felt from the outset.

Given the tragic nature of the play, the designer may decide to make the palace look grey and intimidating. The doors to the palace might be a major feature in the design — perhaps tall, heavy and painted in dark colours. However, the director may prefer the palace to demonstrate the wealth and power of its occupants. Gaudy or ornate decorations could be used to suggest arrogance and over-confidence, as these qualities are demonstrated in Creon's attitudes and behaviour throughout the play.

There is no need for a large amount of detail in the set design, props or costumes in a Greek play. The designer and director might want to preserve some elements of the original staging conditions of Greek theatre, and it should not be assumed that a contemporary audience would ignore these. For example, Nottingham Playhouse's production of *The Burial at Thebes* — an adaptation of *Antigone* by Seamus Heaney (2007) — used a large chorus, a plain set and simple, traditional costume. The lack of obvious attempts to 'update' the story meant that the audience focused on the interplay between characters. No props or other clues as to any particular era were used, and although some features of Greek theatre were used, these were very simple and did not impose a specific historical context.

Costume and make-up

Costume design and the use of make-up are as important as set design. They influence how the status and personality of a character are conveyed as well as how they move and interact with others.

Inevitably, the era in which the production is set will have a fundamental impact on decisions about costume, but so too will characterisation. Antigone and Ismene are sisters and princesses, but they have opposing views about the burial of Polynices. Should their costumes be identical or different? If they were to be different, Antigone's costume and make-up could be used to make her appear older or more intense than Ismene, for example, with a darker or plainer costume to give the impression that she is more mature and resolved.

What costume ideas would you use to realise the chorus? You may — as in original Greek productions — wish to have them looking all the same. However, in a more naturalistic setting, it may be necessary to create a chorus that is representative of the society of Thebes, including women and people of various ages and classes. In such a production, you may want costumes to reflect the variety of the chorus members rather than their uniformity.

Technical features

Lighting

Given that the action in the play is continuous and the set remains unchanged throughout, there is no specific need to blackout or change the lighting at all. However, a variety of lighting effects might be used, depending on the style of the production. Very bright light could emphasise the idea that Polynices' corpse is lying rotting in the sun. This brightness might provide a dramatic contrast to the gloom of the story and the tragic outcome for the characters.

Throughout the play, characters often refer to action that has taken place in the past (e.g. the chorus describes the events that led up to Polynices and Eteocles killing each other). If the director decides to show these events through flashback or mime then lighting could play a specific role here. Seeing an event in a dimmed light or through a colour filter can introduce a sense of surrealism or a dream-like quality. For example, when depicting/describing the deaths of Haemon and Antigone, having a red light fill part of the stage would make the atmosphere seem nightmarish and violent. There are many instances during the play when a character makes a long speech and these moments could be enhanced by intensifying the light around the speaker, making him or her the focus for the audience.

Sound

Sound could also play an important role in a production. It can take the form of human or musical sound, and does not necessarily have to involve electronic amplification.

The chorus may contain many people, and the impact of them speaking some of their lines in unison — particularly when they appeal to the gods — would be considerable.

Music may enhance particular moments in the play, although in a simply staged production, especially one that uses traditional staging techniques, amplified music may seem out of place. It is important that the design aspects of the production do not jar with each other. Electronic, discordant music can be highly effective in a modern production, but may seem incongruous in one that relies on more traditional techniques.

Practical considerations

The designer must keep practical considerations in mind when designing the set and the visual effects of the play. The set must offer a safe and uncluttered environment in which the actors can act effectively. For instance, if the director decides to include a large chorus, the set may have to be limited to a series of flats or backdrops to accommodate the number of people on the stage.

Essay questions

1 Give an account of the design ideas you have for the costumes of two major characters in *Antigone*. Give reasons for your choices.
2 What ideas do you have for the set of *Antigone*? How would these ideas help to reflect some of the major themes of the play?
3 Identify how lighting or sound might be used at two key moments in the play. Ensure that your answer is linked to your vision for how the themes in the play would be expressed.

Considerations for the actors

An actor in *Antigone* will face a number of challenges. Many of these depend on the style of production and the aims of the director. Much will also depend on the size of the chorus and the design of the set and its proximity to the audience. However, there are some specific challenges to an actor, regardless of these factors.

Verse speaking

For the main characters, the demands of verse speaking must be addressed. There are a number of translations of this play; the one quoted in this book, by Sir George Young, is in blank (i.e. not rhyming) verse. Young aimed to preserve the feeling of the original Greek as far as possible. He uses somewhat archaic language in the blank-verse dialogues, with more complex vocabulary in the choruses.

Even where a simpler translation in blank verse is used, demands are still made on the actors. Greek theatre can be static, and the listening skills of the audience are tested during the many long speeches. An actor approaching the roles of Creon or Antigone, for example, will need to develop strategies for addressing the verbal challenges of the role. He or she may break down a long speech into smaller sections and work on the meaning of each section before linking all of them together. The actor may also need to spend some rehearsal time working on projection and ensuring that the different stages of the character's personal journey are communicated clearly.

Varying emotional intensity

Although *Antigone* is not a naturalistic play, there are many moments when characters express emotion. The characters are, at different times, enraged, passionate, heartbroken, resolved, panic-stricken and guilty. There is little subtlety about the characters' emotions or the way they are expressed, but the actors must think about how to express them.

Jonathan Hyde as Creon in *Antigone*, Old Vic Theatre, London, 1999; written and directed by Declan Donnellan

TopFoto

Creon

The danger with Creon is that the character's constant reaffirmation of power and authority and outrage at being contradicted or disobeyed could lead to the actor giving a one-dimensional performance, during which he simply shouts a great deal. It is important for the actor to look carefully for clues in the script that might enable him to vary the performance. For example Creon says:

[…] These orders from the first some people
Hardly accepted, murmuring at me,
Shaking their heads in secret, stiffening
Uneasy necks against these yokes of mine.
They have suborned these sentinels to do it,
I know that well.   (p. 12, ll. 345–50)

This is an angry and megalomaniacal speech, but also one that borders on the paranoid. The suspicion Creon feels about his own countrymen can be expressed without recourse to shouting or over-projection. The actor might even choose to express this in a low and accusatory tone — perhaps directed towards members of the chorus.

It is vital for the actor playing Creon to observe the potential for shifts of tone offered by the text, and to emphasise any change of mood.

Antigone

The actor playing Antigone has a similar problem to that of the actor playing Creon. There are many instances where she laments her fate and expresses distress at her imminent and early death. There is a danger that the audience's sympathy for her may become weakened if the constant expression of her fears, emotions and outrage becomes tedious to listen to.

The actor will need to find the shifts of emphasis in the text so that the range of Antigone's emotions can be observed. Her mood alters from outrage at the beginning of the play (when she explains to Ismene what has happened to Polynices' body) to calm resolve in the face of Creon's wrath and finally to heartbroken distress — but not cowardice — as she confronts the reality of her imminent death.

The range of emotion is, therefore, quite complex and the actor needs to use rehearsals to prepare adequately for these challenges. (The techniques used by Konstantin Stanislavski — discussed in detail in chapter 5 — may be relevant here.) However it is interpreted, an actor will need to consider the most appropriate way not only to communicate the emotion, but also to develop rehearsal techniques to create that emotion in the first place.

Ensemble acting

Antigone relies on ensemble acting. The requirement for a chorus means that a large number of people could be cast, and the action is continuous. Therefore, trust needs to exist between the actors. Trust is important in any production, but perhaps more so when actors are chorusing the same lines and when (depending on the director's interpretation) there is a need to create physical images using only each other.

It is essential that actors work closely and in synchronicity to create a well-timed and coordinated piece of theatre. The actors may well be talented as individuals, but becoming a polished ensemble still requires careful and extensive rehearsal. Moreover, the company of actors would need to develop ideas for rehearsal techniques to help create the ensemble.

Double casting

Some characters would have been double cast in an ancient Greek performance. In a modern production the same device might be used. Alternatively, some of the minor characters such as Eurydice might be played by chorus members.

Summary

♦ *Antigone* is an ancient Greek tragedy. There are some conventions of ancient Greek theatre — such as the number of actors and use of ensemble playing in the chorus — which may still be relevant to a modern production.
♦ The play has a number of striking themes:
   – the rights of a ruler
   – the impact of religion on the behaviour of the individual
   – the rights to protest and disobey the law
   – the use and abuse of power by a ruler
   – the dilemma of loyalty to an individual against loyalty to a principle or idea
This list is not exhaustive and there are many other themes that you may think of. However, aspects of these themes should be reflected in a production of the play.

Discussion questions

1 How might you use your voice to express Creon's response to the Guard's information in the early part of the play?
2 How might an actor playing Antigone develop the emotion needed to express the fear of the character immediately before her final exit?

Essay questions

1 What rehearsal techniques might you attempt with the actors in the chorus in order to help them form an ensemble? Answer with specific reference to one or more of the major chorus speeches.
2 As a director, how would you arrive at a concept for your production of *Antigone*?
3 What value does a play that is more than 2,000 years old have to an audience in the twenty-first century?
4 In common with other plays of this era, there are no scene changes and the action is continuous. What opportunities and challenges does this create for designers?
5 The play is characterised by many long speeches. What techniques might be used by an actor to help prepare for these speeches?

Chapter 3

The Taming of the Shrew

by Shakespeare

Background

Scholars consider this to be one of Shakespeare's earlier plays. A play called *The Taming of a Shrew* was published in 1594 (the 1594 Quarto), and if this is assumed to be a version of Shakespeare's play rather than a source for it, then his play probably pre-dates 1592; from that year onwards theatres in London closed for long periods because of the plague. However, some scholars have suggested that the 1594 version of the *Shrew* is a badly printed text of an older play that formed Shakespeare's source: it includes the duping of Christopher Sly, the 'taming' of Kate, and a variation on the Bianca sub-plot. There is no firm evidence for a more precise date for the play, but the version you study was first published in 1623 (the 1623 Folio) and seems to have been set straight from a manuscript copy, perhaps a transcript by a scribe that retained some marks of Shakespeare's working manuscript.

Inn yard theatres

Before the major theatre-building programme in the late sixteenth century in England, plays were often performed in the courtyards of inns. The architecture of Elizabethan theatres owed much to these origins, with their balconies and central open space for performance. Some inn yards were converted into permanent theatres and existed alongside the larger, more established playhouses. Even high-profile companies used inn yards — for example, the Queen's Men performed at both the Bell Inn and the Bel Savage Inn. The use of scenery and artificial lighting in such theatres was rare.

Elizabethan theatres in London

The theatres that staged Shakespeare's plays were probably like the Swan Theatre in 1596 (see below).

The stage area of an Elizabethan theatre was covered by a canopy and supported by columns. The wall at the back of the stage would have had a number of openings — probably three — with a prominent entrance for royal or high-ranking characters in the middle. The structure at the back of the stage (the equivalent of the *skene* in Greek theatre) was known as the 'tiring house' and was where costumes and props were stored and where actors dressed themselves

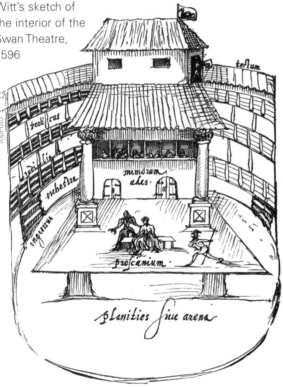

Johannes de Witt's sketch of the interior of the Swan Theatre, 1596

before a performance. The ceiling of the stage was often referred to as 'the heavens' and sometimes decorated with stars.

Seating surrounded the stage in tiered galleries, while the area in front of the stage housed the 'groundlings' — poorer audience members who would pay an entrance fee of one penny. Richer patrons would sit in the covered galleries, paying as much as half a crown for their seats. It is supposed that nobles sat on the stage, nearer to the actors. It seems, therefore, that audience composition was representative of London society. Although the early theatres had part of the stage covered, they were still reliant on good weather and natural light if the audience were to enjoy the performance to the full. However, fully indoor theatres did exist at this time; the boys' company of St Paul's performed in a private theatre — seating only about 200 people — within the precincts of St Paul's Cathedral.

Elizabethan theatre companies

Towards the end of the sixteenth century, two major theatre companies emerged in London: the Lord Chamberlain's Men and the Admiral's Men. The former company was housed initially at a theatre in Shoreditch, then the Curtain Theatre, and later in the Globe, while the Admiral's Men performed in the Rose. Shakespeare joined the Lord Chamberlain's Men as both an actor and a playwright.

It was common for the actors in a theatre company also to part-own it — underwriting the costs and sharing the profits. As the number of theatres increased, so the competition between the companies intensified, and the need to find a playwright with the ability to write a successful drama was essential. *The Taming of the Shrew* would have needed to attract an audience, and its ostensible theme may have been chosen to draw people in.

Elizabethan actors

In *The Oxford Illustrated History of Theatre* (ed. J. R. Brown, 2001), Peter Thomson suggests that the number of players needed to perform in a play during the late sixteenth century rose from around 12 to 16 people. Even so, this would indicate that some doubling of roles was commonplace throughout the century, especially in those theatres where finances were under strain.

In the Elizabethan era, a number of leading actors emerged. Edward Alleyn (1566–1626) was arguably the greatest actor in Elizabethan England, rivalled only by Richard Burbage. Alleyn dominated the London theatre during the 1590s with his performances of Marlowe's great roles. A number of Marlowe's plays such as *Doctor Faustus* (1592), *Tamburlaine* (1587) and *The Jew of Malta* (*c.* 1590) feature a strong principal character who is central to most of the action and appears in nearly every scene. However, although Shakespeare's plays often have a single leading character, many of his plays also contain a number of other pivotal characters. In *Julius Caesar*, for example, Caesar, Brutus, Cassius and Antony are all, arguably, leading roles. This feature is connected with the ethos of the Elizabethan theatre company and the ways in which the group of actors would have grown and matured in their work together. This requirement for group work is evident in the construction of *The Taming of the Shrew*, where there is more than one 'leading' character, and the supporting roles are given a considerable degree of individuality and influence.

Outline of the plot
Act I

The play begins with a drunken tailor, Christopher Sly, being ejected from an alehouse on account of his rowdy behaviour. After he passes out, a group of noblemen decide to play a trick on him. They take him to one of their houses, dress him in finery and when he comes round pretend that he is a nobleman who has lost his memory. Utterly bewildered by his treatment, Sly begins to watch a play that has been provided for his amusement.

The play commences. Lucentio, a young noble, and his servant Tranio arrive in Padua from Florence. They witness an argument in the street between two sisters — Katherina (Kate) and Bianca Minola and their father, Baptista. The argument concerns two other noblemen, Hortensio and the aged Gremio, who are desperate to marry Bianca. However, Baptista makes it clear that no one may woo his younger daughter until his elder daughter is married. The problem is that his elder daughter, Kate, is regarded as a 'shrew' — hot tempered and unmanageable — and she has no obvious suitors. Baptista declares that he will allow no man but a tutor access to Bianca. Lucentio has by now fallen in love with Bianca and resolves to disguise himself as a teacher. His servant, Tranio, disguises himself as his master, as Lucentio is expected in Padua.

Petruchio arrives with his servant Grumio. He is looking for a wealthy wife and is encouraged by his friend, Hortensio, to pursue Kate. Hortensio warns Petruchio about Kate's nature but that does not deter Petruchio. Hortensio persuades Petruchio to take him along to the Minola house where he too is introduced as a tutor. Gremio and Tranio — also in love with Bianca — join the group.

The plot of *The Taming of the Shrew* in context

Both the 'beggar transported into luxury' and the 'shrewish wife' are traditional elements of ballads and folk tales. They are also elements of Classical comedy: the Roman comedies of playwrights Plautus (*c*. 251–184 BC) and Terence (*c*. 190–158 BC) in turn influenced Italian Renaissance plays. Shakespeare's treatment of the courtship of Bianca follows a pattern from one of these plays, Ludovico Ariosto's *I Suppositi* (1509), which was translated into English by George Gascoigne as *Supposes* in 1566.

On the face of it, *The Taming of the Shrew* proposes that a desirable woman is quiet and submissive, and women who are spirited must be 'tamed' through physical and mental abuse. In Shakespeare's time, it was commonly believed that a man was by right of natural order the head of his household, and the laws of succession to the throne of England (which still exist) meant that a son would always assume the title 'King' over an older sister. Although at the time the play was written Elizabeth I was Queen of England (and therefore Head of State), her much younger brother Edward reigned as King Edward VI, before his early death opened the succession to his half sisters, Mary and Elizabeth. It is necessary to bear this in mind when investigating the themes of the play, because close study of the text suggests the possibility of a much more complicated and ironic interpretation of what is happening than first appears. Is Bianca actually the dominant partner in her relationship at the end? Is Kate really subdued or are she and Petruchio just playing a game with society's expectations? Is it all 'only a play'?

Act II

Bianca and Kate are fighting because Kate believes her sister to be the more favoured daughter. Baptista tells Petruchio that he is allowed to marry Kate once he wins her love. The various 'tutors' arrive and are allowed access to Bianca. Kate and Petruchio meet and exchange lively insults. However, Petruchio passes this off as her public behaviour. He assures everyone that she is loving and gentle in private and that they are going to get married on Sunday. Baptista is happy with this outcome and so turns his attention to the question of who will marry Bianca. Tranio — disguised as Lucentio — is his first choice provided he can produce proof of his wealth. However, Bianca clearly prefers the real Lucentio — disguised as a tutor called Cambio.

Vanessa Redgrave as Kate and Derek Godfrey as Petruchio in *The Taming of the Shrew*, Aldwych Theatre, London, 1961

Act III

On Kate's wedding day Petruchio fails to arrive. When he eventually does appear, he is dressed inappropriately and behaves in an extreme and aggressive manner. Once married, he takes Kate away, not allowing her to attend her own wedding reception. They argue for the entire journey and when they arrive at Petruchio's house, Kate is exhausted and hungry. However, to prolong her suffering further, Petruchio refuses to allow her eat anything on the grounds that it is not good enough for her. Furthermore, he is dissatisfied with the state of the beds so she is not allowed to sleep either.

Hortensio realises that Bianca favours Lucentio (as Cambio) over him and angrily declares his intention of marrying a wealthy widow. Tranio — still disguised as Lucentio — persuades a stranger to impersonate Lucentio's father, Vincentio. He needs his father to prove his wealth. Baptista is convinced by Vincentio's 'proof' and Bianca and the real Lucentio are married in secret.

Act IV

Petruchio's eccentric behaviour continues. He declares that they will return to Padua for Hortensio's wedding feast and that they will dress in finery. However, Petruchio finds fault with the tailor's work and throws all the new clothes away.

He then declares to Kate that they will return to Padua and will arrive at noon. When Kate contradicts him and says they will arrive at night he insists that she agree with him before they are allowed to leave. On the journey, he declares the sun to be the moon and will not allow the party to continue on its way until Kate agrees with him. Petruchio's mind control seems to have worked when they meet the real Vincentio (an old man) and he refers to him as a young woman. Kate does not attempt to contradict and agrees that he is, indeed, a young woman — much to the consternation on Vincentio and Hortensio.

Photostage

Sian Thomas as Kate and Alfred Molina as Petruchio in *The Taming of the Shrew*, RSC Regional Tour, 1985/86

Act V

When Vincentio arrives in Padua the various deceptions are discovered and the characters' true identities are recognised. A celebration is held for the three marriages: Petruchio and Kate, Lucentio and Bianca and Hortensio and the widow. At the end of the feast, the women withdraw and the men discuss the relative merits of an obedient wife. They bet each other that they have the most obedient wife and will prove it by each man sending for his wife. Bianca refuses to come, as does the widow. However, Kate arrives and speaks at some length on the importance of a woman being obedient and dutiful to her husband.

Considerations for the director

The Taming of the Shrew is a popular play today (and we might therefore assume that it would have been so for contemporary audiences). The Royal Shakespeare Company (RSC) claims — on the basis of its box office takings — that it is the second most popular of Shakespeare's plays.

This popularity could be explained partly because of the varied opportunities offered for interpretation. Just as with Greek tragedy, Shakespeare's work does not have to be set in the time of its original realisation. Michael Bogdanov's production in 1978 started with Christopher Sly in modern dress behaving like a drunk off the street who was determined to destroy the set. In 2003, Phyllida Lloyd directed an all-female production of the play starring Janet McTeer in the lead male role of Petruchio.

There are many examples of Shakespeare's plays being staged in different eras. An example is the 1995 film version of *Richard III* starring Ian McKellan, in which the character of Richard is reminiscent of a fascist leader and the production values clearly owe much to the pre-war years of the 1930s.

A director of *The Taming of the Shrew* therefore has a complex task. As discussed below, the play can be directed as an energetic farce — almost a sex comedy — or as a play about gender politics. However, a farcical interpretation does not prevent the production from making a statement about gender politics. Farce can help to highlight the ridiculousness of character and situation and, therefore, does not necessarily mean that the important issues of a play are diminished. The Italian playwright Dario Fo (born 1926) built a reputation as a farceur but was clearly a politically motivated playwright, writing controversial works such as *Accidental Death of An Anarchist* (1970) and *Can't Pay Won't Pay* (1974).

Kathryn Hunter as Kate and Janet McTeer as Petruchio, in the all-female production of *The Taming of the Shrew*, Globe Theatre, London, 2003

Issues surrounding the 'taming'

Although the play is a comedy, the theme of a character, particularly a female character, being 'tamed' by a man is controversial today. Some may view the play as sexist or misogynistic, and any director presenting the play in a modern political and cultural context will be aware of the offence that it may cause. After studying the play, you will have your own views on its central theme. However, you should be aware that the decisions made regarding the production will affect an audience's interpretation of the play's themes: the label 'sexist' can be applied as much to the production as to the play itself.

It may be useful to reflect on the following points:

◆ The prologue in which Christopher Sly appears sets up the idea of the play itself being part of a delusion: Sly is duped into believing that he is a nobleman and the whole of the play that follows is shown as part of his delusion. By the end it is possible to have forgotten this, since Sly never reappears after the first scene. Could the director find a way to remind the audience members that they are actually watching a play within a play?

♦ There are many other examples from Shakespeare of female characters who are far from weak or malleable. For example, Lady Macbeth is much more concerned to fulfil the predictions of the witches and murder Duncan than Macbeth is. Lear's daughters — all of whom come into conflict with their father at different points of the play — are strong and determined characters. In view of the fact that Shakespeare created strong-minded female characters in his other plays, is it appropriate to label this particular work 'sexist'? On the other hand, this play is one of Shakespeare's earliest plays and many of his 'great' female roles had yet to be written.

♦ Is Bianca as sweet and innocent as her suitors believe her to be? If she is the model of a good wife, why does she not come when Lucentio sends for her at the end of the play?

♦ The play is unquestionably a comedy. The character of Kate displays a number of unreasonable and intemperate qualities, particularly in regard to her treatment of her sister. It could be argued that both she and Petruchio are extreme characters designed to serve comic functions, and thus are not meant to be taken seriously. A director could decide to play this comedy in such a way that its farcical construction is brought out.

♦ Although attitudes to women at the time the play was written were extremely different (no women would have acted in the play and few would have been in the audience) it should be borne in mind that there was a female Head of State (Elizabeth I) at the time of the play's original production. Given her support of the theatre, it seems unlikely that Shakespeare would have risked incurring her wrath by creating a play that ridiculed women and seriously advocated their 'taming'.

♦ The central character is often seen as the 'hero' of the play and it is expected that we, the audience, will sympathise with him to a certain extent, in spite of his weaknesses. This is certainly true of other flawed Shakespearean characters such as Hamlet, Lear, Hal/Henry V, or Falstaff. However, in *The Taming of the Shrew* there is no reason for the audience to identify or agree with the principal character, Petruchio. His behaviour is eccentric and extreme and, although we may feel he is pretending to be mad in order to 'tame' his wife, his motives in marrying her — at the outset of the play — seem to be largely commercial. He says to Hortensio:

[…] if thou know
One rich enough to be Petruchio's wife —
As wealth is burden of my wooing dance —
Be she as foul as was Florentius' love,
As old as Sibyl and as curst and shrewd

As Socrates' Xanthippe, or a worse,
She moves me not, or not removes, at least,
Affection's edge in me, were she as rough
As are the swelling Adriatic seas.
I come to wive it wealthily in Padua;
If wealthily, then happily in Padua.

(*William Shakespeare, Complete Works*,
ed. Bate and Rasmussen, Macmillan/RSC 2007, I.2.60–70)

Petruchio should not necessarily be seen as the 'hero' of the play. How he is presented by the director will influence how the sentiments of the play are communicated. A clownish, eccentric Petruchio will support the notion that his actions should not be taken seriously or be seen as a credible way to treat women.

♦ The final speech in which Kate discusses the importance of obedience does not have to be delivered 'straight'. It is an extreme evocation of female duty, particularly towards the end of the speech:

My mind hath been as big as one of yours,
My heart as great, my reason haply more,
To bandy word for word and frown for frown;
But now I see our lances are but straws,
Our strength as weak, our weakness past compare,
That seeming to be most which we indeed least are.   (V.1.182–87)

Again, the director and actor could interpret this speech to demonstrate an irony in Kate's words — indicating that she realises what she is saying is ludicrously extravagant.

Whether or not *The Taming of the Shrew* is a sexist play is open to discussion, and anyone directing it needs to evaluate his or her own views on the subject. While *Antigone* is a play with political impact, it is debatable whether *The Taming of the Shrew* is about gender politics or simply a comical farce that uses a battle-of-the-sexes scenario to deliver slapstick entertainment.

Developing themes and ideas

In her production of *The Taming of the Shrew* at The Globe in 2003, Phyllida Lloyd used sixteenth-century costuming and staging (in the reconstructed Globe) — a simulation of the setting of the first performance. However, her use of an all-female company offered a far from traditional interpretation, as the *Daily Telegraph* reviewer noted:

Lloyd is a director with an infectious sense of fun, and the mere fact that all the men here are played by women highlights the absurdities of the male of the species without any need of overt editorialising.

(*Daily Telegraph*, 23 August 2003)

Context

The context of the production (the time in which the play is set) may assist in the development of ideas and themes. A production does not necessarily have to be set in a specific era. If the production is focused on the farcical elements of the play, a director may feel that a timeless quality may be appropriate and he or she may choose, for example, to concentrate on the physical aspects of the comedy.

Physical interpretation

There are a number of scenes that rely on physical interaction and where comic timing and physical skills are important.

The argument between Petruchio and Kate, which dominates the middle of the first scene of Act II, is full of witty word-play and banter. The couple exchange a series of one-liners, each trying to outdo the other. As Petruchio's objective here is to woo Kate and her objective is to reject him, there is the potential for a 'chase' type of movement sequence.

Petruchio: Why, what's a moveable?
Katherina: A joint stool.
Petruchio: Thou hast hit it: come, sit on me.
Katherina: Asses are made to bear, and so are you.
Petruchio: Women are made to bear, and so are you.
Katherina: No such jade as you, if me you mean.
Petruchio: Alas! good Kate, I will not burden thee,
For knowing thee to be but young and light —
Katherina: Too light for such a swain as you to catch,
And yet as heavy as my weight should be.   (II.1.196–205)

This is a fiery and swift exchange, and a director will want to ensure that the physical movement matches the pace of the dialogue.

A moment later, in the middle of their argument, Kate actually strikes Petruchio:

Petruchio: What, with my tongue in your tail? Nay, come again.
Good Kate; I am a gentleman.

Katherina: That I'll try. *[She strikes him]*
Petruchio: I swear I'll cuff you, if you strike again.   (II.1.218–21)

This moment in their exchange specifies a particular physical action — that of Kate striking Petruchio. Petruchio could mirror this action by physically threatening to strike her back as well as verbally doing so.

Using mistaken identity

This play — along with some other Shakespeare comedies, especially *The Comedy of Errors* (*c.* 1594) and *Twelfth Night* (1601) — contains classic scenes of mistaken identity. However improbable this seems, by simply adding an extra garment, characters are mistakenly believed to be different people. We see this in the scenes where Bianca's suitors disguise themselves as tutors in order to pursue her. We also see it where a passing stranger is persuaded to disguise himself as Vincentio and where Tranio disguises himself as Lucentio. The rapid exchange of garments that takes place in order to affect these disguises emphasises the farcical nature of the play. This important element in the action needs to be addressed by the director.

Using ensemble acting

Despite being a very different type of play to *Antigone*, *The Taming of the Shew* still requires a director to create a sense of ensemble acting (see Chapter 2 page 41). The scenes where many characters gather on stage, and where there is much movement, require careful direction and specific staging skills.

Using 'chase' routines

In Act V scene 1, where the cases of mistaken identity and the various plot twists are resolved, there are several instances of characters entering and exiting the stage quickly and from a variety of entrances. This kind of farcical chase routine is to be found in many other plays and types of comedy, including *commedia dell'arte*, a form of improvised comedy originating from Italy in the sixteenth century.

Using stereotyped characters

Commedia dell'arte was built around a series of well-known storylines and stereotyped characters (e.g. the fussy old pedant, and the resourceful servant who makes a fool of the master). Some of the characters in *The Taming of the Shrew* echo these stereotypes (e.g. the character who is persuaded to disguise himself as Vincentio is called a 'pedant', and Tranio is a 'resourceful servant' character). Therefore, elements of traditional comedy craftsmanship can be found in this play, and the director should explore the possibilities they present.

The director's task

A director must address a number of key issues connected with this controversial play. Is it appropriate for a twenty-first-century production to seem to support a 'sexist' philosophy? An audience may perceive a production as such unless it highlights the farcical nature of the play or finds ways of presenting an ironic interpretation. However, if a director becomes too 'hidebound' by the politics of the play, he or she may not focus sufficiently on the comic nature of the piece. The play is still popular precisely because it makes audiences laugh. A successful production will be one where the actors have been well rehearsed in developing the comic potential of their characters and their situations.

Discussion question

Make thorough notes on the points that arise from your consideration of the following question, either from discussion or your own observations.

What advice might you give to an actor playing Kate in the delivery of her final speech? Think especially about how you want an audience to respond to it.

Essay question

Describe how you might stage Act V, scene 1 of *The Taming of the Shrew*. Pay particular attention to the entrances and exits of characters, and explain their significance.

Considerations for the designer

This play takes place in a number of different areas — some of them indoors and others outdoors. Given that the play, in places, is a fast moving farce, the designer must ensure that there are no delays between scene changes.

Set design

In an original production, scene changes would have been minimal, suggested merely by the addition or removal of simple furniture. Today, the design needs to reflect the social and historical context in which the play is set.

The design can influence the comic impact of the piece: for example, a setting that uses garish colours and bright lighting could lend a sense of fun to the production. The set could contain a variety of entrances and exits to reflect the way the characters hurry on and off the stage in the tradition of a farce; indeed, the play contains references to different doors in Baptista's house and windows where certain characters are 'revealed'. Overall, the set must allow the audience to appreciate the full 'chase and final revelation' sequence that provides part of the climax to the play.

Costume and make-up

There is comic potential in the design of the costumes. This is particularly true with the 'disguises' the characters use. The suitors disguise themselves as music tutors, the pedant disguises himself as Vincentio, and Tranio disguises himself as Lucentio. The fact that the other characters in the play are convinced by the transformations while the audience is not could produce comic moments of dramatic irony. The disguises could be made to appear ridiculous to the audience, perhaps reflecting, for instance, the academic credentials of the 'tutors'.

Bianca's suitors disguised as musicians in *The Taming of the Shrew*, RSC, Courtyard Theatre, Stratford-upon-Avon, 2008. Sean Kearns (Hortensio), Amara Karan (Bianca) and Patrick Moy (Lucentio)

The costuming of Kate and Petruchio will depend — as with all the costumes — on the style and era of the production. However, there are specific requirements of both characters' appearances at particular moments. In Act III scene 2, when Petruchio enters to marry Kate, his dress has already been described by Biondello as:

[...] a new hat, and an old jerkin: a pair of old breeches thrice turned; a pair of boots that have been candle cases, one buckled, another laced [...]   (III.2.40–41)

The impact of Petruchio's appearance in the wedding scene should be a comic and outlandish one. Therefore, whatever the historic setting of the production, due heed should be paid to the nature of Petruchio's costume in order for it to reinforce the outrageous nature of his behaviour.

Later in Act IV scene 1, Petruchio dismisses the tailor and haberdasher, who are supposed to provide the wedding garments for him and Kate as they prepare to attend Bianca's wedding. The implication is that he is forcing her to attend her sister's wedding in ragged and old clothes. As Petruchio says:

[...] We will unto your father's
Even in these honest mean habiliments:
Our purses shall be proud, our garments poor
[...]   (IV.1.162–64)

It is important for the full impact of his statement to become clear that over the subsequent journey taken by Kate and Petruchio their clothes show a steady deterioration. This could be achieved by providing the actors playing Kate and Petruchio with two costumes each, one a ragged and soiled version of the other. This costuming will enable the actors to convey the inappropriateness of their dress for a wedding, as well as Petruchio's increasingly eccentric behaviour.

Technical features

Lighting

The action takes place in different locations and at varying times. The lighting should reflect the place and physical nature of the environment, and also influence the mood of the play by providing for a 'sunny' atmosphere or a darker moment.

Sound

Music is often used to accompany comic episodes in drama. You may wish to reflect on the relationship between comic chase sequences and music in early twentieth-century silent movies. Is there scope for music to be used in a similar way here? Does there need to be a theme running through the production, or could characters have particular themes attached to them to punctuate their appearances or give the audience a sense of anticipation as they appear?

Live or recorded music could also be used to heighten the intensity of the romantic interludes in the play. The moment when Kate and Petruchio finally kiss may present an opportunity for the use of more romantic music, as may the moment when the conflict between them is finally resolved. Much depends on the director's interpretation of the final scene of the play, but romantic music might accompany Kate's final speech. However, such an accompaniment would perhaps be unsuitable if the director wished to present the speech as a piece of irony.

Essay questions

1 Describe the features needed on a set of *The Taming of the Shrew* to enable the comic potential of the play to be realised. Answer with reference to one scene specifically.

2 What opportunities might there be to use lighting in *The Taming of the Shrew* to move from one scene to another? Answer with reference to two scenes where the location and/or the time of day changes.

3 How might music enhance a production of *The Taming of the Shrew*? Where in particular might music help to articulate the mood or feeling of the play? Answer with reference to two particular moments in the play.

Considerations for an actor

The timing and delivery of the comedy in *The Taming of the Shrew* rely on the skills of the actor being employed to realise the director's vision. However, there are a number of important issues that the actors themselves need to address.

Petruchio

An actor playing the part of Petruchio faces many challenges. The character is neither essentially heroic nor downright villainous. While Petruchio is motivated by money and indulges in some extreme behaviour in his 'taming' of Kate, an actor cannot approach this role simply from the perspective that Petruchio is a 'bad' man. The actor must create a compelling relationship between Petruchio and Kate, time comedy well, and keep and focus the audience's attention.

When the audience first meets him, he has arrived in Padua with his servant. There is some confusion as Petruchio instructs his servant to 'knock' for his friend Hortensio:

Petruchio: Verona, for a while I take my leave,
To see my friends in Padua; but of all
My best beloved and approved friend,
Hortensio, and I trow this is his house.
Here, sirrah Grumio, knock, I say.
Grumio: Knock, sir! Whom should I knock? Is there any man has rebused your worship?
Petruchio: Villain, I say, knock me here soundly.
Grumio: Knock you here, sir! Why, sir, what am I, sir, that I should knock you here, sir?
Petruchio: Villain, I say, knock me at this gate
And rap me well, or I'll knock your knave's pate.
Grumio: My master is grown quarrelsome. I should knock you first,
And then I know after who comes by the worst.
Petruchio: Will it not be?
Faith, sirrah, an you'll not knock, I'll ring it;
I'll try how you can *sol-fa*, and sing it.
[He wrings him by the ears]

(I.2.1–17)

Comic violence in master–servant relationships

The relationship between Grumio and Petruchio, as shown above in the opening of Act I scene 2, is reminiscent of the relationship that John Cleese's Basil Fawlty has with his hapless servant Manuel in the 1970s BBC television series, *Fawlty Towers*. (Perhaps it is no conicidence that Cleese later played Petruchio in the BBC version of *The Taming of the Shrew* in 1980, directed by Jonathan Miller.)

Another master–servant relationship that includes comic violence is the one between Rowan Atkinson's Blackadder and his stupid but loyal servant Baldrick in the *Blackadder* television series.

In traditional Italian comedy or *commedia*, the servant character — Arlecchino or Pedrolino — may be similarly bullied, but he is usually given the ability to behave resourcefully and often outsmarts his tyrannical masters.

Thus, at an early stage in the play the audience understands that Petruchio can be violent, but that the impact of his violence will probably be comic. In approaching this scene, the actor must consider the likely impact his first appearance will have and the way in which he wishes to perform this early example of quite aggressive behaviour.

Although Petruchio's initial motives for choosing to woo Kate are ostensibly financial, the actor must ask himself whether those feelings change and whether, during the course of the play, he falls in love with her. The actor playing Kate must also ask the same question. Does Kate fall in love with Petruchio (we know by the end of the play she is obedient to him, assuming the final speech is played 'straight') and if so, at what point in the play does this happen? Can we be sure that a loving relationship exists between the two main characters by the end of the play? In Petruchio's final speech at the end of Act III scene 3, there is a suggestion that his feelings towards Kate are becoming more tender. It is clear that his outrage at the apparent negligence of his servants is an act and all part of his technique to 'tame the shrew'. He says:

Ay, and amid this hurly I intend
That all is done in reverend care of her.
And in conclusion she shall watch all night,
And if she chance to nod I'll rail and brawl
And with the clamour keep her still awake.
This is a way to kill a wife with kindness   (III.3.166–71)

The statement that 'all is done in reverend care of her' indicates that his fondness for Kate is genuine. His belief that he set on a path to 'kill a wife with kindness' suggests that his motives may be 'kind' even if his practice is barbaric. If the actor decides that by the time Petruchio makes this speech he is already in love with Kate then it will clearly influence how the speech is delivered. It forms a contemplative, quiet conclusion to an otherwise violent scene in which Petruchio has made several aggressive outbursts towards his servants. The scene provides a rare moment when we see Petruchio in a reflective mood, unobserved by other characters. This challenges an actor to draw the audience's attention to a more complex interpretation of Petruchio's motives and feelings towards Kate.

Kate

For the actor playing Kate, the challenge is no less great but is of a different nature. If we accept that the character has an irrational and volatile temper, can we identify a reason for it? When we first meet Kate in Act I, her father is explaining to Bianca's would-be suitors that until Kate is married Bianca cannot be courted. He then invites either Hortensio or Gremio to court Kate instead. Gremio says, in an aside, that he would rather 'cart' her.

There is a sense of the public humiliation involved for Kate, as she is almost bartered by her father. Baptista then tells Bianca to go into the house and not to let his decision displease her because:

[…] I will love thee ne'er the less my girl.   (I.1.77)

He expresses no such loving sentiments towards his elder daughter. The actor playing the role of Kate must consider the differences in Baptista's treatment of his two daughters and think about whether Kate behaves in an aggressive way to mask her vulnerability. Another interpretation is that Baptista may prefer

Bianca simply because he is exasperated by his elder daughter's continuous caustic and hostile behaviour. The actors and director must consider whether Kate's behaviour is a response to the favouritism of her father, or whether her father's favouritism is a response to Kate's behaviour. The answer to this question could lead to markedly different interpretations in the portrayal of the character.

Understanding Shakespeare's references

Actors in a production of *The Taming of the Shrew* (and indeed any play by Shakespeare) would be well-advised to use a text with authoritative footnotes which provide explanations of the significance or meaning of the language. The RSC always uses authoritative texts.

For instance:

Gremio: To cart her, rather. She's too rough for me.   (I.1.55)

In Elizabethan times, a prostitute was punished by being dragged through the streets on a cart.

Kate: I pray you, sir, is it your will
To make a stale of me amongst these mates?   (I.1.57–58)

The word 'stale' as used in Shakespeare's time meant bait, laughing stock or prostitute (and it also puns on the chess term 'stalemate').

Tranio: That wench is stark mad or wonderful froward.   (I.1.69)

The phrase 'wonderful froward' means 'remarkably obstinate'.

(from *William Shakespeare*, Complete Works,
ed. Bate and Rasmussen, Macmillan/RSC 2007)

In Act 2 scene 1 the tension between the two sisters is expressed violently. Kate has tied Bianca's hands and is trying to get her to confess which of her two suitors (Gremio and Hortensio) she prefers. When Bianca says she has not seen any man she wants, Kate strikes her in frustration. The actors need to consider whether the conflict between the sisters is borne out of Kate's jealousy and resentment of Bianca (fuelled by the insults of men and her father's apparent lack of care) or is the result of Kate's violent and irrational disposition. While it is difficult to excuse Kate's extreme actions in this scene, it may be possible to find reasons for them. The actor must consider her motivations as part of the preparation for the role.

The moment when Petruchio and Kate feel mutual attraction for each other is open to interpretation. Although in their first meeting Petruchio's attempts to woo Kate are spurned by a barrage of insults, there is a sense that the word play they engage in displays the couple's enjoyment of the situation. Shakespeare uses this device of a couple trading witticisms and insults in another of his comedies, *Much Ado About Nothing* (*c.* 1598). In this play, the characters Beatrice and Benedick tell themselves that they dislike one other intensely, but eventually realise they have fallen in love. The point at which there is a genuine attraction between Petruchio and Kate is important, since this will inform the actors' choices in later scenes. It will also influence the way Kate makes her final speech. Is it a genuine submission from a lovestruck and fulfilled young woman who has truly been 'tamed' or is it a piece of sarcasm, delivered with bitterness and irony?

Summary

- While a comedy, *The Taming of the Shrew* has a controversial theme and many judge it to be sexist. A director needs to consider this point when identifying a production concept. However, the comic (almost farcical) nature of the play means that the characters do not have to be taken seriously in their extreme antics.
- The play affords moments of physical humour which need careful choreographing or staging.
- The play can be set in any historical or social context — or, indeed, some design choices might give the play a timeless quality. Its non-naturalistic style allows the production to be flexible. However, the choices must be made with care and with due heed to the comic nature of the play.
- The language of the play may well provide a challenge for the actors. This should be addressed by the director early in rehearsals.

Discussion question

Make thorough notes on the points that arise from your consideration of the following question, either from discussion or your own observations.

If you were playing the part of Kate, what choices would you make vocally and physically in Act 2 scene 1, to demonstrate the character's feelings towards Petruchio?

Essay questions

1 There is much physical humour in *The Taming of the Shrew*. As an actor playing Petruchio, how would you meet the physical challenges of the role? Answer with reference to a specific scene in the play.

2 As a director, how would you deal with the potential accusation of sexism that might be expressed towards a production of the play by a contemporary audience?

3 As an actor playing Kate in Act II scene 1, how would you convey — both physically and vocally — the character's feelings towards Petruchio as the scene develops?

4 In Act III scene 1, explain how props and costumes might be used to enhance the comedy as the 'tutors' attempt to woo Bianca.

The Shadow of a Gunman

by Sean O'Casey

The Shadow of a Gunman was written by Sean O'Casey in 1923 and is set in Dublin during the war of independence in 1920. To gain an appreciation of the play it is necessary to understand something of its historical context.

Background

There have been disputes over the sovereignty of Ireland for centuries. Until the twentieth century, the whole of Ireland was part of the UK. However, the Irish uprising in Easter 1916 led to a period of conflict and civil war that lasted until the settlement of 1921, which saw Ireland divided into two parts. The six counties of Ulster stayed with the United Kingdom; these were (and still are) referred to as Northern Ireland. The other 26 counties became the Republic of Ireland.

This situation led to continual unrest in Northern Ireland for the next 80 years. After the compromised resolution of 1921, a struggle for power developed between the Irish Republican Army (IRA) who were legitimised in the eyes of many by the majority Sinn Fein victory in the 1918 general election, and the British army, assisted by police reinforcements.

The strife, bloodshed and bombings that dominated the life of the province for most of the twentieth century finally ended with the Good Friday Peace Agreement in 1998 (with the exception of the Omagh bombing that took place that summer). Northern Ireland is now ruled over by a devolved government involving representatives from both sides of the community — Republican (who want Northern Ireland to be part of a united Ireland) and Loyalist (who want to remain part of the UK).

The Dublin plays

O'Casey wrote three plays about the politics and the fears of people in Ireland between 1915 and 1923: *The Plough and the Stars*, *The Shadow of a Gunman* and *Juno and the Paycock*. O'Casey was an admirer of Shakespeare's history plays, but although his own plays could also be described as 'histories', they illustrate very different themes: disorder rather than order, labouring men struggling with democracy rather than kings struggling with leadership, and decentralised rather than centralised power.

The Shadow of a Gunman is set in Dublin in 1920, during the post-1916 civil war that eventually led to the division of Ireland in 1921. This war was not purely defined by the notion of the British versus the Irish. Many Irish people were loyal to the British; for example, the character Adolphus Grigson makes it clear that he is an 'Orangeman' (someone loyal to the cause of William of Orange, who led the 'Glorious Revolution' against the Catholic King of England, James II, in 1688). Consequently, the community O'Casey depicts is a complex one — but one united by fear. As Seumas Shields comments in Act II:

Shot in the back to save the British Empire, an' shot in the breast to save the soul of Ireland. I'm a Nationalist meself, right enough [...] I believe in the freedom of Ireland, an' that England has no right to be here, but I draw the line when I hear the gunmen blowin' about dying for the people, when it's the people that are dyin' for the gunmen!

(Act II, p. 40, from *Three Dublin Plays*, Sean O'Casey, Faber & Faber 1998)

Sean O'Casey (1880–1964)

O'Casey was born in Dublin, the youngest of seven surviving children. He had little formal education due to a combination of ill health and poverty, and he worked as a manual labourer until he was over 40 years old. He involved himself both in the struggle for Irish independence and in bettering conditions for the poor. He was secretary of the Irish Citizen Army and wrote for the *Irish Worker*.

Influences on O'Casey

O'Casey's use of apparently easy, natural dialogue and the lack of plot in his plays echo the techniques of naturalism used by playwrights and writers from the nineteenth century, for instance Anton Chekhov (1860–1904) and Henrik Ibsen (1828–96), or French novelist Emile Zola (1840–1902). O'Casey's work reflects his belief, also held by the practitioners of naturalism in drama, that 'environment' controls human 'will'.

The greatest twentieth-century influence on O'Casey was the Dublin-born Irish playwright George Bernard Shaw (1856–1950), whose play *John Bull's Other Island* (1904) changed O'Casey's life when he first read it in about 1912. O'Casey admired Shaw's use of irony and felt that *John Bull's Other Island* depicted the real Ireland rather than a romanticised view of it. He explains this in the introduction to *The Irish Trilogy*. The description of Donal Davoren's character in *The Shadow of a Gunman*, the first of his Dublin plays to be staged, describes him as dedicated to:

> the might of design, the mystery of colour, and the belief in the redemption of all things by beauty everlasting.
>
> (Opening stage directions, Act I)

This is a quotation from Shaw's play *The Doctor's Dilemma* (1906). It reminds readers of the play that O'Casey was not simply reproducing the language of the people around him in documentary fashion; he was conscious of the shape of his work in the artistic sense. Much later in his life, he came to abandon naturalism for a more experimental form:

> To me, what is called naturalism, or even realism, isn't enough. They usually show life at its meanest and commonest, as if life never had time for a dance, a laugh or a song.
>
> (From 'O'Casey's Credo', *New York Times*, 1958)

O'Casey's drama moved towards a form of expressionism, his dialogue tending to a series of word-poems and his plots receiving less emphasis. His anti-war play *The Silver Tassie* (1928) shows this development, and the artistic direction he was moving in is evident in *The Shadow of a Gunman*.

Outline of the plot

The play is divided into two acts, and is set in a room in a tenement building in Dublin. The room is the home of two young men — Seumas Shields (a pedlar), and Donal Davoren (a poet).

Act I

It is 12.30 p.m. and Seumas is only just waking up. He starts to gather together an assortment of cutlery and haberdashery that he is taking out to sell. His roommate, Donal Davoren, sits at his typewriter composing poetry. A man named Maguire, who is supposed to be working with Seumas, arrives and tells him he cannot work that day as he has to go to Knocksedan 'to catch butterflies'. He leaves a bag with the two men and tells them that he will collect it later that evening. They place the bag in a corner of the room.

As Seumas is preparing to leave, there is another knock on the door and the landlord arrives. An argument erupts between Seumas and his landlord because Seumas owes 11 weeks in rent and has sub–let the room to Donal.

After the landlord leaves, Seumas reveals to Donal that the landlord is anxious because, along with many others in the community, he believes Donal to be a gunman on the run.

Seumas: He thinks you're on the run. He's afraid of a raid and that his lovely property'll be destroyed.

Donal: But why, in the name of all that's sensible, should he think that I'm on the run?

Seumas: Sure, they all think you're on the run. Mrs Henderson thinks it. Tommy Owens thinks it, Mr an' Mrs Grigson think it an' Minnie Powell thinks it too.

(Act I, p. 13)

Seumas leaves with his attaché case to do some selling and for a while Donal is alone with his poetic thoughts — he compares himself to the Greek character, Prometheus. A young woman from the tenement, Minnie Powell, comes into the room and asks to borrow a cup of milk. They discuss poetry and music for a while, although it is clear that Minnie does not have much knowledge in these subjects.

Donal quotes one of his poems and Minnie suggests that it was written for a girl. Donal denies this and says that it was written with no one specifically in mind. It is clear that there is an attraction between them but as they go to kiss each other another character, Tommy Owens, enters. Although it is the first time Tommy has met Donal, he speaks to him conspiratorially, as if he is aware that Donal has an important position with the Irish Republican Army (IRA). When Donal denies having any knowledge of the politics of the day, Tommy assures him that he can trust him and that he, Tommy, would be prepared to die for his country. At the height of Tommy's passionate declaration, another neighbour from the tenement, Mrs Henderson, enters and introduces Mr Gallogher. Mrs Henderson is also deeply deferential to Donal, acting as though he is a figure of some authority. She tells Mr Gallogher that Donal can help him with his problem.

Mr Gallogher's problem is presented through a very long-winded discussion and an equally long-winded letter he has written to the IRA. He dislikes the behaviour of his neighbours ('a gang of tramps'), and has

Jane Murphy as Minnie and Aidan McArdle as Donal in *The Shadow of a Gunman*, Tricycle Theatre, London, 2004

TopFoto

decided to turn to the IRA to help him: he requests that they bring their guns to the house. Clearly, the entire neighbourhood believes that Donal is an important figure in the IRA, and that he can solve problems by summoning force.

The news of an ambush in Knocksedan arrives, via Mrs Grigson calling the 'stop press' up to Mrs Henderson. One man by the name of Maguire has been killed. Mr Gallogher leaves the room after giving the letter to Donal. As the stage clears and Donal is left once more with Minnie, he types her name together with his and gives it to her at her request, kissing her as she leaves.

On his own, Donal reflects that Minnie is attracted to him because she thinks he is a gunman, but he recognises that he is attracted to Minnie. As the first act ends, Donal asks himself what danger there can be in 'the shadow of a gunman'.

Act II

Later the same night, Seumas is in bed and Donal is still writing his poetry. Seumas comments that he thinks that Maguire will be sorry that he did not join him in his work since the consequence of the trip to Knocksedan was two bullets through the lungs. The two men argue about the life of a poet, with Seumas arguing that poetry is no preoccupation for a working man:

It doesn't pay a working man to write poetry. […] I think a poet's claim to greatness depends upon his power to put passion in the common people

(Act II, p. 35)

Donal argues:

Ay, passion to howl for his destruction. The People! Damn the people! They live in the abyss, the poet lives on the mountain top […]

(Ibid)

Seumas now announces that he can hear tapping and feels it is a sign of death, especially as only he can hear it. As they prepare to sleep, the sound of gun shots rings out. Their conversation is quickly forgotten as they take stock of the situation.

Mrs Grigson, who lives in the basement of the tenement, enters. She is worried about her husband who is out after the curfew. He arrives a short time later, clearly drunk, and everyone is relieved that he is safe. The sound of a truck is heard outside the tenement. The troops are out in force and Seumas fears that the house could be raided. Panic sets in and Donal remembers the letter addressed to the IRA that Mr Gallogher brought round. He finds it and burns it. Seumas then remembers the bag that Maguire brought that morning. He assumes that it will contain only the goods he sells but Donal checks the bag and discovers that it is full of bombs.

As they panic about what to do, Minnie runs in. She asks Donal what there is in the room that might incriminate them. When he reveals that there is a bag of bombs, she calmly takes them, declaring that the troops might not search her room and even if they do they will not harm a woman. She throws Donal, who is in a state of nervous collapse, a loving glance.

The soldiers break into the tenement and one comes into the room where Seumas and Donal are waiting nervously. He carries a gun and is abusive and threatening. Mrs Grigson appears in distress. She reveals that Mr Grigson's pint bottle of whiskey has been found under his pillow by the rest of the soldiers. This distracts the soldier with Seumas and Donal, who goes off to search Grigson's room.

Mrs Grigson, Seumas and Donal wait anxiously, telling themselves that Minnie's room will not be searched. Then Minnie can be heard off-stage shouting 'bravely but a little hysterically', 'Up the Republic!'

The three of them listen to Minnie being taken away. Then Mrs Grigson runs out to see what is happening. She quickly returns:

Minnie being taken away by the troops, Tricycle Theatre, London, 2004

Mrs Grigson: *(running in)* They're after gettin' a whole lot of stuff in Minnie's room. Enough to blow up the whole street, a Tan says. God tonight, who'd ever have thought that of Minnie Powell?

(Ibid, Act II, p. 58)

Seumas worries that Minnie will say something incriminating, Mr Grigson boasts of his bravery and Donal worries about Minnie being roughly handled. No one does anything.

Next, commotion and gun shots are heard; the army lorry taking Minnie away has been ambushed. Off-stage shouts reveal that Minnie has been shot and killed as she jumped from the lorry, trying to run away.

Donal is appalled by Seumas's fears that their cries of outrage will bring the soldiers back up to the room.

Seumas: For God's sake speak easy, an' don't bring them in here on top of us again.
Donal: Is that all you're thinking of? Do you realize that she has been shot to save us?
Seumas: Is it my fault? Am I to blame?

(Act II, p. 61)

Mrs Grigson mourns helplessly:

[...] poor Minnie Powell, to think of you full of life a few minutes ago, an' now she's dead!

Finally, Donal and Seumas both give their distinctive reactions:

Donal: [...] Oh Davoren, Donal Davoren, poet and poltroon, poltroon and poet!
Seumas: *(solemnly)* I knew something ud come of the tappin' on the wall!

(Act II, p. 62)

Who are the soldiers in *The Shadow of a Gunman*?

The armed men who burst into Seumas and Donal's room are 'Black and Tans' — ex-servicemen from the First World War who were employed as police reinforcements and called upon to assist the British Army. They were also known as 'Auxies'. These men had often been unemployed as a result of the postwar depression and were therefore happy to accept this job. As Seumus says:

'If it's the Tommies, it won't be so bad but if it's the Tans we're going to have a terrible time.' (Act II, p. 53)

The purpose of the raid, by the British Army, was to look for 'Shinners' (Sinn Fein suspects), who were identified with the IRA. Davoren's neighbours think he must be a 'Shinner'. Such raids were commonplace and violent: O'Casey himself experienced one in 1920 and he drew on this when writing *The Shadow of a Gunman*.

Considerations for the director

O'Casey's work was often the subject of controversy and protest because of his refusal to create work that was entirely in favour of the Irish Republican cause. Minnie is killed by people on her own side, and Donal is revered because the characters think he is a gunman — a misapprehension that he does nothing to dispel.

The violent, poverty-stricken world that O'Casey presents us with can make a powerful impact on an audience if the moments of terror and the humour and warmth of the characters are both fully developed to create a striking contrast. The director should bear in mind that, while the play is rich in comic dialogue and characterisation, its playwright described it as a tragedy.

Issues surrounding the setting

Unlike the other two plays discussed in this section, *The Shadow of a Gunman* has to be set in its own social and historical context. It is not possible for the play to 'travel', because it is too naturalistic and contains too many references to a specific time and place. The director's task is to convey the world in which the play is set — a 1920s tenement in Dublin.

Why should a twenty-first-century audience want to know about the events of Dublin in 1920? Why should the strange and often comical array of characters appeal to an audience now? While the issues surrounding Irish sovereignty are not fully resolved, they are of a more peaceful nature than they have been for centuries. Although poverty still exists in Dublin, it is a far more prosperous city than when the play was set or written. The issues presented by the play are, then, surely resolved? Does that make the play obsolete? For the following reasons I would suggest not.

* Modern audiences will be able to appreciate the wider issues raised by the play: the implications of the use of terrorism to overturn political systems; the danger of military organisations who are stronger than their state; the inability of most people to see beyond their own immediate concerns, even in matters of life and death (Donal thinks he is able to do so, but he fails Minnie just as everyone else does); the impetus for brave actions being rooted in the personal, not in the abstract.

* The events of this play are from the relatively recent past and the impact of those events has a bearing on the political life of Ireland and Northern Ireland today. Anyone interested in the social and political history of Ireland and its relationship with the UK will gain a fascinating insight into the attitudes of people living in 1920s Dublin.

* There are many examples of plays being set in the past which still have resonances for modern audiences, and such plays often prove to be popular. Recent examples include *The Madness of George III* (1991) by Alan Bennett and *Our Country's Good* (1988) by Timberlake Wertenbaker. Of course, the difference here is that both of these works were written more recently about events from the past. O'Casey's play, however, offers an insight into the lifestyle of Dubliners in the early part of the twentieth century and is, therefore, valid as a piece of social history.

Developing themes

The use of irony

How would a director point up the many ironies in the play, such as this scene?

Donal: No man, Minnie, willingly dies for anything.

Minnie: Except for his country, like Robert Emmet.

Donal: Even he would have lived on if he could; he died not to deliver Ireland. The British Government killed him to save the British nation.

Minnie: You're only jokin' now. You'd die for your country.

Donal: I don't know so much about that.

Minnie: You would, you would, you would — I know what you are.

Donal: What am I?

Minnie: *(in a whisper)* A gunman on the run.

Donal: *(too pleased to deny it)* Maybe I am, and maybe I'm not.   (Act I, p. 18)

Treatment of the tragedy

While it is clearly different in tone and style from a Greek tragedy, there are features of this play that are common to the 'rules' of Greek tragedy and adhere to the principles of Aristotle. For example, the play takes place across one day and in one place.

The deaths, when they occur, do so off stage. This heightens the claustrophobic atmosphere of the play — the sense that the characters are trapped by the violent events of the play and that they are victims of events that they are powerless to control. The room may seem like a refuge from the violence of the conflict between the factions involved in the uprising, but we see at the end of the play that it is easily penetrated by invading forces.

A director wishing to enhance the impact of these principles of tragedy has to focus his or her attention on the clarity of the production. Despite the panic of the characters and the sudden death of Minnie, the audience must be absolutely clear about the order and nature of events. Furthermore, the tragedy can only make an impact on the audience if the director has developed a credible sense of fear expressed by the performers. This can be achieved through the actors' own research into the conditions and the use of rehearsal techniques devoted to the expression of emotion, particularly fear.

Treatment of the comedy

There is a marked contrast in the style of comedy used in *The Shadow of a Gunman* from that of *The Taming of the Shrew*. Whereas much of the comedy in the *Shrew* is physical (comic violence meted out on recalcitrant servants, for example) and has a visual dimension (the various disguises, for example), the comedy in *The Shadow of a Gunman* is always tempered by the context of tragedy. There are moments that may well make an audience laugh (Grigson's drunkenness, Mr Gallogher's letter and Mrs Henderson's introduction of it, for example). The irreverence with which Seumas treats his landlord and the paying of his rent may also be amusing to an audience. However, these incidents are always set against the background of the prevailing situation of violence and conflict.

The comedy of *The Taming of the Shrew* is uncompromised by any realistic social context; that of *The Shadow of a Gunman* is not. This is not to say that serious issues cannot be given a farcical treatment without diluting the sense of seriousness. Dario Fo, in *Accidental Death of An Anarchist* (1970), uses farce to intensify the stupidity and the corruptness of the police and government in Italy in the 1960s. The humour in Fo's farce is a savage one, which ridicules the figures of authority. *The Shadow of a Gunman* is not presented as a farce in this way. The characters have a greater sense of reality, the reality of the violence they face is more evident and they show compassion towards one another. The humour may mock their naïve beliefs and their vanity but it is not a cruel humour.

The director's task

In bringing the world of the play to life, the director has to work carefully with the actors to develop their understanding of the political and social circumstances in Dublin during the 1920s. The rehearsal process should therefore involve the actors researching political situation and social conditions of the time.

Staging the play presents many challenges. There are moments of quiet and intimacy, such as the conversations between Seumas and Donal, and the romantic climax to Act I between Minnie and Donal. Directing these moments requires sensitivity to the pace of the dialogue and an ability to inspire the actors to find the heart of the relationships and convey them truthfully and meaningfully. The naturalistic feel to the play might encourage a director to use ideas from Stanislavksi (see Chapters 5 and 6) in order to develop emotionally believable performances. However, a director also has to stage the end of the play carefully, because it involves high-speed action and a large number of actors invading the stage as the premises are searched. A play that has such dynamically contrasting moments, and which is alternately gentle, sentimental, comic, tense and finally tragic, requires a sure directorial hand to guide it through all these contrasts.

Discussion question

Make thorough notes on the points that arise from your consideration of the following question, either from discussion or your own observations.

How could a director of *The Shadow of a Gunman* ensure that the comic and tragic elements of this play remain balanced, so that the tragedy of the characters' lives and attitudes is brought to the fore at its conclusion?

Essay question

As a director, explain how you would meet the challenge of staging the final scene of the play. Identify in particular how you would achieve the moments of dramatic contrast in the scene.

Considerations for the designer

Set

The design of the set is one of the most important features in a production of this play. Achieving a sense of the dingy, poverty-stricken room and the rest of the unseen tenement is essential to the feel of the play and the depiction of its social context. The use of colour and shade, and accuracy of props will help to communicate the reality of the characters' daily lives. Unlike *Antigone* and *The Taming of the Shrew*, the set is described by the playwright in some detail. It does not change during the two acts, so there is no need to plan for quick scene changes and the level of detail can be painstaking.

Achieving an impression of a dingy and cramped room is important in a production of *The Shadow of a Gunman*. Aidan McArdle (Donal) and Frank McCusker (Seumas), Tricycle Theatre, London, 2004

The main challenge of designing the set for this play is to create a cramped, ugly room that also conveys a sense of the world beyond its walls — parts of the rest of the house and the street. Since many characters enter and leave the room, the set also has to be large enough to adapt to the physical demands that are made of it. The designer must therefore create a set that is detailed, intimate and cramped but, when required, convenient and spacious to move about in.

Costume and make-up

Costume and make-up can help to communicate the context of the play. For example, many of the characters live their lives in a dark, dingy environment and are probably fearful of venturing too far from the tenement. Make-up can be used to create pale, sallow complexions. Costumes can be tattered and dull-coloured to enhance the audience's sense of the characters' poverty and deprivation.

Technical features

Sound

Sound is the area of design that requires particular emphasis in this play. The world beyond the stage imposes itself on the events in the play mostly through sound effects.

A successful climax to the play depends on the audience's appreciation of the events that are taking place outside the tenement. The sounds of gunshots, lorries arriving, shouts of protest, bombs going off, and the cries of shocked, injured and dying people need to be heard. These must be credible if the tragic dénouement is to be effective.

The sound effects must therefore be harsh, shocking and violent. However, there are also moments of calm — almost stillness — in the play. For example, before the first gunshots are heard, the two main characters are having a peaceful discussion about religion and philosophy. Their conversation is interrupted in a brutal and uncompromising manner, and the audience is alerted to the bleak tragedy that awaits the characters beyond their room.

Lighting

For a lighting designer, there are a number of opportunities to create the atmosphere of the play. In common with Greek tragedy, the structure of the play condenses the action into the span of a single day. At the start of Act I, it is midday and there is no warning of the approaching tragic events. A light, almost optimistic effect might be achieved through the use of warm, straw-coloured lighting to suggest the sun coming through the tenement windows.

Having areas of contrasting shadow on the stage could be used to suggest that this sense of warmth and optimism is, quite literally, clouded. It could also help to indicate that, in spite of the midday sun, the room is dingy and deprived of light. Later, at the start of Act II (which is set in the dead of night) the sense of dinginess and claustrophobia can be intensified through the lighting. This can be achieved by the use of steel gels, which cast a colder, almost blue, light on the acting area. Levels of light can also be reduced to create an overall dimmed effect.

Discussion question

Make thorough notes on the points that arise from your consideration of the following question, either from discussion or your own observations.

Explain how your ideas for design would help to convey the sense of poverty inherent in *The Shadow of a Gunman*.

Essay question

Explain the challenges of designing a set for *The Shadow of a Gunman*. Specify moments in the play where the set has a particular use.

Considerations for an actor

Acting in *The Shadow of a Gunman* presents a number of challenges and opportunities.

While there may be moments where solo performers can 'shine', it is more important that an ensemble feel is created throughout the production. Although the play is not an ensemble piece such as *Antigone*, with its reliance on a chorus, the actors need to convey the sense of the community within the tenement — a group of people who live in close proximity to one another. It is this closeness, and the fact that people are acutely aware of each other's presence without actually communicating, that has led to the rumours of Donal being a gunman.

Donal and Seumas

Donal and Seumas know each other well; indeed, all the inhabitants of the tenement are familiar with each another's day-to-day lives. Actors playing these two roles therefore need to focus on the ways in which living in such close proximity have affected their relationship. Their characters are described in some detail by O'Casey: for instance, we are told that Donal's life 'would drive him mad were it not for the fact that he never knew any other'.

The characters cannot escape the circumstances of their strife-torn community, because that same community removes their resourcefulness. The actors need to find ways to communicate the characters' acceptance of their lifestyle and the comfortable but static relationship the two men have. They also need to know in detail what each finds irritating about the other.

In rehearsals, the actors should aim to become familiar with the set as if it were their own home, knowing where everything is.

Relationship between Minnie and Donal

Perhaps the most poignant aspect of the play is the doomed relationship between Minnie and Donal. The development of this relationship is important as a tragic aspect of the play. The actors may wish to explore the spatial elements of the relationship and the focus of the characters — through eye contact — as they pursue their courtship.

This is a feature which needs to be explored in the first act. When Minnie is questioning Donal about his poetry and — in particular — whether it has been written for a woman, she could look enquiringly at him and with an intense stare. He could, in turn, avoid her gaze, although becoming increasingly aware of and perhaps pleased at her growing interest in him. The staging could allow the characters gradually to move closer together, instilling in the audience a sense of anticipation, before Tommy Owens enters and breaks the moment between them.

This moment is then resurrected when the other characters leave at the end of the act and they do indeed kiss. Their embrace should be thought about carefully. After all, their society is strongly dominated by religious faith and it is unlikely that either character would have had much experience of relationships with the opposite sex. The kiss should, therefore, be more romantic than sexual and naïve rather than practised. The romantic link between them, and Minnie's growing feelings for Donal, are the trigger for her actions later when she saves Donal from arrest. It is important that the romantic and emotional climax of the first act is played with intensity and utter conviction.

Creating comic impact

A number of characters have a comic impact on the play. Often, these characters appear for one scene and the audience does not see them again. Mr Gallogher is one such character. It is important, therefore, that his appearance makes a strong and memorable impact. Characters such as Mr Gallogher or Mrs Henderson can be described as 'cameo' roles. They are not on stage for long, but during the time they appear they provide a significant focus for the action.

Mr Gallogher's letter shows him to be portentous and self-important but vulnerable. Mrs Henderson's overbearing introduction of Mr Gallogher and his letter shows her to have a highly simplistic view of life.

> Mr Davoren is wan ov ourselves that stands for govermint ov the people with the people by the people. You'll find you'll be as welcome as the flowers in May.

> (Act I, p. 23)

The actors' challenge is to play the comedy but with a belief in the situation. It is important to express Mr Gallogher's and Mrs Henderson's outrage with credibility; it is, after all, an outrage deeply felt.

We should always remember that the characters are explored within a serious social context that mitigates against interpreting them in too stereotypical a manner. So, for example, although the reading of Mr Gallogher's letter might be very funny, the treatment of the characters by the actors is a serious one. This is an outrage deeply felt and it is important that, while the complaint may be articulated in ridiculously convoluted terms, we do not see the people involved simply as buffoons.

Conveying fear

Towards the end of the play, the stage is occupied briefly by the British troops. The impact of this invasion is vital to the climax of the play, and these scenes make significant demands on the actors involved.

The occupants of the house are plunged into fear as they react first to the noise of gunshots, then the realisation that they have a bag of bombs in the house, and finally the invasion of the troops. The actors playing the main characters will need to consider how they might convey these intense feelings of fear to the audience.

The troops are depicted as violent, abusive and threatening. The actors playing these characters need to develop a persona that is very different from those of the characters living in the tenement. This could be achieved through the use of a different accent, and making aggressive and decisive movements. They should show contempt for the Irish characters and behave as if the house is theirs to abuse and destroy. Throughout these scenes, the reality of invasion and occupation should be felt by the audience.

Summary

- *The Shadow of a Gunman* depicts life among tenement dwellers in Dublin during the struggle for Irish independence. As such, the context is a realistic one. This factor must be borne in mind by all personnel involved in a production — designers, directors and actors.
- While the play is described as a tragedy, there are many comic moments. It is important, however, that the characters at the centre of the comedy are acted without lapsing into caricature or stereotype. The context is a deeply serious one and the comic moments are set against a background of tension and conflict.
- Anyone mounting a production of the play should give thought to its significance/relevance to a modern audience. A director must consider whether he or she would want the audience to draw the links between the conflict depicted in the play and conflicts in the world now.
- The play is one of contrasts: tenderness followed by violence, tranquility followed by chaos. There are moments when Donal is on stage alone and occasions when the stage is, quite literally, invaded. These contrasts need to be observed by the director if the audience is to appreciate the potential impact.

Discussion question

Make thorough notes on the points that arise from your consideration of the following question, either from discussion or your own observations.

Fear is an important dramatic ingredient of *The Shadow of a Gunman*. As an actor, how might you approach the conveying of fear in the second act if you were playing either Mrs Grigson, Donal or Seumas?

Essay questions

1 How would you approach the role of Donal in the opening scene of *The Shadow of a Gunman*? What relationship with Seumas would you want to convey through your performance and how would you achieve it?

2 As a director, what features of the play would you emphasise in production to make it meaningful for a twenty-first-century audience?

3 As an actor playing either Mr Gallogher or Mrs Henderson, how would you explore the comic potential of the role?

4 Explain how the use of costumes and props might contribute to the dramatic impact of the final scene of the play.

Unit 2

AS: Practical presentation of a play extract

Chapter 5

The work of Konstantin Stanislavski

Konstantin Stanislavski (1863–1938)

Konstantin Stanislavski came from a wealthy family in Russia. He was born Konstantin Sergeievich Alexeiev. 'Stanislavski' was a stage name that he adopted in 1884, in order to keep his performance activities secret from his parents. The prospect of becoming a professional actor was unthinkable for someone of his social class; at that time, actors had a low social status in Russia.

From childhood, he developed an obsession with acting and the theatre, performing initially in a converted building on his family's estate. He founded the Society of Art and Literature in 1888 and later the Moscow Art Theatre in 1897 with Vladimir Nemirovich-Danchenko. Stanislavski is credited with being the originator of naturalistic acting and he strove to create a sense of truth on stage, adapting and revising his ideas constantly. His system of acting is often linked with, but should never be confused with, the 'Method', whose practitioners include Lee Strasberg and Stella Adler.

There is probably more written about the ideas and work of Konstantin Stanislavski than any other theatre practitioner. This chapter aims to distil the available information down to a manageable size. However, it is essential that you use the chapter as a springboard into further research, rather than reading it as an end in itself.

An ambition to act

Stanislavski's career as a director is inextricably linked with his aims as a teacher of acting. In order to gain a true appreciation of his theatrical endeavours, it is essential to understand the historical and social context into which he emerged and in which he worked. You should also note that Stanislavski was, principally, an actor and a director. He was not a playwright.

Stanislavski was born into great wealth in the latter half of the nineteenth century and his family fortune enabled him to practise his art. In his youth, Stanislavski performed in many plays and sketches, and his desire to be a good actor — often the source of painful frustration in his adolescence — became a lifelong ambition.

Stanislavski's initial attempts to refine his talent as an actor through drama school in the 1880s brought nothing but further frustration. The training was largely imitative, delivered with the idea that there was only one way of rendering poetry, only one acceptable manner of sitting on a chair or playing a particular 'type' of character. It did not offer him what even at this early stage he felt he needed — an approach to understanding and conveying the internal forces and feelings of the characters.

It has been argued that if Stanislavski had possessed a natural talent in acting then he might not have spent most of his life trying to hone and develop an approach to acting. However, the failures and successes he experienced in performance served to set him on course to identify a defined system to help actors in the preparation of roles.

The Society of Art and Literature

In his twenties, Stanislavski founded the Society of Art and Literature, which sought to promote an ambitious repertoire of plays and to develop a more realistic style of acting. Stanislavski describes the state of Russian theatre in the late nineteenth century in his autobiography *My Life in Art* (1924). According to his account, and the accounts of others, the world of theatre was paralysed by a 'star' system and by the emphasis on declaiming speech beautifully, often with substantial help from the prompt.

The idea that Russian theatre had always been a vehicle for the vain 'ham actor' is, however, far from the truth. A generation earlier, the great actor Mikhail Schepkin (1788–1863) and the novelist and playwright Nikolai Gogol (1809–52) had both emphasised the need to create a greater sense of truth and realism in theatre.

Schepkin had been the lead actor at the Maly Theatre — the national theatre of Russia — for nearly half a century. However, since his death (he died coincidentally in the year Stanislavski was born, 1863),

Star system

In the star system, individual talents dominated the theatre, often to the detriment of a production. In Britain, the staging of a play was often built around the celebrated appearance of a star individual, such as Edmund Kean or Henry Irving. In such productions, the performances of other actors were subjugated to the needs of the star player and his relationship with the audience.

Such an approach runs counter to Stanislavski's emphasis on the importance of ensemble. He referred rather disparagingly to the star system he saw in evidence in the Russian theatre at the start of his own career: 'In spite of my great admiration for individual splendid talents, I do not accept the star system; collective creative effort is the root of our kind of art.'

the standard of Russian theatre had seriously declined. Through his work at the Society of Art and Literature, Stanislavski sought to recreate the spirit of Gogol and Schepkin by emphasising a more considered approach to acting.

Although technically an amateur institution, the society eventually became a focal point for quality theatre in Moscow. High-profile actors and directors such as Aleksandr Fedotov and Fiodor Kommisarjevsky were attracted to the society to work, and Stanislavski's own reputation as an actor grew throughout the 1890s.

Moscow Art Theatre

In 1897, Stanislavski and his colleague Nemirovich-Danchenko (1858–1943) founded the Moscow Art Theatre. This offered them the opportunity not only to produce excellent theatre but also to identify and practise a disciplined philosophy in acting and repertoire.

The decadent days of the Russian theatre — with its emphasis on ornate décor, actors and audience arriving fashionably late and its upholding of the 'star' system — were now over. The ambitions of the two men were nothing less than to create the most professionally rigorous theatre in the land. However, they were not intellectually or socially elitist and despised the way the theatre had become a club where wealthy Muscovites could meet and socialise. Their initial idea was to call the theatre 'The Moscow Art Theatre — open to all'.

Konstantin Stanislavski with the Moscow Art Theatre troupe of actors in the 1930s

TopFoto

Naturalism and realism

Naturalism as an artistic movement came to prominence initially in the nineteenth-century French novel; the term was invented by the French novelist Emile Zola. His works were a conscious refutation of romantic fiction and often depicted low-born characters struggling to survive in adverse environments.

The classic example of this is *Germinale* (1885), the story of a group of miners in northern France struggling against starvation and oppression. Conveying a sense of 'gritty' realism, Zola explored the idea of inherited characteristics. The central character, Etienne, is shown to possess strengths and weaknesses bequeathed by his ancestors. Zola deliberately took a more scientific approach to the creation of characters and the exploration of their behaviour in specific environments.

The scientific advances of the nineteenth century, most notably the evolution theories of Charles Darwin, inspired novelists and playwrights to take a more analytical, often harsher view of humanity and its ability or inability to survive. Thus it is that plays of the nineteenth century that can be said to be part of the naturalistic movement often take a deeply unromantic, even if sympathetic, view of humanity.

It is essential to acknowledge the inherent problems with terminology such as 'realism' and 'naturalism': these terms are not always used with consistency and are subject to individual interpretation (and, in this case, translation). Stanislavski himself drew a distinction between the terms. He used 'naturalism' as a more pejorative expression, meaning merely the imitation of surface-level behaviour, whereas 'realism' described 'natural truthfulness'. He wrote in *An Actor's Handbook*:

> Those who think we sought naturalism on the stage are mistaken. We never leaned toward such a principle… We sought inner truth, the truth of feeling and experience.

However, those who believe that Stanislavski is a slavish exponent of realism at the expense of imagination should recognise the distinctions he makes between 'scenic' and 'literal' truth. Stanislavski was at pains to point out that what happens on a stage is not real but the product of an imagination. Therefore, when attempting to create truth in acting (scenic truth), the preoccupation is with the sense of purpose and believability established by the actor, not with making sure that the props are authentic or the set completely realistic. Furthermore, it is entirely possible to create a sense of truthful acting in a piece that is surreal (not bound by the limits of realistic truth), hence the distinction between scenic and realistic truth.

For Stanislavski, the danger of applying a philosophy such as naturalism to acting was to threaten the potential individuality of a character and, therefore, the truthful playing of that character. He identified the need for an actor to avoid extremes of theatrical excess and exaggeration of the truth.

As he went on to say in *An Actor Prepares*:

> Naturalism on the stage is only justified by the inner experience of the actor.

Stanislavski stressed that even if a character is described as 'peasant', it is the inner characteristics of that particular peasant rather than the outer stereotypical, instantly recognisable characteristics of the concept of peasantry that should be of concern to the actor.

In *An Actor's Handbook*, he draws a useful example from the 'death scene', which he says should not be concerned with 'cramps, nausea, groans, horrible grimaces' at the expense of preoccupation with 'the last moments of the human soul'. He says that:

> Truth on stage must be real but rendered poetic through creative imagination.

The Duke of Saxe-Meiningen and the Meiningen Players

The Duke of Saxe-Meiningen George II (1826–1914) was a wealthy aristocrat and head of a small German principality. In 1866, he established his own court theatre group, known as the Meiningen Players. He recognised the importance of central artistic control and undertook several roles: producer, director, financial backer and costume and scenery designer. Influenced by contemporary English theatre, he insisted on realistic lighting, speech and stage mechanics and historically accurate costumes and sets. The Meiningen Players toured Europe from 1874 to 1890, inspiring theatrical reforms wherever the group performed.

A director's theatre

Stanislavski, as a director and a coach of actors, as well as an actor himself, had to find a system which could lead to convincing and credible productions through this subtle approach to playmaking and characterisation. He was interested in the work of the Meiningen Players, particularly in their ensemble playing and coherent production methods. He was aware that he was watching a company that was disciplined, organised and concerned to demonstrate the authenticity of a play through accurate design features created specifically for each new production. By contrast, in the Russian theatre of Stanislavski's youth it was not unusual to see the same elaborate sets and costumes brought out time after time.

The Meiningen Players' acting, which was workmanlike rather than vain and did not include a specifically emphasised star performer, could perhaps be more accurately described as a 'director's theatre' than an 'actor's theatre'. This too attracted Stanislavski's attention. His detestation of the star system and the kind of simultaneously overblown and amateurish production commonly to be seen on the Russian stage in his youth emerges clearly in his autobiography *My Life in Art*:

> These performances seemed to be created for the purpose of showing the primary importance on the stage of the actor himself and the entire lack of necessity of the whole production and all beautiful scenery in the absence of the most important person — the actor… What is important to me is that the collective creation of all the artists of the stage be whole and complete and that all those who helped to make the performance might serve for the sake of the same creative goal and bring their creations to one common denominator.

Stanislavski's ideas

Many of Stanislavski's ideas on acting can be found in his published works *An Actor Prepares* (1937) and *Building a Character* (1938). However, two points must be borne in mind when reading these:

TopFoto

*   Much of Stanislavski's writing is still unpublished and in its original Russian.
*   There is substantial evidence to suggest that his ideas on acting were constantly changing. Revision notes found after publication of these works and after Stanislavski's death confirm this. While *An Actor Prepares* was published during his lifetime, other works were published posthumously and reflect thoughts and ideas at specific moments during his life and career. According to those with whom he worked, these were always subject to revision.

Consequently, Stanislavski's writings should never be seen as a rule book or a dogma, as many of his critics have sought to insist. They are, instead, a guide, an attempt to help the learning actor. Stanislavski's need to provide theatrical works of distinction and, above all, to impart

Stanislavski's writing should not be seen as a rule book or a dogma authenticity and a sense of truth meant that his work as a director at the Moscow Art Theatre combined with the role of acting coach.

It would be a mistake to believe that at its inception the Moscow Art Theatre brought with it a coaching programme consistent for every production and adhered to by all the practitioners in the theatre. Stanislavski's work as a director, actor and acting coach over the decades provides many examples of trial and error.

However, accepting that the written guides we possess are not definitively reflective of Stanislavski's practice — since it was constantly changing — there is still a sufficiently robust philosophy for practitioners to apply.

Seeking ways forward

By 1906, Stanislavski had reached something of a crisis point in his work. He had just played Thomas Stockmann (the central character) in Ibsen's *An Enemy of the People* (1882). Response to much of the theatre's repertoire over the 9 years since its foundation had been positive and the Ibsen production was likewise well received. Stanislavski and Nemirovich-Danchenko's ambition of a theatre dedicated to excellence was on its way to being realised. However, for Stanislavski these apparent successes were not enough. He constantly sought ways to improve his practice.

He had established — under the directorship of Meyerhold — the 'First Studio' company, dedicated to experimental work in both styles of acting and repertoire. However, this had not been a success and he was afraid that the company would stagnate unless new and successful ideas could be implemented. In particular, he was concerned with how to identify a process for actors which could help them to achieve a successful performance, even if it could not *guarantee* such an accomplishment. He recognised the moments of success in his own and other actors' careers but could not define *how* that success had been achieved. Too often it was a matter of luck whether a performance was successful or not.

He was also concerned that, as the senior actor and director at the Moscow Art Theatre, his work was imitated. He knew from his disastrous time in drama school in the 1880s that learning through copying a demonstration of another's work could only be a partially successful activity, lacking in creativity and depth.

Realistic sets

Much of the way in which Stanislavski tried to activate a sense of truth in the imaginations of his actors was by providing the stimulation of a realistic set. Russian theatre often used and reused the same artefacts to create sets. Part of the philosophy of the Moscow Art Theatre was to make theatre design a central concern. This approach, however, had once again achieved only partial success. According to Stanislavski's biographer, Jean Benedetti, one notable production of Shakespeare's *Julius Caesar* (1599) succeeded in achieving archeological and historical authenticity while failing to offer anything but dull drama. Instead, students of history were reputedly taken to see the production simply because of its accuracy in recreating the environment of ancient Rome.

Development of emotional or sense memory

Stanislavski became aware that in order to create believable acting it was necessary to stimulate feeling — that is, to work on the internal thoughts and motivations of the actor. His problem was to find a way of stimulating feeling that an actor could use at will. To dictate to an actor what he or she should be feeling would be counter-productive: the actor could simply demonstrate the required feeling through behaviour without genuinely connecting with the sentiment.

Stanislavski realised that the strength of an individual's will and his or her ability to concentrate on personal performance without being distracted by an audience or other external forces were crucial. This in turn prompted his interest in psychology, although the subject was in its infancy. The work of the French psychologist Théodule Armand Ribot (1839–1916) had particularly caught his attention, as it put forward the theory that all memories are stored in the nervous system rather than forgotten and that stimulation can reawaken those memories. Such stimulation may be merely a touch or a smell or a sound: the memory comes flooding back, bringing with it the associated emotion.

Stanislavski felt that if an actor, through will, could find ways to trigger appropriate memories during acting, then the emotion produced would be genuine. It was important for the actor to be fully aware of the emotions attributed to the dramatic persona, in order to associate with them and create the appropriate response.

Emotional memory versus incoherent emotion

The process of recalling emotional memory is not, as some have interpreted it, the ability to cry copious tears on cue. The challenge of the process is in fact for actors to understand the emotion of their character, to use their will to reawaken the appropriate personal memory and to draw on that memory to express the emotional dimension of the character without exaggeration. Mere histrionics result in a lack of truth and the kind of 'over-naturalism' to which Stanislavski frequently refers.

It is important to understand the distinction between the disciplined, creative process of drawing on emotional memory and the somewhat indulgent method of producing hysterical, incoherent emotion for emotion's sake. There have been many 'successors' to Stanislavski, most of whom have defined their allegiance in the context of the execution of emotional- or sense-memory acting. However, this is perhaps one of the most common areas of misunderstanding and misinterpretation of Stanislavski's system. Emotional truth does not necessarily mean emotional outpouring; indeed, the canon of plays produced by the Moscow Art Theatre in most instances demanded a subtle, discriminate and measured application to acting.

In *So You Want to be a Theatre Director?* (2004), Stephen Unwin argues that while there has been much mystification of the process, emotional memory is an essential part of acting and is constantly used by good actors and good directors alike.

The 'circle of attention'

Through his meticulous note-taking and scrupulous awareness of his own fallibilities and strengths as an actor, Stanislavski realised the important link between concentration and successful performance. He also realised that the more he concentrated his focus on himself during performance, the more relaxed he was. If he allowed his attention to wander to extraneous matters, such as distractions from the auditorium, his muscles tensed and his performance became nervous and artificial.

Stanislavski therefore defined the 'circle of attention' — the confined and specific area of focus with which the actor should be concerned, the world of the play on stage. If an actor can maintain that focus, Stanislavski argued, the audience members will be drawn into the world of the play and the actor's hold will 'force them to participate actively in his artistic life' (*An Actor's Handbook*, p. 24).

This 'circle of attention' can be enlarged or reduced depending on the nature of the action taking place on stage. However, if an actor is to be successful, he or she must control the nature of the circle and not allow anything to distract his or her attention.

Units, objectives and obstacles

During rehearsals, Stanislavski would break up a play into 'units'. Each unit would be defined by a piece of action or an event. As Stanislavski put it in *An Actor's Handbook* (p. 154) 'a core…a thing without which it cannot exist'.

Within each unit, an actor will have to meet a particular objective for the character he or she plays. In Act I scene 2 of Shakespeare's *A Midsummer Night's Dream* (*c.* 1595), for instance, the unit may be said to concern the casting of the play. The actor playing Peter Quince must realise his character's objective of seeing to it that all the other characters know the role they are to undertake and are supplied with the script. However, it may be the case that another character's objective might be to provide an obstacle to Quince's objective — and so it proves to be. Bottom, who has been cast as Pyramus, has the objective of playing all the other parts too. This hampers Quince, who ultimately has to assert himself vigorously:

No, no. You must play Pyramus.   (I.2.42)

It would be impossible for both characters to achieve their objectives, as they are mutually frustrated by the disparate intentions. It is Quince who wins the argument, although his subsequent mollifying words to Bottom suggest that perhaps he has an additional objective, that of ensuring that Bottom is happy with his role and not sulky:

You can play no part but Pyramus, for Pyramus is a sweet-faced man, a proper man, as one shall see in a summer's day: a most lovely gentlemanlike man: therefore you must needs play Pyramus.   (I.2.63–65)

It is important for actors to understand the objective of their character, in order to appreciate their motivation and to recognise whether the objective is finally achieved or whether an obstacle — usually another character's objective — has prevented it from being accomplished.

Super-objective and through-line of action

The super-objective is the ultimate ambition of the character and may be linked to the fulfilment of immediate objectives. Thus, to use the example of Peter Quince again, it may be argued that while his immediate objective in the unit of Act I scene 2 is to cast the play, his super-objective is to put on a fine production for the entertainment of Duke Theseus. The objective of Act I scene 2 is merely a small part of that super-objective.

Stanislavski explained how the fulfilment of each objective leads to the next objective as the 'through-line' of action. The actor must navigate his or her way through the play using the immediate objectives and individual units almost as a sailor might use marker buoys. However, as Unwin has argued in *So You Want to be a Theatre Director?* (2004), the super-objective is by no means certain in each case and is often subject to change. Quince's super-objective may not just be the achievement of a fine production; he may also wish to become a full-time poet so that he no longer has to work as a carpenter.

Hamlet's ultimate super-objective is to avenge his father's death by killing his uncle. However, at the beginning of the play he is not aware of the circumstances

While the immediate objective of Peter Quince in Act I scene 2 of *A Midsummer Night's Dream* is to cast the play, his super-objective is to put on a fine production for the entertainment of Duke Theseus. (Linbury Theatre, November 2005)

of his father's death and his initial super-objective is to find any means possible to end what he sees as a desperate and heartbreaking existence. His only means of escape — having discounted suicide — is to go back to Wittenberg University. However, even this objective cannot be achieved, as his uncle and his mother both put pressure on him not to return.

Recognition of the super-objective is a useful way for an actor to determine the character's ambition and motivation. The fact that this may be linked to how the actor interprets the role, as well as how the playwright has written it, makes the notion of the super-objective no less valid.

Given circumstances

Stanislavski felt that an actor must have a fundamental awareness of 'the story of the play'. This awareness should take in not only the facts that are contained within the script, but also the context of the character — social, historical and political — and his or her specific condition. Knowledge of these 'given circumstances' cannot be achieved without a thorough exploration of the text and a sound understanding of the director's interpretation.

Arthur Miller's *Playing for Time* (1980) — a play based on the autobiography of Fania Fenelon, a Parisian Jewish singer who was deported to Auschwitz during the Second World War — tells the story of how she and other inmates survived by forming an orchestra to entertain the Nazi hierarchy. The context here, therefore, is not only specific but also particularly graphic and violent.

Obviously, it is vital for everyone in the company of actors to understand and appreciate the extreme nature of the context, but not just in political or historical terms. In addition, the actors need to have a sense of the characters in terms of their backgrounds before entering Auschwitz. They must explore their characterisations beyond the label of 'Jewish prisoner'.

Actors must also explore the more visceral of the given circumstances, such as how it must feel to be permanently hungry and to know that each day could well be your last. In this sense, the given circumstances of the character are linked with the emotional preparation that the actor must make and the development of truth and credibility in performance. It is not possible to 'bluff' through a script which offers so many challenges and which deals with the bravery of individuals in one of the most appalling episodes of human history. In plays such as *Playing for Time*, the assimilation by the actors of the given circumstances of the characters is necessarily a respectful as well as a professionally expedient practice.

Magic or creative 'if'

The idea of 'magic if' is concerned with the actor's appropriate and effective use of imagination. While a situation such as the one cited above in *Playing for Time* may be beyond his or her experience, the actor must try to imagine what life would be like 'if' he or she was in that situation.

Inevitably, this idea is linked to that of emotional memory. It is highly unlikely that any actor taking part in this play can compare experiences in his or her own life with what he or she is being asked to enact. Actors may be able to conjure memories of fear through the emotional memory technique but they will need to engage a developed sense of imagination to place themselves in that specific situation. Imagination will need to be supported by research — led by the director — into the historical details of the situation.

The notion of the 'magic if' comes with a health warning. It is sometimes argued that it is necessary to lose all sense of self and to believe that you *are* the character that you are playing. For an actor to render a role with complete believability, it is vital for him or her to believe that he or she is genuinely inhabiting the world of the play, rather than simply performing on a stage.

It should be stressed that while there may be exponents of the above method who believe such a theory, Stanislavski was opposed to such a technique. He did not believe that the actor should 'give himself up to hallucination...quite the contrary... He does not forget that he is surrounded by stage scenery and props' (*An Actor's Handbook*). To try to indulge the kind of hallucination Stanislavski refers to is to lose control as an actor and to move from a process of creativity to one of abandoned self-deception. On the contrary, it is the word 'if' that acts as a lever to lift the actor from the real world into the world of his creativity. Stanislavski did not engender any notion in his actors or his students that they were to believe they had actually become the character they were playing.

Stanislavski and politics

When Stanislavski's work is discussed, comparisons are often drawn with the work of other practitioners, most notably Bertolt Brecht. One important and obvious distinction, however, is that Brecht was principally a playwright and Stanislavski was not. It is also often argued that while Brecht was a political and theatrical revolutionary, Stanislavski was a more establishment bourgeois figure, from a background of privilege and wealth, who had no interest in politics.

Such a judgement is partial and unfair. Stanislavski lived and worked in a politically volatile society: early twentieth-century Russia. During a performance of Ibsen's *An Enemy of the People* in 1905, Stanislavski, playing the lead role, experienced an unusual audience reaction. Earlier in the day, a troop of imperial guards had opened fire and massacred unarmed civilians protesting over food shortages in Kazansky Square in Petrograd (now St Petersburg). The audience in attendance at the Moscow Art Theatre's production in Petrograd that night was largely made up of middle-class, middle-aged members of the intelligentsia who were in angry mood and revolutionary spirit. They identified with many moments of the production. When the principal character Stockmann (played by Stanislavski) put on his coat — torn during an assault on him — and declared 'One need not put on a new coat when one fights for truth and freedom', this was too much for them. In *My Life in Art*, Stanislavski relates:

> The spectators in the theatre connected this sentence with the massacre in Kazansky Square, where more than one new coat must have been torn in the name of truth and freedom. Unexpectedly my words aroused such pandemonium that it was necessary to stop the performance... The entire audience rose from its seats and threw itself towards the footlights... I saw hundreds of hands stretch towards me all of which I was forced to shake... That evening I found out through my own experience what power the theatre could exercise.

Russia was subjected to two further revolutions in 1917, resulting initially in the removal of the tsar as head of state and ultimately in the success of the Communist Party led by Lenin and later Stalin. As the head of the foremost theatre company in Russia, Stanislavski would have been subjected to the keenest scrutiny by government officials. That both he and the company survived through this time when many did not (his successor at the Moscow Art Theatre, Vsevolod Meyerhold, was tortured and shot by the authorities in 1940) is a tribute to Stanislavski's considerable skill and courage when dealing with the Communist Party and, on occasion, Stalin himself.

In his biography of Stanislavski, Benedetti points out that his approaches to Stalin smack of political naïvety. However, it is unfair to suggest that he was in any sense a 'part' man or a mouthpiece of government propaganda. In fact, Stanislavski did not pursue an overtly political line in either the choice of repertoire at the theatre or in his interpretation of the repertoire as a director. Indeed, he was clear that the actor should not try to project a political message. He felt that while political messages may emerge from the work, there should be no attempt to compromise the artistic integrity of the production by substituting honest and truthful acting with preaching. However, by promoting the work of Chekhov, Gorky and Ibsen, among others, he was consciously placing an emphasis on the work of the most prominent playwrights of the era who, as we have seen, were part of the naturalistic vision. As such he was presenting plays which were often critical of both society and its leaders.

With regard to the work of Chekhov, the official party line was to interpret the plays as being critical of the old tsarist order. However, Stanislavski often found himself at odds with the aims of the official censor. There is no doubt that as a theatre director, Stanislavski saw that he had a spiritual and educative duty to the ordinary people of Russia; that he used this position to promote some of the finest and most socially-conscious playwriting in theatre's history should not be overlooked.

Summary

As we have seen, it is misguided to interpret Stanislavski's ideas on acting as a permanent and rigid set of training principles. Even in the area of emotional memory, which some see as being the defining element of his ideology, Stanislavski moved in the later part of his life towards a belief that emotion could be more effectively triggered by a method of physical actions:

External action acquires inner meaning and warmth from inner feeling, and the latter finds its expression in physical terms.

(*An Actor's Handbook*, p. 8)

Nonetheless, irrespective of his ability to move on to other ideas, the principles of acting we have inherited from Stanislavski are enormously useful, especially in approaching a work of realism. The next chapter is devoted to attempting to apply these principles to a proposed production of a suitable play.

Activity

Select a scene for performance from either a play you are studying or one of personal interest to you. The play needs to be of a realistic nature and involve rounded characters. Before you attempt the scene, focus on your character (A) and another character (B) with whom he or she is particularly close, for example Hamlet and Ophelia, Romeo and Juliet, or Proctor and Elizabeth. Go through the script, asking the following questions:

- What does character A say about character B?
- What does character B say about character A?
- What does character A say about himself or herself?
- What does character B say about himself or herself?
- What does character A say to character B about him or her?
- What does character B say to character A about him or her?

While this may seem an exhaustive and almost fussy process, it requires you to consider how characters respond to one another and reveals the honesty or frankness with which they address one another about their feelings. On this basis, you can start to consider your character's motives with regard to the other character, and perhaps engage in some emotional preparation.

Chapter 6

Applying Stanislavski's principles

An Inspector Calls by J. B. Priestley

An Inspector Calls was written in 1944 by J. B. Priestley. It is probably his most famous play, although *Dangerous Corner* (1932), *Time & The Conways* (1937) and *When We Are Married* (1938) are all well known and respected standards of British theatre, albeit less frequently performed.

J. B. Priestley

John Boynton Priestley (1894–1984)

J. B. Priestley was an author, novelist, playwright, broadcaster, scriptwriter and social commentator — a 'man of letters' whose career spanned the twentieth century. His first theatrical venture was an adaptation of his novel *The Good Companions* in 1931. This was followed by the thriller *Dangerous Corner*. A committed socialist, his best-known play is *An Inspector Calls*, which depicts a complacent and well-to-do family, all of whom have contributed to the death of a local girl but fail to take responsibility for their actions. However, Priestley was also an adept writer of comedy, and his farce *When We Are Married* is still frequently performed.

The plot

An Inspector Calls is set in the fictional industrial town of Brumley on a spring evening in 1912. A well-to-do family, the Birlings, are finishing dinner, and the mood is clearly one of celebration. Sheila, the daughter of the household, is getting engaged to Gerald Croft, a similarly well-to-do young man but from an even more important local family. There is an atmosphere of cheerfulness, and perhaps even smugness, about their situation.

After proposing a toast to the happy couple, Mr Birling begins to make a speech. He tells his family that they are lucky to be living in such a time of progress and prosperity and that, despite all the rumours and scaremongering, there is no chance of war. There is simply too much at stake and the Germans are as unenthusiastic about war as the British. Furthermore, one of the signals of progress is the building of a new and unsinkable ship of over 40,000 tons, equipped with every luxury and named *The Titanic.* Later in the same scene, he tells his son and prospective son-in-law to ignore all the nonsense spoken about community because a man has to make his own way in the world.

Into this complacent world a police inspector named Goole unexpectedly arrives. He is investigating the death of a young girl named Eva Smith, who has killed herself by drinking disinfectant. Finding letters and diaries in Eva's room, the inspector is pursuing an inquiry which involves all the members of the Birling family and Gerald Croft too. One by one, the inspector reveals how each of them has contributed to Eva's downfall and suicide. Mr Birling sacked her from his factory when she was one of a group of young women who led a strike for higher wages; Sheila, his daughter, had her sacked from her next job working in a clothes shop. Gerald had a relationship with her after she fell into prostitution and kept her as his mistress, but ended the relationship when it no longer suited him. Eva then met Eric, the Birlings' son, and had a brief relationship with him, which he ended when she became pregnant by him. Finally, Mrs Birling rejected Eva's appeals for help when she came to her charitable organisation pregnant, abandoned and destitute.

The inspector warns that unless people like them learn the lesson that we are not alone, that our fates intertwine, that we are all part of one community and responsible for each other, there will come a time of 'fire, blood and anguish'.

We discover ultimately that there is no Inspector Goole (possibly a play on 'ghoul', meaning ghost) and that no girl has died. As Mr and Mrs Birling and Gerald all breathe a sigh of relief on the assumption that they have been the victims of an elaborate hoax, the phone rings. Mr Birling receives the news that a girl has just died from drinking disinfectant and that an inspector is on his way to ask some questions.

A piece of naturalism?

In many respects, the play is a piece of naturalism, most notably in that it explores the behaviour of people in a specifically defined social context. The historic context of the play is in fact not 1912 but the mid-1940s at the end of the Second World War, also a time of 'fire, blood and anguish'.

Some would argue, however, that *An Inspector Calls* is not a wholly naturalistic play because of the 'supernatural' quality of the inspector's character and because of his polemical statements about society and shared responsibility. His involvement gives the play something of a didactic, political quality.

The play does not attempt to break with the conventions of naturalism and the reality of the inspector is completely accepted by the other characters, even if they find his behaviour unorthodox.

Applying Stanislavski's system

Stanislavski's system can help actors in a production of *An Inspector Calls* in a number of ways.

Working with emotion and sense memory

Each of the characters endures an emotional journey during the course of the play, with the possible exception of the inspector. Even though he differs from the other characters in this way, it is clear that he becomes increasingly impatient with Mr Birling's blustering defence of his actions and the others' attempts at excusing their behaviour.

All the characters experience a moment of recognition when they remember what has happened between them and Eva Smith. Each actor must therefore consider carefully his or her character's reaction to the news that Eva is dead.

Sheila

When Sheila is shown the photograph of Eva and recognises the young woman she has caused to be dismissed, the stage direction reads:

She looks at it closely, recognises it with a little cry, gives a half stifled sob, and then runs out.

The stage directions do not necessarily have to be followed exactly here, but there is a clear expectation that Sheila reacts to the photograph with extreme shock. Later she discovers that her fiancé, Gerald, has been unfaithful to her with Eva and she gradually learns of the involvement of the rest of her family in the death of the girl.

If this emotional journey is to be played with a convincing sense of truth and with credibility, the emotion which the actor playing Sheila displays must be genuine. While the actor in question will probably not know what it is like to discover that she has contributed to a young girl's suicide, it is possible to isolate the emotion of shock she experiences at this point by remembering a time when she personally received shocking news. If the memory can be recalled vividly, this will make the effect all the more potent. In order to evoke a powerful recollection, the actor should aim to recall the place where the shocking news was received, the way in which the news was delivered, the smells in the air and so on. In this way, the shock is stimulated from distinct memories rather than from vague recollections.

Gerald

The way in which an actor experiences shock or grief may differ from the way his or her character does — it is not just a case of reliving the emotion, but of recounting it and making it part of the creative process. Thus the actor playing Gerald must assimilate the information that his character has had a close relationship with Eva, may even have been a little in love with her, and admits to being:

rather more upset by this business than I probably appear to be.

Gerald perceives himself to be responding to the news of his former lover's death with stoicism, but there is still a need for the actor to stimulate emotion — in order to then conceal it. That is why it is important — as stated earlier — that emotional truth is not simply about emoting liberally on stage. Far more important is the task of cultivating the appropriate level of emotion and using knowledge of the context (the character and his or her situation) to judge how that emotion should be expressed.

The inspector

The role of the inspector is more challenging. Can emotional or sense memory help an actor to play a character who is supernatural? Much depends on the interpretation made by the actor playing the role and the director of the production. If there is something of the mystic about the inspector — a figure of authority with a spiritual message he feels impassioned to communicate — that could lead to a delivery of some emotional intensity. The actor could draw on experiences of frustration or impatience, or of trying to convince a sceptical audience of a deeply-held conviction.

There is an unsettling and disturbed quality to the frequency with which the inspector recalls seeing the dead body of Eva Smith — an image he recalls quite graphically. Although we discover that, at the time of the inspector's visit, no girl has been brought into the infirmary, we infer that the inspector has foreseen this event and knows the harrowing nature of the image he describes. The description may be enough to enable the actor to visualise what he describes so that no extra help is needed from his emotional memory. However, recalling a response to a distressing image — even an image of death from television news — might help the actor recreate the sense of anger and helplessness required here.

There is something of the mystic about the character of the inspector, and this can influence an actor's delivery. (Niall Buggy at the Playhouse Theatre, London, September 2001)

Using the 'circle of attention'

Unlike a musical or a play with narration, this is a play which requires no acknowledgement of the presence of the audience. The audience should be drawn into the world of the play and, therefore, the actors' concentration should be directed entirely within the stage environment.

The circle of attention for the actor playing the inspector may enlarge sufficiently to encompass all of the other characters, as it does immediately before his final exit early in Act III. However, it may also be limited to a direct address to one character, as during his interrogation of Mr Birling or Gerald for example.

When Mr Birling makes his optimistic and complacent speech about progress at the beginning of the play, his circle of attention is still the world of the play, but more the world — or his interpretation of it — beyond the immediate action of the stage. At this point, Mr Birling's attention is focused on the world of business and enterprise, of unsinkable ships and eternal optimism, of prosperity and triumphant capitalism. Although still focused on his dramatic audience (the other characters on stage), the actor playing Mr Birling can afford to allow his imagination to conjure the images the character describes and to create a focus which assimilates the world of the play with the world beyond the confines of the stage.

Identifying units

The play has a three-act structure, but there are clear and almost predictable units as the plot progresses. After a while, we almost anticipate that the inspector will move on to the interrogation of another member of the family. It is as if each character is assigned a personal unit in which his or her relationship with Eva and the portion of his or her guilt are revealed.

The plot has something of a murder mystery about it. Agatha Christie's stories — Poirot or Miss Marple — work in this forensic way to investigate each of the suspects until the identity of the murderer is revealed. However, there is little mystery about *who* is responsible for Eva's death; the mystery is *how* they were responsible and how one person's responsibility links to another's.

Identifying objectives

Since the behaviour of each character alters drastically during the course of the action, it is challenging to identify each persona's objective.

At the outset of the play, the immediate objective of each character seems to be simply to enjoy the occasion, and in each instance that objective is being fulfilled. However, there is perhaps a little more detail to be drawn into these objectives; much depends on the interpretation of the actors and the director.

Mr Birling

Mr Birling is concerned to make a good impression on Gerald, being conscious that Gerald is of a higher ranking family than his own. He is also aware, perhaps, that his son is inclined to drink too much and that he is a likely source of embarrassment. Eric's behaviour is, therefore, a potential obstacle to Birling's objective.

Eric

Eric may have a different objective from simply enjoying himself. As we see later in the play, he has stolen money from the firm in order to help Eva as he knows she is pregnant. His level of anxiety is therefore more intense than anyone else's at the outset of the play. Both he and Gerald know that they have done something which must remain secret if a way of life is to be sustained and its relationships are to remain unaffected.

Alteration of objectives

The arrival of the inspector alters each of the characters' objectives. Mr Birling's initial objective is to see to the inspector as quickly as possible and then go back to enjoying himself. Clearly, the inspector's behaviour provides an obstacle to that objective being achieved.

As the inspector works through the characters' accounts of their personal acquaintance with Eva Smith, his objective is to get each individual to tell the truth. In each case, he succeeds in eliciting confessions from the characters about their involvement with Eva, even if they remain resolutely unrepentant, as do Mr and Mrs Birling. Indeed, there are few real obstacles to the inspector realising his investigative objective, apart from Mrs Birling's rather feeble accusation of impertinence and Mr Birling's somewhat superfluous interjections of 'Now, look here, inspector'.

Arguably, it is a weakness of the play that the inspector extracts the confessions too easily, and that at no point is any witness accused of committing a crime. However, it is clear from Sheila's response to the inspector that any actor undertaking the role should give him qualities which prompt each of the characters to

TopFoto

The inspector's objective is to get the other characters to tell the truth. (Diane Fletcher, Niall Buggy and Emma Gregory; Playhouse Theatre, London, September 2001)

disclose information about their involvement and face up to their responsibilities in contributing to Eva's death.

Following the exit of the inspector, the objectives of each character change again. Mr Birling is concerned with how to avoid a scandal and protect his prospective knighthood. Eric and Sheila, however, have radically different objectives from their father. Their social consciences have been awakened and they are concerned that the inspector's words are heeded. They demonstrate sincere regret over what has happened and they feel frustration and anger towards their parents as they witness Mr and Mrs Birling's efforts to disprove the inspector's words and confute his authenticity. The realisation of the children's new-found objective is frustrated by the attempts of Gerald and Mr and Mrs Birling to protect themselves and solve the mystery.

Staging objectives and obstacles

Making observations about characters' objectives and obstacles is only of use if interpreted practically for work on stage. For example, a director recognising the ways in which the inspector's objectives provide obstacles for other characters should allow this realisation to influence staging ideas.

On his entrance, the stage directions describe the physical presence of the inspector as 'creating a sense of massiveness, solidity and purposefulness', although it also mentions that he need not be a big man. During the play, the inspector dictates a lot of the action, at points allowing people to leave the room and at others preventing them from doing so, particularly Eric. Although it would be inappropriate to have the inspector using any physical force in his dealings with the Birling family, his physical presence could be used in such a way as to present a physical obstacle to a character's exit. Certainly the stage direction offered by Priestley — that he stares at a person before asking them a question — is a useful device in meeting the objectives discussed.

There are also other methods of staging that can be used to explore the dynamics between the characters and their objectives. There is a sense of binary opposition between the inspector and the other characters, and this should be explored on stage. For example:

* The inspector is the hunter — the other characters are the hunted.
* He is shabby — they are glamorous.
* He is direct and purposeful — they are noncommittal and obfuscating.

This binary opposition would translate well into physical terms, for instance:

* The inspector is sitting — the other characters are standing.
* He is calm and still — they are moving and gesturing.

Super-objectives

The inspector's super-objective is to hold all the other characters accountable for the death of Eva Smith and to make them acknowledge their involvement.

The super-objectives of some characters alter following the unexpected arrival of the inspector: while Mr Birling's super-objective at the beginning of the play could be interpreted as the securing of his daughter's engagement to Gerald, by the end it is to rid himself and his family of the inspector and to avoid a public scandal.

Characters' super-objectives do not change immediately with the arrival of the inspector, however. For a time, Mr Birling sees his unexpected guest merely as a temporary inconvenience — an obstacle, perhaps, but not a permanent obstruction to the achievement of his super-objective.

Subtext super-objectives

It may also be argued that Mr Birling's (and Mrs Birling's) super-objective at the outset of the play is to use the evening to better his chances of receiving a knighthood or of being re-elected as Lord Mayor.

It is important to realise that such a super-objective is reliant on personal interpretation and decisions made by actors and the director. The script is not the ultimate determinant. In this regard, there is an element of subtext in the establishment of both objective and super-objective. The text itself, as Stanislavski argued, is a piece of work in progress and can only be completed when given life on a stage. A play, therefore, may lead to many varied and diversified productions, dependent on actor and director interpretation.

The through-line of action

In this play, there is really only one character with a clear through-line of action, and that is the inspector. However, the through-line of action is important in order to establish for each actor a sense of purpose and urgency in the communication and achievement of their character's super-objective:

* How urgent is Mr Birling's desire to secure the partnership with Gerald and/or his knighthood? How does the audience witness this degree of urgency in the actor's performance?
* How important is it to Eric to get through the evening without detection? Is it his super-objective just to anaesthetise himself with alcohol and to leave at the earliest possible moment? If that is his super-objective, how urgent is it for him to achieve it and how will the urgency show in the actor's performance?

Ultimately, the character's objectives and super-objective will only be of cursory interest to the audience if the portrayal of them is not linked with the physical, vocal and emotional decisions of the actor.

Given circumstances

An Inspector Calls has a specific set of given circumstances and it is impossible to act in or direct this play appropriately without a thorough understanding and awareness of its backdrop.

The play is set clearly in 1912; there are references in the play to dates and events of the era, making it virtually impossible (and pointless) to set the play in any other period of history. Moreover, there can be no doubt about the intentions of the playwright in writing the play at the end of the second of the major world wars and setting it on the eve of the first: the setting of the play might be 1912, but the historical context is 1945. Priestley's point is that the attitudes and social injustices of the early part of the twentieth century are so entrenched that they have led to more than 30 years of 'fire, blood and anguish'. There is a didactic message here: that the reign of 'fire, blood and anguish' is reaching its height at the time of writing (1944–45) and that it will not die away until lessons of the past have been learned.

However, if the play is actually set in 1912, should the performances — according to a Stanislavskian interpretation — show any kind of awareness of the social upheaval to come? Not only would this be rather difficult to achieve, it would also seem to run counter to the ideas of Stanislavski that the actor should invest belief in the circumstances of the play. The 'magic if' requires actors to assimilate the given circumstances of their characters within the social context of the setting.

Nevertheless, setting and interpretation are ultimately down to directorial adaptation.

Given circumstances: character versus setting

Stephen Daldry's landmark revival of Priestley's play in 1992 for the National Theatre afforded a revision of the usual naturalistic delivery set in the Birling family's dining room. Instead, Daldry embraced both historical eras and set the Edwardian world of the Birlings in a doll's-house-like structure on stilts on the stage, while ragamuffin children from the 1940s played in bomb craters around it. At the moment of the inspector's 'fire, blood and anguish' speech, the doll's house spectacularly collapsed and the speech was delivered straight to the audience.

Can Daldry's interpretation, or indeed any expressionistic interpretation of a play, remain consistent with Stanislavski's principles regarding realistic performance? Certainly it seems feasible. Despite the imaginative and unorthodox setting of the play, the reality for the characters remains the same. We have seen how Stanislavski's attempts to stimulate realistic performances from his actors by supplying a completely authentic set ended in frustration and partial failure.

Stephen Daldry (1961–)

Stephen Daldry entered the world of the stage via a traditional route, spending part of his formative years performing youth theatre in Taunton. While at Sheffield University he excelled in dramatics, becoming chairman of the university drama society. After graduation, while most of his friends sought jobs as assistant stage managers, he took up an apprenticeship with Italian clown Elder Milletti and worked alongside him in a Romany circus in southern Italy. From 1985 to 1988 he served an apprenticeship at the Crucible Theatre in Sheffield, before heading to London, where he trained at the East 15 Acting School. While there, he began to garner attention for his work at the Gate Theatre (1990–92).

In 1992, Daldry was appointed artistic director at the Royal Court Theatre. He went on to direct the long-running, Tony-Award-winning revival of J. B. Priestley's *An Inspector Calls* and David Hare's monologue *Via Dolorosa*. He has also directed several films, including *Billy Elliot* (2000) and an adaptation of the Michael Cunningham novel *The Hours* (2002).

The acceptance of the given circumstances for each character does not undermine or challenge a more experimental array of choices for design or production. Daldry's production proved this: critical reactions to his interpretation pointed out that the complacency of the Edwardian world of the Birlings coupled with the devastation of the 1940s, when the play was written, served to underpin rather than detract from the play's major themes.

Therefore, whatever the nature of the production, the facts the actors need to assimilate for their characters remain the same. The characters' circumstances are in most cases quite clear.

Mr Birling

The actor playing Mr Birling must identify himself with the specific circumstances of the character in the play. He is a wealthy industrialist with no reason to be anything other than completely happy. He sits at the head of his table, having enjoyed a good dinner, and is now indulging himself with speech making. One assumes that as he has had experience in local politics, speech making is not something he finds difficult. He is confident in his opinions and clearly enjoys airing them.

Eric and Gerald

In the cases of Eric and Gerald, their guilty secrets are an important part of their given circumstances. Gerald is celebrating an engagement, knowing that he has cheated on the girl he intends to marry. Eric is aware that his theft could be discovered by his father at any moment. Therefore, their happiness is possibly tainted.

The inspector

It is more difficult to establish the inspector's given circumstances, since he is possibly an unearthly or ghostly figure. How can an actor interpret Stanislavski's ideas when the character he is playing arguably does not occupy a reality in the pragmatic sense? Can we think in terms of motivation and given circumstances for a character who, in all probability, is not a real inspector?

Again, it is important to think of reality in the context of the play. The inspector certainly has a stage reality that is accepted by the other characters until he leaves, and the conviction of his arguments leaves the audience in no doubt that he is heartfelt in his determination to secure the confessions of the Birling family. The circumstances that necessitate his visit are real, even if his character is a supernatural or mythical presence. It is the social evils committed by the Birlings that provide the actor with the important given circumstances on which the reality of his character is based.

Summary

J. B. Priestley's *An Inspector Calls* can lend itself to interpretations other than the purely naturalistic, as Daldry's expressionistic revival demonstrates. If Stanislavski could have directed *An Inspector Calls* (he died 7 years before it was written), his production would almost certainly have looked different from Daldry's. However, it would be a mistake to assume that because a production embraces techniques or design ideas that take it beyond the province of naturalism, its conception is inconsistent with Stanislavski's ideas.

The importance of the sense of scenic truth, which needs to be projected in this play, and the need for psychological understanding of the characters by the actors still hold good and are consistent with Stanislavski's key principles.

For both actor and director, Stanislavski's advice on concentration, units, objectives, obstacles and sense memory will surely prove useful.

Summary of Stanislavski's ideas

- Stanislavski was the first practitioner to identify a form of actor training. It was embedded into his work as artistic director of the Moscow Art Theatre.
- He believed in a theatre which promoted a sense of truth in acting.
- He drew clear distinctions between naturalistic theatre and realism. When discussing Stanislavski, it is important to distinguish the two.
- His ideas about acting and his dramatic practices changed and developed across a career spanning almost 60 years. It is essential not to interpret his ideas as a rule book.
- He and the Moscow Art Theatre promoted the work of some of the most important playwrights of the day, for example Chekhov, Ibsen, Gorky and Bulgakov, as well as revivals of Shakespeare plays.
- Although not politically motivated, Stanislavski felt a sense of social responsibility as a director and believed that theatre had educational and spiritual virtues. He often directed the works of playwrights who were politically motivated.
- He sought to create a style of theatre which undermined the 'star' system and the vanity of theatre.
- He set up studios to experiment with more expressionistic and non-realistic styles of acting.

Discussion questions

Make thorough notes on the points that arise from your consideration of the following questions, either from discussion or your own observations.

1 Reflecting on the plays you are studying, which of Stanislavski's ideas might prove useful in the preparation of one or more roles?

2 What plays have you seen where you think the director or actors may have used some of Stanislavski's ideas in their preparation?

3 Have you seen a play where you have been critical of aspects of the acting? Would the application of any of Stanislavski's ideas have helped? If so, which ones and with which performance(s)?

Essay questions

1 Plan a rehearsal of a play you are working on. Show how you might introduce some of Stanislavski's ideas, either through text or off-text work.

2 Focusing on one of the plays you are studying, make the case for a director requiring a realistic approach to the acting but not necessarily to the design of the set.

3 Name a style of play where the ideas of Stanislavski might not be useful. Explain your answer.

Chapter 7

The work of Bertolt Brecht

Aside from Konstantin Stanislavski (and possibly Antonin Artaud, see Chapter 9), Bertolt Brecht is the most influential figure in twentieth-century theatre. Brecht and Stanislavski are often contrasted with one another, since it is generally supposed that their intentions and their ideas were in complete opposition.

TopFoto

Bertolt Brecht (1898–1956)

Bertolt Brecht was a German poet, playwright and theatre director. He studied philosophy and medicine at the University of Munich before becoming a medical orderly in a German military hospital during the First World War. After the war, Brecht returned to university but eventually became more interested in literature than medicine.

His first play to be produced was *Baal* (1922). This was followed by *Trommeln in der Nacht* (1922), a play about a soldier returning from war, *Im Dickicht der Städte* (1923) and *Mann ist Mann* (1926).

Bertolt Brecht in 1954

Brecht developed a new approach to the performance of drama, trying to dispel the traditional make-believe of the theatre. Brecht required detachment from the audience, so that he could communicate his version of the truth.

The Berliner Ensemble

Despite the supposed polarity of their aims, what Brecht and Stanislavski have in common is that they were both outstanding directors who cultivated a particular tradition and discipline with specific theatre companies — in Brecht's case with the Berliner Ensemble, which he founded in 1949.

Brecht's rebellion against the established theatre was not necessarily a rebellion against the specific ideas and practices of Stanislavski, although there were many elements of the theatre of realism that he criticised. Neither is it the case that all his work as a playwright and director makes use of his theories about theatre.

John Willett — generally acknowledged as the foremost British scholar on Brecht — makes the valuable point that some of Brecht's later productions with the Berliner Ensemble achieved critical acclaim without being specifically 'Brechtian' in style. In *The Theatre of Bertolt Brecht*, he cites Sam Wanamaker (1919–93, the actor and restorer of the Globe Theatre in London), describing the performance by Brecht's wife Helene Weigel (1900–71) in *Mother Courage* (1939) as 'indistinguishable from a superb Stanislavski-trained actress'. Just as with Stanislavski, it is important not to adopt a formulaic or rigid approach when exploring Brecht's ideas for theatre.

The principal difference between the two men — not in terms of their political aspirations, which we shall come to, but in their practical activities — is that whereas Stanislavski was an actor as well as a director, Brecht was primarily a playwright, essayist and poet.

This is a crucial consideration. Although Stanislavski wrote daily, and copiously, he did so for the purpose of personal reflection, self-analysis and observation, in order to improve his own practice and the practice of those in his charge. His work was essentially note-taking. Brecht, on the other hand, was a writer of academic essays. He was a Communist and a supporter of the revolutionary ideals of Karl Marx. He wrote about theories of performance and presentation in order to contribute publicly to a political debate as much as to express coherent practical ideas of theatre procedure. There has, therefore, been a tendency by some teachers and directors to interpret his ideas too literally and ignore the political context in which he offered them. Stephen Unwin states the situation succinctly in *So You Want to be a Theatre Director?*

> Brecht is his own worst enemy. His essays have led generations of actors and directors into a theoretical jungle, in which superficial aesthetic ideas have been mistaken for substance — above all the much disputed 'alienation effect' — and crude demonstrative acting is excused on the grounds that it's 'Brechtian'. But Brecht's writings on theatre need to be seen as provocations at a particular time and place, a reaction against the headlong embrace by half of Europe's theatre-goers of the ghastly stupidity of fascism. And they can be exceptionally useful.

Brecht's ideas

If Brecht's ideas are to be 'exceptionally useful', as Unwin suggests, then they must be applied with understanding and discrimination. This means, as much as anything, the realisation that those ideas will not work for every play and that, indeed, they will not even necessarily work for every play by Brecht.

Before we identify a suitable text which might be explored effectively in production using Brechtian theory, we will first pinpoint the major elements of the theory and then explore how they were developed in practice.

Epic theatre

Brecht's style of theatre is often referred to as 'epic theatre'. 'Epic' is a term originally coined by the Greek philosopher Aristotle with reference to poetry. The poetic tragedy, Aristotle argues, should consist of one series of events taking place over a definable and contained period of time. On the other hand, the epic poem may depict a number of events that happen simultaneously, to 'add mass and dignity to the poem'.

The epic poem

An epic poem is a long narrative poem, often detailing the heroic exploits of an individual. The first epic poems would have been created and transmitted orally, often by travelling poets, and were not written down. Many ancient Greek epics (for instance Homer's *Iliad* and *Odyssey*, poems centred around the siege of Troy) date from between the eighth and the sixth centuries BC, and were probably originally oral. The Old English poem *Beowulf* is an example of a Dark Ages epic poem that was probably oral in origin (*c.* 700 AD) but later written down (*c.* 1010 AD). It is over 3,000 lines long. A more recent example is John Milton's famous epic poem in ten books, *Paradise Lost* (1667).

There is in the 'epic' creation, therefore, a sense of scale or a 'capacity for enlarging its dimensions'. It is this sense of scale that has meaning for us today when we describe a play — or more usually now a film — as epic, referring to its length or the complexity of its setting. Many of the films of the mid-twentieth century made by the British film director David Lean have been described as epics, for instance *The Bridge on the River Kwai* (1957), *Lawrence of Arabia* (1962), *Doctor Zhivago* (1965) and *Ryan's Daughter* (1970).

Doctor Zhivago (1965) has been described as an epic film

Brecht's use of the term 'epic' bears only some relation to Aristotle's definition, in that he did not wish to be constrained by the unity of time, which Aristotle had identified as being an essential ingredient of tragedy. He wished to have the freedom to depict events happening in an irregular time frame. This is why many of Brecht's plays contain a large number of short episodic scenes that do not necessarily take place in a chronological order.

Part of Brecht's desire in moving away from the unity of time was to eliminate what he saw as the hypnotic qualities of theatre — those elements that might seduce an audience into becoming too engrossed in the story rather than engaged by its social issues. Short, punchy scenes, often punctuated by music and covering a series of events that might be taking place simultaneously, would keep an audience's attention and 'jerk' its members into the role of observers rather than passive witnesses.

Brecht and silent film

Brecht was impressed by early silent cinema (from around 1895 to the late 1920s), particularly some of the comic work of Charlie Chaplin (1889–1977) and Buster Keaton (1895–1966). Silent film comedy shows episodic structure and the use of strong, immediate physical humour.

Epic theatre versus dramatic theatre

Brecht used the term 'epic' to distinguish his work from 'dramatic' theatre. In his introductory notes to *Rise and Fall of the City of Mahagonny* (1927) — a political-satirical opera by Kurt Weill to which he wrote the libretto, first performed in Leipzig in 1930 — Brecht usefully offers definitions to clarify his understanding of the two types of theatre. Some of them are reproduced in Table 1.

Table 1 Epic theatre versus dramatic theatre in Brechtian terms

Epic theatre	Dramatic theatre
Narrative	Plot
Turns the spectator into an observer	Implicates the spectator in a stage situation
Arouses the spectator's capacity for action	Wears down the spectator's capacity for action
Forces the spectator to take decisions	Provides the spectator with sensations
The spectator is made to face something	The spectator is involved in something
Argument	Suggestion
The spectator stands outside, studies	The spectator is in the thick of it, shares
The spectator is alterable and able to alter	The spectator is unalterable
Social being determines thought	Thought determines being

If you compare the two sides of the table, you will begin to understand the essential differences between Brecht's own epic theatrical aims and his perception of the theatre of realism ('dramatic theatre').

The importance of audience

The aims shown in Table 1 are particularly useful for a discussion of the importance of audience. It is interesting to note that while Stanislavski, in his writing, clearly respects the audience and takes seriously his role as a provider of culture and education, he does not make the audience a part of the dramatic process. Brecht, on the other hand, views the audience as a pivotal part of the process of theatre, and this process is geared towards making the spectator respond. Not only should man be seen as a being who can reach decisions as a result of witnessing theatrical productions, the theatre that he sees should force him to make such decisions.

Brecht's aim, therefore, is to inspire his audience to take action. Having identified in simple terms the aims of epic theatre, what techniques does Brecht employ in order to achieve these aims?

The alienation effect

Of all the techniques and theories propounded by Brecht, undoubtedly the so-called 'alienation effect' is the most controversial and often the subject of misunderstanding or misinterpretation.

The word 'alienation' in this context is a translation from the German term *Verfremdung*, thus the concept is often referred to as the *Verfremdungseffekt* or the *V-effekt* (you should note that 'alienation' is an imperfect translation for *Verfremdung*).

In essence, we should see the alienation effect as being the means by which we can look critically at events and people in a fresh and perhaps unfamiliar light. To illustrate the idea, Brecht gives the example of regarding one's mother as a wife:

> To see one's mother as a man's wife one needs a *V-effekt*; this is provided, for example, when one acquires a stepfather. If one sees one's form-master hounded by the bailiffs a *V-effekt* occurs: one is jerked out of a relationship in which the form-master seems big into one where he seems small.
>
> (Willett, *The Theatre of Bertolt Brecht*)

Practical application in performance

The common misperception of the alienation effect is that it requires an actor to perform without emotion or even expression. Reflecting on Wanamaker's view of Helene Weigel's performance in *Mother Courage* (see page 109) — a performance captured on film and clearly one of emotional complexity and depth — it is difficult to sustain the view that the alienation effect somehow means that the actor should emotionally neuter his or her performance. What then is meant by 'alienation' in the context of performance, and why is it misinterpreted in this way?

The alienation effect does not entail estranging the audience in the sense of making its members hostile to the performance they are watching or the views being expressed by the play. Rather, it is an attempt to reveal drama in a fresh light, where events and relationships should not be taken for granted. Therefore, Mother in *Mother Courage* should not simply be seen as a mother who loses three children in the war but as a woman who puts business before her children and loses them as a consequence. The alienation here is an attempt to distance the audience from the obvious interpretation of the character as a grief-stricken mother. The emotional complexity of the role should not deter the actor from exploring the social implications of the play and the strong political message that underlies it. The playing of the role should reflect this 'concrete truth' and not become a performance that is purely about the bereavement of a mother.

The alienation effect, then, prevents an audience establishing too intimate or one-dimensional a relationship with an actor's interpretation of a character. An actor should explore the social elements of the character — in conjunction with the director — to ensure that his or her interpretation demonstrates an understanding of the character as a feature of society, not just a figure of human emotion. That is why one of the major distinctions between the 'epic' theatre of Aristotle and the 'epic' theatre of Brecht is the lack of empathy between audience and actor: for Brecht, members of the audience must not be hypnotised into losing themselves in the performance of the actor and so surrendering their critical faculties. They must remain alert to the issues of the play, make decisions about them and then act on those decisions.

This does not preclude the idea that the action may be presented with emotion by the actor, but this emotion should not distract from the playwright's message, the substance and content of the play.

Gestus

Gestus is, perhaps, an even more difficult German term than *Verfremdung* to translate into an equivalent English expression. As the word suggests, it is connected with the gestures an actor might make. However, it also describes the attitude and gist of a scene or a role and is, therefore, expressed in a number of ways.

Gestus, either through words or movement, helps the actor to simplify the role and condense it into its recognisable essential elements. It defines appropriate action rather than subtext and psychological preoccupation.

Practical application in performance

The sense of distilling a role to its essentials is reflected in Brecht's craft as a writer, choosing as he does to adopt an economic poetic style rather than create expansive or elegant speeches and dialogue. A good example is Peachum's opening song in *The Threepenny Opera* (1928):

You ramshackle Christian awake!
Get on with your sinful employment.
Show what a good crook you could make.
The Lord will cut short your enjoyment.

Betray your own brother, you rogue
And sell your old woman you rat.
You think the Lord God's just a joke?
He'll give you His Judgement on that.

The language in this extract is simple, the meaning and attitude abundantly clear, assisted by a punctuated, sharp rhythm. There is no subtlety in these lines and they leave little room for doubt about the character and motives of Peachum.

However, in its crudest and most misguided interpretation, *Gestus* has been used to suggest character through a series of limited and repeated gestures. In a recent production of Brecht's 1937 play *Señora Carrar's Rifles*, the director had clearly instructed the actors to choose about three gestures each and stick to them rigidly. Given that this particular play is, arguably, a rare example of Brecht experimenting with a more Aristotelian approach, the sight of actors constantly having to repeat a series of awkward and contrived gestures was alienating to the audience in precisely the manner Brecht did *not* intend.

Gestus can be helpful to actors and director alike in attempting to discover the essential heart of a scene or an onstage relationship. To impose the notion of *Gestus* as a rule which restricts movement or gesture is to miss the point entirely. At its best, it can be used as tool of discovery and simplification; at its worst, it can confuse, obstruct and over-complicate.

Music

Brecht often used music in his plays. His most notable collaboration was with the composer Kurt Weill in *The Threepenny Opera* (1928), an adaptation of *The Beggar's Opera* written by John Gay in the early eighteenth century. The role of the music here is not to hypnotise or charm the audience, as is often the case in the modern musical, but instead to jerk them into consciousness.

The songs in *The Threepenny Opera* have been described as 'interruptions', and the actors in the original production were chosen because of their acting ability and not their prowess in singing. In his notes for *The Threepenny Opera*, Brecht writes:

> Nothing is more revolting than when an actor pretends not to notice that he has left plain speech and started to sing… As for the melody, he must not follow it blindly: there is a kind of speaking-against-the music which can have strong effects; the result of a stubborn, incorruptible sobriety which is independent of music and rhythm.

For Brecht, music is not there to provide an emotional peak to a play or scene but instead to create a moment when a character might speak messages or tell stories through the song. We must not confuse Brecht's use of music, therefore, with the use made of it by writers of popular musical theatre, where music is used to seduce or thrill an audience — for example, the title theme in Andrew Lloyd Webber's *Phantom of the Opera* (1986).

It is open to question whether the intention not to seduce or thrill was truly realised, given the success and appeal of some of Weill's music — most notably 'Mac the Knife' from *The Threepenny Opera*, which has since been recorded by Bobby Darrin, Ella Fitzgerald and Frank Sinatra. The big production treatment afforded to this and numerous other versions of the song would have appalled Brecht, who used a simple chamber orchestra production sung by an actor with an untrained singing voice. For him, the music had to deliver the text and was, therefore, subservient to it. Brecht's lyrics were part of his notion of *Gestus*; they were economical and poetic but efficient and constrained. They were not lyrically expansive and beautiful.

Among other collaborators, Brecht worked somewhat unsuccessfully with the composer Paul Hindemith on the *Lehrstück* (1929), a series of short didactic plays. While Hindemith's work is often far from easy listening, it can be chillingly atmospheric and Brecht was concerned that it might interfere with or overwhelm the sharply didactic nature of the text. Hindemith, on the other hand, was reluctant to provide music which was always going to be subjugated to the text — designed to deliver the written word rather than to enhance it as an equal partner.

Practical application in performance

In Brechtian theatre there should be little or no attempt to disguise the musicians from the audience. Hence musicians can appear on stage beside the actors, rather than being hidden away in an orchestra pit. In some Brechtian productions, the actors may also serve as musicians, ensuring that the illusion of their characters' reality will be broken for the audience as soon as they pick up their instruments.

Music in Brecht's plays, it has been argued, is part of the alienation effect, since it cannot fail to remind the members of an audience of the theatrical nature of what they are seeing and subvert any temptation they may feel to accept that the representation they are witnessing is fact — it is an obvious part of the mechanics of theatre. However, the role of music is more profound and defining than simply that of a reminder to the audience of the theatrical devices at work. Rather, it is an attempt by Brecht to punctuate his language — sometimes quite harshly — and affords characters the opportunity to report on the action and to tell stories to the audience that are relevant to the action and often didactic in tone.

Education and 'entertainment'

Many people assert — understandably, given the nature of some of his essays — that Brecht firmly believed the theatre should be a place of education and not of entertainment.

In his notes on *Mahagonny*, he identifies the distinctions between dramatic and epic theatre and also expresses the need to redefine the theatre generally:

> Thus to develop the means of entertainment into an object of instruction, and to change certain institutions from places of amusement into organs of public communication.

This statement has a somewhat authoritarian tone to it and perhaps provides us with an example of how Brecht's theory can differ from his practice. There is little doubt that his plays of the time *were* entertaining — often containing significant elements of verbal and physical humour — and it seems strange that he would advocate the complete scrapping of the role of entertainment. Brecht's theories do at times differ from his practice, and it is necessary to remember that he was writing from the viewpoint of a polemicist and his expressed views are, therefore, deliberately provocative.

Auditorium atmosphere

In his notes to accompany *The Threepenny Opera*, Brecht describes the auditorium atmosphere he aspired to have as:

> ...that boxing-ring attitude of smoking and observing.

Clearly Brecht felt that the audience should be relaxed and in an informal environment, conducive to discussion and reflection. The members of the audience should be able to see all the mechanics of theatre — musicians, stagehands, all the work of acting and singing. No attempt should be made to persuade them that the theatre experience is mimicking reality. The theatre, in other words, should be a place of representation rather than illusion, and the theatrical environment one in which the working man should feel comfortable, not awkward.

Changing theory of entertainment

In 1949 Brecht wrote an important document called 'A Short Organum for the Theatre', in which he refers once again to the theme of entertainment. The 'Organum' was deliberately written in the style of Aristotle, whose original 'Organon' had been his treatise on logic.

Just as Aristotle had sought to define areas of theatre, so too did Brecht, offering revised versions of his earlier ideas. Instead of suggesting the scrapping of entertainment, as he had once done in the introductory notes of *Mahagonny,* he now wanted to embrace it:

> Let us treat theatre as a place of entertainment…and try to discover which type of entertainment suits us best.

However, this new emphasis on entertainment was not quite the radical shift which it first appears. Nor should it be thought that by embracing entertainment Brecht now saw theatre as a place of frivolity. In the postwar era, Brecht was concerned that theatre should be seen as part of the new scientific age. Willett argues in *The Theatre of Bertolt Brecht* that the pleasure gained from the entertaining elements of theatre is the pleasure one might feel from seeing a highly efficient and beautiful piece of mechanics at work, or from hearing a social issue expressed with clarity and analytical precision: 'Science and art meet on this ground, that both are there to make man's life easier…'

The Organum is a development of Brecht's earlier writings, being rather less polemic and less politically motivated. This is understandable, since it was written after the defeat of the Nazis. Many of his earlier ideas regarding the use of lighting and singing remain unchanged. However, it is important to point out that even the Organum contains elements of theory that Brecht did not try out. The majority of Brecht's productions were not held in factories or centres populated by only working people. They were often performed in the centre of Berlin or on tour, and frequently to appreciative middle-class audiences. So far as his untried theories were concerned, Brecht put this down to a lack of readiness in the audience. Although the members of his audiences lived in a scientific age, he said, they themselves were not scientific enough to be exposed to his new ideas.

Brecht's theories applied

The point should be clear now that one should not apply the work of theorists formulaically. When you visit the theatre, although you might do so with a critical perspective, your first response to a production will probably *not* be to ask yourself whether it has been influenced by the ideas of either Brecht or Stanislavski. It is not contradictory for a production to be influenced by both practitioners. The practice of trying to force Stanislavski and Brecht into a 'boxing ring', where the work of one is diametrically opposed to the work of the other, is as pointless as it is inaccurate. However, there are principles and practices of Brecht which may be applied usefully and successfully. To illustrate this idea, we will look at two plays, one of which is unmistakably Brechtian in tone and style and another which is open to broader interpretation.

Approaching a production of 'Oh! What a Lovely War'

In preparing any text for production, it is important for a director to consider his or her concept for the play. *Oh! What a Lovely War* (Joan Littlewood, 1963) is a play with a number of specific requirements. It is the story of the First World War, staged as an 'end of the pier' Pierrot show. All the actors, therefore, are intended to be dressed in white clown-like costumes over which they add extra elements of theatrical attire.

Oh! What a Lovely War is staged as an 'end of the pier' Pierrot show. (Regent's Park Open Air Theatre, 2002)

It is, of course, possible to vary this presentation. In 1963, when the play was first performed, Pierrot shows would have been in the living memory of some members of the audience — such shows were on the rise at the time of the First World War (1914–18). However, a modern director may feel that Pierrot is too remote an image for an audience of the twenty-first century and therefore wish to adapt or amend the nature of the play's presentation.

Oh! What a Lovely War depicts the major events of the First World War in a series of episodes, and delivers its message through music and dance as well as dialogue. In what ways could this play be seen as typifying the elements of Brechtian theatre?

'Character' in the play

It is impossible to become embroiled in the fate of one major character in this piece — there aren't any. At the start of the play, the members of the cast sing a well-known 'music hall' song of the era, 'Johnny Jones'. The Master of Ceremonies enters, wishes everyone a good evening, tells a few corny jokes and introduces 'the ever popular war game'.

The 'characters' of all the major countries involved in the war now enter and explain their tense relationships. Germany believes it should have more say in world affairs. The MC blows a whistle and announces the second part of the war game, and — against the background of German music — the German generals discuss their plans for war. As they do so, an image of the 'Schlieffen Plan' (Germany's ultimately disastrous blueprint for winning the war in a matter of weeks) is projected onto a screen by a slide projector. One by one, the other nations announce their plans for war and for striking the all-important knockout blow.

As the play continues, we see the progress of the war through a series of scenes, some more realistic than others.

Towards the end of the first half, the scene is set in the trenches of the Western Front on Christmas Eve 1914. A dialogue develops between the soldiers from the German and the British trenches and eventually they meet and shake

Pierrot shows

The character of Pierrot, in his familiar white baggy costume, was created by Giuseppe Giratoni in France in the middle of the seventeenth century. Pierrot arrived in England in 1891, and his popularity was established by his appearance in a French mime play which ran at the Prince of Wales Theatre. The first English Pierrot troupe was set up around 1895.

Pierrot shows pioneered a new form of public entertainment in England, consisting of songs, dances, comic sketches and occasional monologues. The shows were performed in the open, and gained the English name 'concert party'.

By 1910, troupes were taking their Pierrot shows on tour rather than remaining in one resort for the summer season. By the end of the 1920s, permanent wooden staging was often used for the alfresco shows, offering proper seating for the audience. These shows continued to flourish through the 1930s and 1940s, after which their popularity waned.

hands in the middle — in 'no man's land', the patch of ground between the two sets of trenches. The famous First World War song 'Goodbyee' is played. The end of the first half seems to arrive at a tranquil, almost ironically peaceful mood when the sound of an exploding shell is heard and the last line of the song is rendered inaudible.

The following links with Brechtian theory are important:

- During the play, the projection of images and statistics relevant to the war involves modern technology. The use of powerful factual imagery and information underpins the dramatic action, and serves to remind the audience that the performance on stage represents a reality that reaches far beyond the world of the theatre.

- Although written nearly half a century ago and depicting events of nearly 100 years ago, the play is still remarkably popular, particularly with community and youth groups. It is not uncommon for modern productions of *Oh! What a Lovely War* to use photographic and video images from more recent wars and to employ multiracial casts in order to afford a more contemporary feel to the piece. Thus Brecht's ideal of a play which does not constrain its audience within an individual plot is preserved, and a modern audience may still bear witness to the narrative of an anti-war statement.

- Although there is a chronology to the war, to which the slogans and on-screen projections largely adhere, the episodic structure of the play prevents an audience being drawn into a plot line. The arms dealers' shooting scene at the start of Act II is not significant from the perspective of plot (this scene could have been placed almost anywhere in the play); it is the potential impact on the audience that is important.

- The first act ends with the scenes in the trenches on Christmas Eve 1914, demonstrating the basic humanity of the soldiers — the men are not naturally enemies. The opening of the second act is almost a parody of this revelation, showing arms dealers from the various sides in the war enjoying the camaraderie of the grouse hunt and celebrating the wealth that the continued hostilities bring them.

- In the second half of the play we meet the only character other than the Master of Ceremonies who could be said to have a major role. Field Marshall Haig was the commander of all British troops from 1916 to the end of the war, and we see him frequently throughout the second half. However, he is presented as a compassionless individual, ordering men to certain death and contemplating that 'the loss of say another 300,000 men could yield some really great results'. There is little danger of an audience being drawn into his story or identifying with him — quite the reverse. This undoubtedly one-sided view of Haig's character (and indeed of other characters and events) led some to criticise the play. But again, this is a reason why it is suitable for a Brechtian treatment. Brecht's theatre is not balanced — there is always a strong political or social message. The message of *Oh! What a Lovely War* is clearly an anti-war statement, and there is no attempt to create a balanced piece of theatre. It is in the nature of political theatre that it presents a cogent viewpoint, not a representation of all sides of the argument.

♦ Further examples of characterisation in *Oh! What a Lovely War* are also consistent with Brecht's style of presentation in that they are described by their functions — 'officer', 'nurse', 'chaplain' etc. The characters are immediately recognisable and relevant to the social and violent context in which they are presented. An ensemble of actors would be expected to play all the parts and would be identifiable in each role they played.

Practical application in performance

How might a performance of *Oh! What a Lovely War* demonstrate elements of Brecht's theories as previously discussed?

First, a production should not be created as a vehicle or showcase for any practitioner's work; such elements should be used only if they help to enhance the production. This was the case for the original adaptor and director of *Oh! What a Lovely War*, Littlewood, and her Company of the Theatre Workshop. They had a clear artistic policy, underpinned and defined by a socialist view of the world. In this regard, they therefore had much in common with Brecht and the work of the Berliner Ensemble. Indeed, Littlewood would almost certainly have seen examples of the ensemble's work when it toured Britain. The broad ideological aims and the nature of the piece they wanted to create meant that many of Brecht's devices for presentation were relevant. For a company producing this play today, there are equally many elements of Brecht's theories which might be useful.

The alienation effect and *Gestus*

The alienation effect is found in the nature of the characterisation, in the use of music and singing and in the short *Gestus*-orientated scenes. *Gestus* is employed in the sense that every scene has a particular gist to it, making it distinctive. For example, the scene featuring Mrs Pankhurst clearly articulates the suffragettes' view of the war and the abusive response of many of the ordinary men and women to her. The sight and sound of her embattled pleas as she speaks to an increasingly dubious and hostile crowd gives the scene a specific dimension and angle.

There is no attempt to explore the psychological impact of the crowd's hostility towards the character of Mrs Pankhurst, nor is there an intricate description of the motivations of each of the characters on stage with her. Such features are unnecessary because it is easily discernible within the action of the scene that one of the effects of the war was to polarise the spirit of patriotism and the aims of the suffragettes, so that the suffragettes were seen almost as traitors and, as a consequence, their cause lost momentum.

There is a definite *Gestus* character to the party scene involving the generals, as they dance with their wives or mistresses to the gentle sound of a palm court orchestra and play power games with and against each other. Such an event may never have taken place, but the purpose here is not to recreate or replicate reality. Rather, there is a higher reality or 'concrete truth', which is that titled and wealthy generals vied for positions of power and influence while sending other men to the Western Front, where they died horrible and premature deaths. The *Gestus* is clear, and a director and actors will find this helpful in developing the characters.

While the nature of the *Gestus*, in this particular context at least, may lead to choices that are stereotypical (for instance, making the character of a general an 'upper-class twit'), that does not make the anger of the piece any less valid or dramatically justified.

The 'boxing ring' atmosphere: audience reaction

It would surely be impractical to stage *Oh! What a Lovely War* in a boxing ring atmosphere, with audiences smoking, observing and commenting on the action; perhaps this would be taking Brechtian theory a step too far.

However, the important quality for a production of this play is that the anger and anti-war sentiment are made abundantly clear to the audience. Even though it is a piece about the First World War, the message should be relevant to the modern world, and the audience should feel a strong reaction.

The director might feel, for instance, that the absurdly nationalistic arguments of the generals professing that 'God is on our side' are reminiscent of the attitudes of a number of politicians over recent years. The members of an audience may well make that connection for themselves, but a director — perhaps one known for his or her strong political stance — might use imagery, scenery and costume to make that connection more concrete for them.

Just as performances in Brechtian-style theatre may have an emotional content, the audience response may legitimately be emotional too. Ask yourself why the audience of *Oh! What a Lovely War* might be weeping. To weep for the loss of a fictional character — for example the death of Leonardo DiCaprio's character in the film *Titanic* (1997) — is an example of the kind of cathartic response that Brecht found repellent. On the other hand, for the audience to weep at the injustice and horror of war is a sign of the play's success, since it is that emotional reaction which may lead the audience to want to change the society that brought about the war in the first instance.

The use of technology

While the original productions of Brecht's plays were given simple settings by his designer, Caspar Neher, Brecht valued the use of technology. His belief in the aesthetic pleasure of seeing efficient technology at work could be incorporated into a modern production of *Oh! What a Lovely War*. Of course, the sophistication of theatre technology has increased enormously since the first production in 1963. It would not be necessary, therefore, to use excessively complicated and expensive technology to enhance such a production, in order for it to qualify as 'Brechtian'. However, it is arguably illogical not to use computerised lighting boards, digital sound systems and PowerPoint-generated images, following a misguided view that any invention that has emerged since Brecht's death is not 'Brechtian'.

Effective use of lighting can certainly support specific moments in the play. For example, a change in lighting, which Brecht advocated when a character sings, could be used to dispel any notion of reality. However, this play is performed successfully in a variety of venues by companies with vastly different budgets. In production, its effect depends more upon clarity of performance and swiftness of scene change than technical wizardry.

Comparison with 'Journey's End'

Does *Oh! What a Lovely War* make its point more effectively than *Journey's End* (1928) by R. C. Sherriff (1896–1975) — a much more naturalistic play on the same subject?

Journey's End is set in a dugout on the Western Front, and the action takes place over the period of a few days in March 1918 during the German offensive. In the course of the play, we become familiar with each of the characters. Stanhope, the young but prematurely aged captain, presides over the officers in his platoon as one by one they fall victim to the enemy onslaught. Does the audience's emotional involvement with the lives and deaths of the officers in *Journey's End* mean that it might lose sight of the issue of the rights and wrongs of war? Some would argue that the naturalistic style of *Journey's End*, in allowing the audience to witness the suffering of individuals, brings home the horror of war more effectively than the Brechtian style of *Oh! What a Lovely War*.

It is ultimately a matter of individual audience experience and the skill of those involved in particular productions as to which play is regarded as more successful. It is not possible to argue conclusively that an issue-based piece of theatre which avoids naturalism is definitely more successful at communicating a 'message' than a piece of 'epic' theatre.

What can be argued with these two examples is that while the element of human suffering is uncompromisingly clear in both plays, the anti-war politics of *Oh! What a Lovely War* are unmistakable. It would be tenable, therefore, to draw the conclusion that *Journey's End* is more of a humanist play and *Oh! What a Lovely War* more of a political one. The message conveyed is no less powerful; it is simply that the emphasis is different.

Does the naturalistic style of *Journey's End* bring home the horror of war more effectively than the Brechtian style of *Oh! What a Lovely War*?

Summary

When evaluating Brecht's theatrical ideas, it is important to remember that he was principally a playwright and a director, not an actor. Furthermore, he did not always put his own ideas into practice. As an essayist, he put forward theories of theatre and staging that were, at least in part, defined by a belief in Marxist ideology. Brecht argued his Marxist standpoint most vociferously while his native Germany was under the tyranny of Nazism.

Brecht identified comparisons between his own works and theories of performance and those of Shakespeare, specifically in the use of verse and soliloquy, and the extensive use of epic action. During his career, Brecht directed a number of Shakespearean productions and was critical of many standard productions of the time.

Group activities

1 The best way to explore Brecht's ideas is to rehearse a scene from one of his plays: look especially at *Mother Courage* and *The Caucasian Chalk Circle*, or at some of the shorter plays in *Lehrstücke*, such as *The Exception and The Rule*.

2 If you are using Brecht's ideas as a model for devising, you could attempt the following activity about the story of the Good Samaritan in the Bible (Luke 10:25–37). In this story, a Jewish man is set upon by thieves and left for dead. A lawyer and a priest pass him by, but a Samaritan helps him and takes him to a place of rest.

It is important to note that Samaritans were despised by the story's target audience, the Jews. To recast the story in a more recognisable modern setting, instead of a Jew being helped by a Samaritan, one could have a racist helped by a member of the race he or she hates, or a sexist man helped by a woman.

Rather than concentrating on the graphic reality of the attack, play the scene ensuring that the views of the participants are clearly known. Each character should use narration to explain his or her actions or the lack of them. An audience should be left in no doubt as to (a) the motives of the individuals in their actions and (b) where the sympathies of the group lie.

Do not necessarily follow the religious implications of the story. For example, you may want to slant the story to the thieves' point of view and focus on their motivations. Or you may wish to suggest that the Samaritan has reasons other than simple 'goodness' in carrying out his actions. The important feature should be that the members of the audience are engaged in a debate and feel challenged by what they have witnessed.

Chapter 8

Applying Brecht's principles

Macbeth by Shakespeare

Brecht directed a number of Shakespeare's plays in addition to his own work, and it has been argued that there are some interesting links between the crafts of the two men. These were links which Brecht himself identified:

- Brecht argues that his plays *Life of Galileo* (1938/1945) and *Mother Courage* owe elements of their structure and their use of clear historical contexts to some of the great works of Shakespeare. Many Shakespearean plays are set in specific time periods or based on real characters from history.

- Shakespeare's use of monologue or soliloquy, usually in verse and addressed directly to an audience, is echoed in some of Brecht's rhythmic verses, likewise delivered directly to the spectators. Shakespeare used soliloquy to confront an audience with a particular view or a passionate declaration, designed to provoke an unexpected response. For example in *King Lear*, the audience does not expect to sympathise with 'the bastard' Edmund when he confides his plotting against his brother and his father. However, having heard Edmund's soliloquy, the audience is forced to take a view about his behaviour. Is he simply a devious and malicious villain, or should we have some sympathy for his case?

In *The Theatre of Bertolt Brecht* the translator and scholar John Willett (1917–2002), who is famous for translating Brecht's work into English, identifies the qualities which drew Brecht to Shakespeare:

Actual events, actual relations, clearly-defined actions, a sort of running fight in which each successive issue is plain: Brecht had aimed at such goals…and in Shakespeare he saw them attained. In Shakespeare but not in the average Shakespeare production.

Brecht also described how he considered Shakespearean plays to be more 'epic' than 'dramatic'. When discussing the structure of *Coriolanus* (*c.* 1608), Brecht claims:

> …all these great and small conflicts thrown on the scene at once; the unrest of the starving plebeians together with the war against their neighbours the Volsci; the plebeians' hatred for Marcius, the people's enemy — together with his patriotism; the creation of the people's tribunes — together with Marcius's appointment to a leading post in the war. How much of that do we get in the bourgeois theatre?

Presumably Brecht believed that most Shakespearean productions did not meet the demands of the play because they failed to reflect 'these great and small conflicts' all at once.

Brechtian elements in productions of Shakespeare
Barrie Rutter

Since the early 1990s, Barrie Rutter's company Northern Broadsides has produced a large number of Shakespeare's plays. Rutter usually employs actors from the north of England who use northern accents. His settings are simple, with plays staged in real working environments. Such an approach has definite links with the aspirations of Brecht and the kind of settings he wished his plays to have.

Productions of Shakespeare often have a specific political flavour, which gives the plays an earthy, angry pugnacity. Rutter's 1992 production of *Richard III* (*c.* 1592–94), for instance, opened with an argument between Richard (played by Rutter) and the Lady Ann which had a fierce, gutteral, confrontational quality about it — a ringing, uncompromising clarity and an unmistakable *Gestus* of anger and guile.

Barrie Rutter often employs Brechtian elements in his productions of Shakespeare's plays

Barrie Rutter (1946–)

Born in 1946, the son of a Hull fishworker, Rutter grew up in the fishdock area of Hull. At school, an English teacher frogmarched him into the school play because he had 'the gob for it'. Rutter's future direction was thus determined.

After leaving school, he studied at the Royal Scottish Academy of Music and Drama and then spent many years in the National Youth Theatre, culminating in his role as Douglas Bagley in the television drama *The Apprentices*

(Peter Terson, 1968), a role specially written for him. His natural talent for acting has resulted in many other roles being written for him throughout his career.

Seasons at the RSC in Stratford, London and Europe completed the 1970s. In 1980, he joined the National Theatre; at this time he met and worked closely with the poet Tony Harrison. Rutter performed in all three of Harrison's adaptations, all written for the northern voice: *The Oresteia* (1981), *The Mysteries* (1985) and *The Trackers of Oxyrhynchus* (1988). In *Trackers*, the part of Silenus was written especially for Rutter. It was this experience of performing in the northern voice that germinated the idea for his company, Northern Broadsides.

Northern Broadsides was founded in 1992 and has developed a reputation for high-quality productions of Shakespeare and classic adaptations. The productions are often simply staged, sometimes using working settings such as textile mills or boatyards, to emphasise a 'workman-like' approach. The style has endured; Northern Broadsides is one of the country's most respected theatre companies, and Rutter himself has emerged as an important director in British theatre.

Michael Bogdanov (1938–)

Michael Bogdanov has produced, written and directed for both theatre and television during his successful career, but his primary interest is in the theatre. He received a Director of the Year award in 1979 for his RSC production of *The Taming of the Shrew*. He has also directed productions of Shakespeare's plays internationally, including *Hamlet* at the Abbey Theatre in Dublin, *Romeo and Juliet* at the Imperial Theatre in Tokyo, *Measure for Measure* at Stratford, Ontario and *Julius Caesar* at the Deutsches Schauspielhaus in Hamburg. In 1992, he directed a pioneering version of *Macbeth*, which travelled to four African countries.

He also created and directed a 12-part series for Channel 4, *Shakespeare Lives*. He co-founded the English Shakespeare Company with actor Michael Pennington in 1986.

Bogdanov was instrumental in establishing the Wales Theatre Company and has continued to enhance his reputation through successful productions of *Under Milk Wood* (2005) and Mal Pope's *Amazing Grace* (2006).

Michael Bogdanov

An example of a political approach to Shakespeare is Michael Bogdanov's production of *The Merchant of Venice*, staged by the English Shakespeare Company (1991).

In this production, the distinguished actor John Woodvine played a tall, dignified Shylock in a Venice set in Mussolini's fascist and anti-Semitic pre-war Italy of 1938. The persecution of Shylock at the hands of the Christians was therefore lent extra venom and political savagery.

Ian Brown

Ian Brown's 2002 production of *Hamlet* at the West Yorkshire Playhouse was not specifically set in a particular period of history, but the use of silent film and uniforms suggested an inter-war setting — perhaps the 1920s or 1930s. The gloomy high walls of the set, with many entrances set at different levels, suggested a place of secrets, rumours and paranoia. Claudius, the king, was dressed in a grey military uniform, suggestive of a totalitarian regime such as Hitler's Germany or Mussolini's Italy. Hamlet himself, played by Christopher Eccleston, was angry, ill at ease and seemingly stifled by an atmosphere of suppression and claustrophobia; he was a trapped poet, suffocating in the politicised, military environment of his uncle's court.

The character of Hamlet in this production, therefore, is not realised simply as a grieving son lamenting the loss of his father and the traitorous actions of his mother. Instead there is a realisation of Hamlet — an emotionally and intellectually vigorous individual — finding himself in a context where individuality may be regarded as dangerously subversive. As such he is a threatened and depressed figure. The production thus had a political as well as an emotional dimension to it.

Macbeth

We will examine here some of the questions which you might consider as the director of a production of *Macbeth* (c. 1606) who wishes to make use of Brechtian ideas.

Your production need not, of course, obey all the 'rules' of what is sometimes seen as a traditional Brechtian production. These include actors getting changed in view of the audience, slogans being projected on screens, actors wearing black and white costumes and musicians being visible on stage. The reality of a production can be far more subtle and may share features with the work of other practitioners.

Background

The plot of *Macbeth* is convoluted. We are first presented with the setting: Scotland, a country ravaged by war from a combination of Norwegian forces and the traitorous Thane of Cawdor. Before any of the political plot-laying commences, we are confronted with the witches' scene, presaging their meeting with Macbeth 'on the heath'.

The swift-moving opening, which takes us from the witches to the king to Macbeth and Banquo, presents us with a series of simultaneous events; the audience is not introduced

'Deadly theatre'

If a production of Shakespeare offers only beautiful spoken verse and the starring performance of a famous actor, the potential strength of the play with its complex social message can be lost. It becomes what the British theatre and film director Peter Brook (1925–) referred to in *The Empty Space* as 'deadly theatre'. A successful production should be a living theatre experience, where members of an audience become involved, where they identify with the characters' emotions, and where they emerge with a heightened awareness of important universal themes.

to a single plot. While we may subsequently be drawn into the world of Macbeth, it is clear from the events of the play that it is about far more than one man's demise — it is concerned with the consequences of abuses of power and the social destruction those abuses wreak.

With its themes of power, ambition and tyranny and the use of violence to achieve political ends within greater and smaller conflicts, this play is potentially a revolutionary piece.

Historical context

Do you wish the production to use images and settings from a specific period in history? If you create a specific setting, do you want the war which is being fought at the beginning of the play to be a recognisable war from the past or, indeed, the present?

Presenting the context on stage

Given the multiplicity of scenes and different environments of the play, how will you treat your setting? How will your set be more conceptual than realistic, and how will it serve the aims of the play and the production? How will you achieve part of the *Gestus* of your production through setting? (Hint: remember the high walls of the set in Ian Brown's production of *Hamlet*, referred to on pages 128–29. Consider how that set decision influenced the play's themes and how the audience might have received these themes.)

Advising the actors

Macbeth

What is the driving force of Macbeth's ambition that makes him kill a king? This question must be linked to the world of the production, not just to individual psychological motives. So, the question for the actor and the director becomes not 'What kind of a man will kill a king to achieve his ambitions?' but rather 'What kind of world is it — and how has that world affected Macbeth — where a man will kill a king?' The character of Macbeth should not simply be presented as a Scottish nobleman who decides on the basis of a supernatural encounter with witches to kill his monarch; crucially, he is part of the violent political world of the play.

The alienation effect is useful to both the actor (not just the actor playing Macbeth — this applies to other roles as well) and the director when considering the elements of the character that society has shaped and how this affects behaviour.

The witches

It is important that the witches are related to the world of the setting — one of political intrigue, violence and ambition — rather than resembling an absurdist 'add on'.

- How do the witches connect with Macbeth, and what is it about them that exerts influence on him?
- Are they part of his nightmare, for example, or a manifestation of sexual fantasy?

These are not psychologically-based questions, but rather a prompt to consider what part of the world of the play the witches occupy. Are they part of its belief system?

The witches in a 1996 production of *Macbeth* at the RSC. Janet Whiteside, Susannah Elliot-Knight and Jan Chappell

Showing social consequences

How do you ensure that this play shows the social consequences of the behaviour of the rulers?

The implication of this question is not that you should contrive a series of vignettes revealing beggars and perpetrators of street violence. On the other hand, it is important to find ways to show how the tyranny of Macbeth has infiltrated society.

How, for example, do you portray the violence of the play? The murder of Lady Macduff and her young child is probably one of the most brutal scenes in Shakespeare. Do you want the audience to feel that this is a terrible one-off event or symptomatic of the world in which the Macduffs are living? How, in other words, do you present violence as a daily reality?

Using technology

Your decisions about the social and historical setting will influence your use of technology.

- How could you use lighting not just to illuminate the events, but also to affect and influence audience perception?
- How could lighting contribute to the *Gestus* and alienation effect of each scene and of the whole production?
- Is technology a part of the play as well as a contributing element of production? For example, do you want the technological influence of armaments to be a perceptible part of the production?

Using sound and music

Remember that music in the world of Brechtian theatre is important not as a means by which to charm or seduce an audience but rather to jerk its members into a response and to allow a character to tell a story or share his or her thoughts.

The link has already been made between Brechtian song and Shakespearean verse and soliloquy. Is there a similar role for music in your production, to punctuate or intensify moments in the play?

Summary of Brecht's ideas

- Brecht developed a theory of performance, referred to as 'epic theatre', that challenged Aristotle's concept of 'dramatic theatre'. Epic theatre aimed at disputing the dramatic unities of Aristotle and presenting an audience with a series of simultaneous events rather than a single plot line.
- Brecht's ideas were aimed at motivating the members of an audience to action, rather than seducing them with an intricate plot or emotional hypnosis.
- Brecht's theatre is not, as some suggest, devoid of emotion. However, the audience should not feel emotion in the sense of emotional empathy with a character. The emotion conveyed should motivate the audience to take some action.
- Brecht's theories acknowledge and proclaim the social function of theatre — the ability to change things by changing people.
- Brecht had important (and, over the years, changing) views about the role of entertainment in theatre.
- Brecht used music and singing extensively in his plays, not to charm the audience with beautiful melodies but to interrupt the play and allow his characters to tell stories.
- Science and technology played important roles in Brecht's productions.

Discussion questions

Make thorough notes on the points that arise from your consideration of the following questions, either from discussion or your own observations.

1 Reflecting on the plays you are studying, which of Brecht's ideas might prove useful for a director preparing a production?

2 What plays have you seen where you think the director or actors may have used some of Brecht's ideas in their preparation?

3 Have you seen a play where you have been critical of aspects of the production? Would the application of any of Brecht's ideas have helped? If so, which ones?

4 Are there any styles of play where the ideas of Brecht might not be useful? Explain your answer.

Essay questions

1 Plan a rehearsal of a play you are working on. Show how you might introduce some of Brecht's ideas on alienation effect or *Gestus* to your cast, either through text or off-text work.

2 Do you believe it is possible to incorporate the ideas of both Brecht and Stanislavski into one production? How would this work and with what play(s)?

Chapter 9

The work of Antonin Artaud

There is an important difference between Antonin Artaud and the two practitioners we have studied so far: while Stanislavski and Brecht achieved recognition as great artists in their lifetime, Artaud — aside from a small, intensely loyal following — did not. Indeed, most of his experiments with theatre ended in failure, and his ideas were not accepted by his theatrical contemporaries. However, his influence on modern theatre practice is significant.

A 'disease of the mind'

In his early twenties, Artaud submitted some poetry for publication to Jacques Rivière, editor of *La Nouvelle Revue Française*. Rivière rejected the submission. He liked Artaud and thought him talented but was critical of the poems' literary merits and commented on their 'divergent images'. Artaud informed Rivière that he was wrong about the literary merits of the poems, and that the problem was in fact a 'disease of the mind'. The ensuing correspondence revealed Artaud's ability to analyse his own deficiencies. Rivière was so captivated and impressed by the content of these letters that he chose to publish them instead.

What is Artaud's style and why did he struggle so much to convey his ideas to both his audiences and his peers? What is his impact today and how might his practice be implemented?

Self-obsession and genius

It might seem an insult to refer to someone as being self-obsessed, as it implies complacency, but the nature of Artaud's self-obsession did not cause him any pleasure. At times during his life he was in a state of tortured and unrelenting anguish. As a child, he had suffered a near-fatal attack of meningitis, and although he recovered he was blighted by headaches for the rest of his life.

However, it was Artaud's anguish and mental torment that provided, in many respects, the source of his genius as well as his frustration and — at least during his lifetime — his failure. These elements are also at the heart of his work, in both his performance and his writings.

It is important to understand Artaud's frustration with the inadequacy of language: for him, words were not enough, even though he used them powerfully to explain his own mental illness. He wrote copiously but still was unable to express clearly either the agonies of his existence or his theories of theatre practice.

However, in his compendium of essays and articles *The Theatre and Its Double* (1938) he did articulate his theatre manifestos, and from these it is possible to discern the essence of his approach.

Antonin Artaud (1896–1948)

Antonin Artaud was a French playwright, poet, actor and director. Born in Marseilles — his father a wealthy shipbuilder, his mother of Greek heritage — he suffered a lifetime of ill-health, both physically and mentally debilitated by a near-fatal case of meningitis when he was 5 years old. He was educated at the Collège du Sacré Coeur in Marseilles, and at the age of 14 founded a literary magazine. Still in his teens, he began to suffer from depression and experience sharp head pains, which continued throughout his life. Around his early twenties, he began taking laudanum (a solution of opium in alcohol) for his pains, and continued to use opium, heroin and other drugs until his death.

Antonin Artaud's influence on modern theatre practice is significant

As an avant-garde theorist of revolutionary theatre, Artaud is famous for his influence on the way writers, directors and actors comprehend the production and the purpose of theatre. He was the progenitor of a provocative form of theatre, the aim of which was to disconcert and radically transform its audience. He sought to dispense with rational drama, masterpieces and psychological exploration, instead advocating a 'theatre of cruelty', drawing on psychoanalytic theory and the Balinese Theatre.

Early career

Artaud worked briefly as a stage performer for the French actor and director Aurelien Lugné-Poe (1869–1940), but this was not a success. He was too consumed by his own agonies to be able to assume another role effectively. He attended classes with Charles Dullin (1885–1949), an actor, theatre manager and director who trained a whole generation of French actors. Dullin admired Artaud's presence and fervour but found nothing but frustration in attempting to direct him. Artaud found it almost impossible to interpret a role in a realistic manner and on one occasion played the Emperor Charlemagne by crawling on all fours. When Dullin upbraided him, Artaud exclaimed in exasperation 'Oh, well if you want the truth!'

The Théâtre Alfred Jarry

At the time of Artaud's first theatrical experiments, Paris was playing host to the fledgling surrealist movement. Surrealism sought to give form to the inner realm of humanity rather than its outer casing (the province of realism), and this was achieved mainly through painting. You can see examples of surrealist art in the works of Salvador Dali and Max Ernst. Their philosophy was that if art was to reflect the reality of the world, it must embrace the unconscious and not be restricted to the realm of the conscious.

For Artaud, obsessed with his inner demons, surrealism was a school of thought with which he could identify and work. However, although presenting work of an experimental anti-naturalistic nature was no longer an outrageous concept, Artaud's efforts in the theatre still failed to find critical favour with many in Paris.

Meanwhile, the surrealist movement (particularly its leader, the painter André Breton) was increasingly moving towards a formal acceptance of communism. Artaud broke away on the grounds that it had simply swapped one set of restrictions for another. He believed that art should be free of political allegiance.

In partnership with Roger Vitrac and Robert Aron, Artaud founded the Théâtre Alfred Jarry in 1926. Subsequently, adherents of the surrealist movement thwarted Artaud's work at the theatre, particularly by protesting at one of his few critical successes, a production of the Swedish dramatist August Strindberg's *Dream Play*, which had received subsidies for its performance in Paris from wealthy expatriate Swedes.

The failure of the Théâtre Alfred Jarry was a further source of frustration to Artaud, particularly as personal failure only intensified his periods of depression and torment. However, he continued to write about his theoretical approach to theatre.

Alfred Jarry (1873–1907) and *Ubu Roi*

The playwright Alfred Jarry was a significant influence on Artaud. His most famous play, *Ubu Roi* (1896), had caused a storm when first performed in Paris in the year of Artaud's birth. The sight of the monstrously fat Ubu waddling onto the stage and emitting his first word '*Merde*!' ('shit') evoked howls of protest. *Ubu Roi* was an anarchic work, a crude parody of *Macbeth* featuring a vengeful, grotesque and murderous central character. Jarry's language was harsh and experimental, employing seemingly obscure rhythmic patterns and alliteration. Jarry's work stripped down the world of respectability and pomp and displayed Ubu in all his obscene vulgarity.

Balinese Theatre

Just as Stanislavski had a moment of revelation when he saw the Meiningen Players in Moscow in the 1880s, so too did Artaud when he saw the Balinese Theatre at the Colonial Exhibition in Paris in 1931. He was struck by the quality of the visible action and the non-verbal communication. In the Balinese Theatre he saw a fresh importance accorded to such features as facial expressions, mimetic devices and gesticulation, triggering in his mind the idea of a new language of theatre, where movement and gesture were of equal importance with words.

This emphasis on movement was extremely important to Artaud, who had found words to be a restrictive rather than a liberating force when attempting to describe or explain his feelings. He felt that movement conveyed the unconscious mind more successfully than words — a fundamental consideration for a surrealist. Seeing the Balinese Theatre confirmed Artaud's opinion that words were incapable of expressing certain thoughts and feelings and that a language of gestures or hieroglyphs with their visual impact was a far more potent and meaningful method of communication.

Antonin Artaud was inspired by the visual impact of the Balinese Theatre

Ralph Paprzycki/Alamy

Artaud's ideas

Over the next 4 years, inspired by the Balinese Theatre, Artaud formulated his ideas on theatre through a series of essays and articles:

- The actor should not just be an emitter of words, reduced to playing a mundane character. Myth and ritual rather than characterisation should lead theatre.
- An ensemble of actors using their bodies and chanting, singing and gesturing as well as using words is far more powerful in communicating with an audience.
- 'Reality' does not necessarily mean 'truth' — indeed, reality often obscures the truth. To get to the truth one has to expose humanity and show its inner being.
- The human soul should be laid bare on stage to show humanity's unconscious state, stripped of its sophistication and societal pretensions. The audience must recognise this and be affected by it.

Where Stanislavski wanted a theatre that drew the spectator in and Brecht wanted a theatre to motivate the spectator into action, Artaud wanted his spectator to be 'cured'. The cure was spiritual and not necessarily a pleasant or relaxing experience. Indeed, Artaud likened a trip to the theatre to a visit to the dentist.

Theatre and the plague

Artaud likened his conception of theatre to the plague. Plague can ravage a civilisation and attacks indiscriminately. Wealth or position cannot protect you, and catching it means that you are out of control.

For a society to suffer the plague is a visceral, painful experience, but its overall effect may, bizarrely, be one of cleansing, providing an opportunity to move forward in ways that are new and different. Artaud felt that a theatrical production should evoke the same extremes of response from an audience, leaving it breathless and shocked but ultimately healed and cleansed.

'No more masterpieces'

Artaud felt that the written text was the overriding and most significant element in traditional theatre. As a result, other theatrical elements were subjugated to the text and could only be partially used. Moreover, he felt that many of the plays hailed as masterpieces and great art were now redundant.

In his essay 'No more masterpieces' (from *The Theatre and Its Double*), Artaud explained that the great works of the past, although literary masterpieces, could not move, thrill or terrify an audience in performance as they may have done when they were first created. This was because modern man was no longer of the culture of the Greek tragedians or Shakespeare. In order to develop a new theatre for the twentieth century, Artaud considered it necessary to create fresh and modern ways to inspire and excite an audience, as the classics had done when they were first performed. Tragedy and epic themes of war, tyranny and cruelty would still be the subject matter of drama, but new forms of presentation were needed.

Artaud's new theatrical language would encompass the ancient and the modern in terms of artefacts and images but remain topical. The topicality of his theatre was not like that of Brecht, who wanted to communicate and evoke a response to a variety of political issues. Artaud was interested in creating a universal topicality of existence itself — of man's struggle with himself and his world. The new language of theatre that Artaud sought to identify promoted all aspects of the theatre on an equal level.

Voice

In his attempts to break theatre's subjugation to text and reveal a language somewhere between gesture and thought, Artaud claimed that 'theatre can still derive possibilities for extension from speech outside words, the development in space of its dissociatory, vibratory action on our sensibility'. In other words, Artaud believed that the actor should not rely solely on the meaning of words to communicate a message. The sound of words was also important, and the actor should use his or her voice like an instrument, in order to articulate the underlying emotions.

Using words like this, in an almost primordial manner, made considerable demands on the actor's breathing and vocal control. During Artaud's production of *The Cenci* (which is discussed on pages 141–43), he suffered considerably from loss of voice, such were the gruelling demands he made on it.

Sound effects

Sound was a hugely significant aspect of Artaud's new style of theatre. This sound should not be perceived as merely an accompaniment or an embellishment; it was part of the whole visceral theatrical experience and often required intricate and detailed orchestration.

A combination of instruments would be used in conjunction with the actors' voices to create the required disturbing sounds. There should be no confusion of this approach with the concept of 'musicals'. The sound effects Artaud experimented with were neither soothing nor realistic. They were — in common with many of Artaud's ideas for theatre — the kinds of sound we might associate with dreams and nightmares: distortions and sounds layered upon sounds.

Lighting

Artaud thought that lighting should be a fundamental part of the theatrical experience. Indeed, he was one of the first practitioners to demonstrate that lighting could create different moods and atmospheres. He explored the interplay of lighting effects, paying particular attention to colours, angles and intensity.

Lighting for Artaud was a theatrical force capable of evoking terror or passion in an audience. He was also aware that these experiments with lighting influenced performance too. A scene from a play feels different to actors performing it under natural light and under stage lights. The intensity, colour and direction of light are all factors that can influence performance.

Role of the audience

While we sometimes discuss the genre of 'total theatre' in relation to the works of Steven Berkoff and other playwrights and directors who adopt a largely physical approach to production, it is a concept that has come about largely as a consequence of Artaud's theories. Quite apart from the concept of all the theatrical elements coming together to create a total and sensory experience (as opposed to an intellectual one with Brecht, or an emotional one with Stanislavski), Artaud wanted to establish the idea that in the theatre there was no barrier between audience and performer. This would be achieved by putting the audience in the centre of the performance on swivel chairs, so that the action could be experienced not just on a stage but at all the surrounding levels.

The audience should be immersed in the action, feeling what it is like to be caught in a world of sensations from which there is no escape. This experience was intended to stimulate the inner existence and spirit of the audience.

Use of set and costume

Artaud maintained that the theatre should not be a place of ornamentation or decoration but of spirituality, like a temple. Simple, symbolic sets should be used, with a suggestion of place rather than a realistic representation of it. The skills of the actors should be sufficient to convey context to the audience.

Costume and masks were also a fundamental component of Artaud's approach, as they were part of the beauty, colour and dream-like world of the theatre. Modern dress was not advocated, as it would fail to stimulate the audience's imagination. However, masks — comical, grotesque, beautiful, garish or terrifying — would enhance the sense of the surreal and the totality of the theatrical experience.

Artaud's failed experiments

In his lifetime, Artaud was afforded few opportunities to see his ideas put into practice. Although he submitted a variety of projects to the leading Parisian directors of the day, they were constantly rejected. His frequent bouts of illness had gained him the reputation of unreliability, and his mental anguish, though undoubtedly at the root of his genius, made him difficult to work with. His ideas were regarded as too extreme, and directors were reluctant to stage theatrical ventures which were intended to cause anguish and terror in an audience.

Although a number of drafted *mise en scènes* are still in existence, Artaud was only able to attempt one major production that utilised the theories he had spent 4 years formulating and writing up in the series of essays eventually published as *The Theatre and Its Double*. This production was *The Cenci*.

The 'theatre of cruelty': Artaud's 'The Cenci'

Artaud attempted to realise his ideas in 1935 with his own adaptation of Percy Bysshe Shelley's tragedy *The Cenci* (1819). *The Cenci* tells the story of Francesco Cenci, a historical figure who plotted the murder of his two sons and raped his daughter. In turn his daughter, surviving son and wife hired assassins to kill him, which they did by driving one nail into his eye and one into his throat. His wife and daughter were then brought to trial and, along with his son, were executed.

This violent story appealed to Artaud as a suitable vehicle for his newly identified 'theatre of cruelty', which was to provide a visceral experience for the audience. He described the action he envisaged in his own version of *The Cenci* as a 'devouring hearth' and he wanted the audience 'to be plunged into a bath of fire'. Here was a story of murder, incest and rape which lent itself to the special theatrical language Artaud had fashioned, with its emphasis on incantatory and rhythmic words, gestures, movements and imaginative uses of sound and light. It was supposed to be his greatest experiment and herald the dawn of a theatrical revolution. If the theatre establishment of Paris was not prepared to hire him or incorporate his ideas, he would commission the theatre and the actors and take the risk personally.

However, the play ran for only 17 performances and then closed. It was a financial and critical disaster.

Antonin Artaud (just left of centre stage) in a performance of *The Cenci* at the Théâtre des Folies-Wagram, Paris, in 1935

The Cenci in performance

It is difficult to imagine the nature and the effect of the original production from looking at the annotated script, but some idea can be gained from reading through it. Notable moments include the following:

- The sound of footsteps at the Cenci banquet was amplified in order to heighten the sense of violence and obsession as the guests, motivated by fear and greed, rushed towards the banquet.

- Later in the play, as the assassins approached Cenci, they did so using gestures to express their fear and their guilt. No words were used, since the impending horror of the moment rendered words inadequate. As the scene heightened in foreboding and violence, the word 'CEN–CI' was heard chanted using human voices and recorded sounds at varying and harshly contrasted pitches. The effect of this would have been a human, yet simultaneously dehumanised, sound — a discordant and violent assault on the audience's senses.

- During the banquet scene involving nobles and priests, the sound and effect of a great wind, like a 'cosmic breath', was used to indicate the idea of a force belonging to the 'world beyond' invading the real world. To enhance the celestial nature of the moment, Artaud used recordings of the peal of the great bells of Amiens Cathedral. To increase the effect even further, he used what must have been one of the earliest examples of quadraphonic sound by placing speakers behind the seats in the four corners of the auditorium. The sound was so loud and oppressive that audience members were subjected to considerable discomfort by the cacophony. However, this was partly the effect that Artaud wanted: to attack the senses of his audience, to reach them beyond a purely intellectual or emotional level.

◆ The play focuses on the cosmic battle of good and evil, and Cenci's sense of his own evil and consequently his awareness of the existence of God. To become closer to the 'One', or the creator, Cenci feels he must commit yet more acts of unrelenting evil. In order to express this sense of spiritual confusion and chaos, the actors were required to breathe and speak in a rhythmic and forced manner. However, the effects of this vocal control (as explained in Artaud's essay 'An Affective Athleticism', first published in *The Theatre and Its Double*) caused the actors to put great strain on their voices, particularly Artaud, who started to lose his voice towards the end of the run.

As we have seen, the essence of Artaud's genius was also partly the origin of his downfall. His amazing gifts as a visionary were not matched by his practical skills as an organiser. Furthermore, the demands the production made on both him and his fellow actors meant that a run of more than 17 performances was probably a physical as well as a financial impossibility.

After *The Cenci*

The failure of *The Cenci* was a grievous disappointment to Artaud. He departed for Mexico, where he found some spiritual fulfilment away from the materialism of the Western world.

Many of Artaud's theatrical quests attempted to discover a form that explored the spirituality of the world as well as the sources of his own torment. The unspoilt, dramatic landscape of Central America and the rituals and religious ceremonies of its people now helped Artaud to find an excitement and sense of spiritual destiny that had eluded him so far. However, he continued to earn a living through writing articles and essays for a variety of artistic journals.

An expedition to Ireland in 1937 ended in disaster when he was arrested for breach of the peace outside a monastery and deported to France. On arrival, he was immediately committed to an asylum and remained in a variety of such institutions until 1946. By this time, although only 50 years old, Artaud was a frail old man. In the last 2 years of his life, Artaud returned to work and embarked upon a number of writing and broadcasting projects. However, he was by now suffering from cancer and died on 4 March 1948.

Summary

Although he was frustrated by failure in his lifetime, there is little doubt that many of Artaud's ideas have found currency in the work of modern practitioners. For example, a strong sense of rhythm and incantation is clear in the language patterns employed by Steven Berkoff in his play *Metamorphosis*.

While it is difficult to prove precise levels of influence, both Artaud and Berkoff valued the sound and structure of language, perhaps considering these to be more important than the content. Both explored the sensory impact that language can make through dialogue, chorus work and amplifications.

Summary of Artaud's ideas

- Artaud's vision for theatre differs from Brecht's and Stanislavski's; he wanted to create a sensory assault on the audience.
- Artaud's work coincided with the era of the surrealists, and for a time he was a part of their movement. The rejection of the rules of realism and the scenic possibilities of a theatre inspired by dreams are points for comparison between the work of surreal artists and Artaud's vision for theatre.
- Artaud was significantly influenced by a visit to the Balinese Theatre in 1931. The emphasis on physical performance, movement, dance and gesture helped Artaud to clarify and identify his own theatrical ideas.
- Artaud rejected the reverence in which 'masterpieces' are held. For example, the impact of Greek tragedy has lessened because modern audiences no longer subscribe to the same belief system, nor are they afraid of the same things. Modern theatre must focus on the spiritual world of humanity so that its effects can be as profound as in the past.
- Artaud wanted to create a theatre which explored the inner spiritual truth of humanity, rather than just the outer trappings of realism.
- Artaud regarded all the individual theatrical elements as having equal status. There were particularly important implications for the use of sound and light.
- The function of the actor in the 'theatre of cruelty' was to be fundamentally different from that in the theatre of reality. Rather than just repeating words, the actor's whole body was to be used as an instrument of expression.
- Artaud promoted new breathing techniques which would vocally dehumanise some of the text as well as allow a more graphic method of expression.
- There should be no physical barrier between actor and audience. The audience should be in the midst of the action and, therefore, part of it.
- Artaud suffered from mental illness during much of his life. The torment that he felt, as well as his frustrations at failure, contributed to the deeply introspective and spiritual dimension he gave to his vision of theatre.

Group activity

The poem *Dulce et Decorum Est* by Wilfred Owen graphically depicts the death of a soldier during a gas attack in the trenches in the First World War. As a group, try to adapt the poem using some of Artaud's ideas. Bear the following points in mind:

* You should not necessarily adapt the poem so that it presents a logical sequence of events. Artaud was concerned to depict a visceral and violent world, where the audience was subjected to a sensory experience. The aim, therefore, is not to create a historically accurate adaptation so much as to realise the essence of the horror of the piece. Explore the sounds of the language as well as the content, and perhaps use repetition of the sounds to intensify the disturbing nature of the scene.

* Find ways in which you can physically — as an ensemble — portray the graphic horror of the poem. Do not try to act it out as a story, but rather look for moments of striking physical imagery.

* Use lighting in a variety of ways to accompany the scene. Evaluate the difference it makes to you as an actor, as well as to an audience watching the scene.

Chapter 10

Applying Artaud's principles

Woyzeck by Georg Büchner

Eugène Ionesco was born in Slatina, Romania, the son of a French mother and Romanian father. He is considered one of the foremost playwrights of the 'theatre of the absurd', an innovative form of theatre designed to startle the members of an audience and shake them out of their comfortable, conventional conception of life. It revolves around a distrust of language as a means of communication, believing that language fails to express the essence of human experience.

Inspired by the repetitive and nonsensical phrases of his textbook while attempting to learn English, in 1948 Ionesco conceived the idea for his first play, *La Cantatrice Chauve* ('*The Bald Soprano*'), produced in 1950. It is composed mainly of the type of clichés found in a foreign-language phrasebook and a series of meaningless conversations between two couples.

The work of the absurdist playwright Eugène Ionesco contains ideas that may have been inspired by the theories of Artaud. In *The Lesson* (1951), for example, a professor stabs a pupil with an imaginary knife, chanting and screaming the word 'knife' as he does so. This is a play which shows the tyrannous power of words and language translated into a weapon of murder.

Perhaps one of the greatest exponents of the ideas of Artaud has been the director Peter Brook (see p. 157), who, with the American director Charles Marowitz, created a 'Theatre of Cruelty' season at the RSC in 1964. His subsequent production of Peter Weiss's *The Persecution and Assassination of Jean-Paul Marat as Performed by the Inmates of the Asylum of Charenton Under the Direction of the Marquis de Sade* (1964) — normally shortened to *Marat/Sade* — was a masterpiece of visceral and explicit theatre, assaulting the sensibilities of its audience in a variety of ways that could not fail to leave a sensory impact.

The 'in yer face' playwrights

The bold theatrical experiments of the 'in yer face' playwrights of the 1990s, such as Sarah Kane and Mark Ravenhill, demonstrate the force with which social issues and values can be explored in theatrical form. Even the title of Ravenhill's first play *Shopping and Fucking* (1996) was designed to create an impact on an audience. Sarah Kane's *Blasted* (1995) shows the violent impact of war — but in a hotel bedroom in Leeds. The journalists who watch and report from the safety of distance suddenly find the war and its plague-like, indiscriminate assault in their midst.

Critical reactions to these productions echo some of the responses to Artaud's work. Kane particularly received mixed reviews for *Blasted*. However, it remains a provocative work of tragic, violent theatre and should not simply be dismissed (as some were keen to do at the time) as gratuitous filth.

TopFoto

Sarah Kane's *Blasted* remains a provocative work of tragic, violent theatre. (The Barbican Theatre, London, November 2006)

Technical theatre: sound and light

While his philosophical and spiritual ideals are being realised by modern playwrights, Artaud's influence also extends to the use of technical elements of theatre by designers and directors. Sound and light are now a fundamental part of the theatre experience, rather than just a supporting feature. Again, the work of Berkoff is a useful example, as his stage directions give specific, detailed and complex instructions as to how both sound and lighting effects should work.

Another example might be Peter Schaffer's *Royal Hunt of the Sun* (1964), which charts the story of Pizzarro's conquest of the Inca empire led by Atahualpa (coincidentally, Artaud drafted but never produced the story of Cortez and the destruction of the Aztec civilisation of Montezuma). In *Royal Hunt of the Sun*, much of the action takes place in the South American jungle and mountains. The lighting required is ambitious in its technical scope, illuminating the actors' bodies to create for the audience the impact of the vast landscapes.

In this kind of total theatre, the aim is not to convince the members of an audience that what they are watching is real, but that a real sense of the physical and spiritual essence of the world is being depicted. The scenes involving the worship of Atahualpa and the incantation offered up by the Incas are strongly reminiscent of Artaud's ideas on rhythmic and choral speaking.

Georg Büchner (1813–37)

Georg Büchner was a German playwright who had completed only three plays by the time of his death in 1837 at the age of 23. He died before ever finishing *Woyzeck*, leaving behind four unpolished manuscripts and a series of notes, so it is impossible to possess a definitive version of the work. It has been pieced together posthumously by scholars, who have passionately scrutinised issues such as which scenes to include, the order of the scenes and the ending. It was not published until 1879 and even then the result was regarded as being somewhat unsatisfactory. It was only when photographic techniques had been developed to a sufficient level that Büchner's writing could be deciphered accurately. Consequently, the play did not reach the stage until 1913 and was subject to some argument as to its genre.

Woyzeck

Just as with Stanislavski and Brecht, there is no virtue in applying the ideas of Artaud as a rule book when interpreting plays, nor should the ideas of one theorist be explored to the exclusion of others. You should note that when Brecht and Artaud were writing essays and journal entries, they may well have rejected the ideas of others; in practice, however, they were clearly influenced by the principles of other theorists. Nonetheless, it is useful to consider how the theories of Artaud might be of interest to a director of the play *Woyzeck* by Georg Büchner.

The plot

The eponymous protagonist, Franz Woyzeck, a poor military barber stationed in a provincial German town, is the father of an illegitimate child by his mistress, Marie. In order to support his family,

Woyzeck earns extra money by undertaking menial work for the Captain and participating in medical experiments conducted by the Doctor. As part of one of these experiments, Woyzeck is forced to eat only peas.

The constant diet of peas causes Woyzeck's physical and mental health to break down and he begins to experience a series of apocalyptic visions. Meanwhile, Marie turns her attentions to an arrogant but handsome Drum Major who, in an ambiguous scene taking place in Marie's bedroom, appears to rape her.

With his jealous suspicions growing, Woyzeck confronts the Drum Major. A fight breaks out, which the Drum Major easily wins. Finally, Woyzeck stabs Marie to death beside a pond. The fragment of script left by Büchner ends with Woyzeck disposing of the knife in the pond, although some scholars maintain that the original conception of the play involved a trial in the third act. However, most productions (including Werner Herzog's 1979 film) conclude with Woyzeck drowning while trying to clean the blood from his hands.

A 'theatre of cruelty' experience

In the intervening years between the writing of *Woyzeck* in the 1830s and its first performance over 70 years later, the schools of realism and expressionism emerged. Although Büchner predates both of these movements, one can detect certain ingredients in his work which are common to both. You should always bear in mind, however, that it is rarely the playwrights themselves who coin the names of the schools of thought into which they are sometimes all too neatly fitted.

The play is based loosely on the true story of Johann Christian Woyzeck, a former solider convicted for the murder of his mistress, despite the defence mounted at his trial to spare his life on grounds of diminished responsibility. Perhaps linked to these real-life influences, it certainly has elements of social realism. However, in exploring the central character's descent into paranoia and his subjection to eccentric and cruel experiments, it also offers a 'theatre of cruelty' experience of disturbing extremes of human behaviour and psychology. There are moments of graphic violence, sexuality and even defecation.

The play is structured into short, powerful scenes that are not necessarily placed in chronological order. It also has something of an 'epic' feel to it, particularly as some of the characters are quite stereotypical and named after their function, e.g. 'Doctor' or 'Drum Major'.

Without necessarily taking a political stance, the play explores the nature of humankind and the injustices it imposes on itself. Büchner had strong links with revolutionary movements in his youth, but by the time he was writing *Woyzeck*, at the end of his life, he had largely abandoned his political aspirations. However, his awareness of social injustice and the effects of poverty on human behaviour and relationships are clearly concerns explored in the play.

Managing the setting

The nature of *Woyzeck* is such that unless revolving scenery is available, it is practically impossible to set each scene in a naturalistic context. The set design, therefore, has to convey a conceptual interpretation. It would not be out of place to devise a surreal style of set, incorporating images and objects from the play — doctor's apparatus, military iconography or the knife which Woyzeck uses to kill Marie.

The use of surrealistic artwork — nightmarish, graphic, colourful and distorted — could provide a suitable backdrop for the action.

Graphic physicality

There are many scenes in the play when the action is dominated more by physicality than by dialogue. Early in the play, a scene takes place in the fairground when Marie first sees the Drum Major. The Showman is inviting people to 'roll up' and see his array of animals:

Showman: Roll up, ladies and gentlemen! Come and see a monkey walking upright like a man! He wears a coat and trousers and carries a sword.

Art improving on nature: our monkey's a soldier. — Not that that's much. Lowest form of animal life in fact.   (I.3)

Later, the Showman introduces the horse, describing its virtues while it defecates on stage. The Showman comments that the lesson to be taken from this act is:

Man, be natural!   (I.3)

The absurdity of this section is apparent, as well as its uncompromisingly graphic nature. Since it is extremely difficult to stage realistically, the opportunity for physical theatre work here could extend the notion of the play's surrealism.

Nightmare

For Artaud, sound and light were fundamental parts of the language of the theatre. They could certainly enhance the quality of many scenes in *Woyzeck*, helping to define the play's nightmarish quality. For example, the scene with the horse quoted above offers opportunities to create distorted and disturbing images.

Later in the play, Woyzeck is taunted by the Captain, who knows of Marie's sexual encounter with the Drum Major. The use of music and/or sound effects, accompanied by an intensifying light focused on his face, could help to suggest the disquieting intensity of Woyzeck's growing jealousy.

When Woyzeck sees the Drum Major and Marie dance in the peasants' scene, his sense of jealousy and frustration reaches fever pitch. The dance and the music could reflect not only the lustful reality of the Drum Major and Marie's relationship, but also the agonised state of Woyzeck's mind. The music could become louder and more hurried (almost like the *Danse Macabre* by Saint-Saëns), more sensual and more ritualistic, and Woyzeck's response to it could accordingly become increasingly enraged and emotional. Lighting too could focus on the couple in such a way as to reflect the distress Woyzeck is experiencing as he watches them. It could become more intense, perhaps tinged with red to portend the inevitable oncoming violence.

When Woyzeck (Edward Hogg) sees Marie (Myriam Acharki) and the Drum Major (Tim Chipping) together, his jealousy reaches fever pitch. (Gate Theatre, London, November 2004)

Absurdity

The Doctor — who is dispassionately observing Woyzeck's changing behaviour — is a figure of cruel absurdity. The dress and make-up of this character (and other absurd characters, such as the Captain and the Drum Major) could be colourful and outlandish to enhance their surreal qualities. The Doctor's use of voice might accentuate his absurdity too. As he presents Woyzeck to his students, his speech is both pompous and deranged:

If we take one of those creatures in whom, gentlemen, capacity of the divine for self-affirmation most clearly manifests itself and we examine its relation to space, the earth and the planetary universe. If, gentlemen, I take [producing a cat] this cat, and throw it out of the window — what will be its instinctive behaviour relative to its centre of gravity?

— Woyzeck! — Woyzeck!!

(He runs back in as the **Doctor** throws the cat at him which he catches.)   (l.8)

Use of language

The Doctor exploits Woyzeck and equates him with the lowest forms of animal life. His lecture to the students gives him an opportunity to use his voice in an overbearing and self-regarding manner. The actor and director could experiment with vocal pitch and pace to enhance these qualities. For Artaud, the language of the Doctor would demonstrate his tyranny and lack of humanity. The vocal projection, therefore, must immediately and graphically reflect those traits, perhaps through a harsh, brittle-sounding oration. The physical sound of the words is more important than their precise content in revealing the Doctor's contempt for Woyzeck in this impersonal and cruel lecture.

After the peasants' dance scene, the crowd falls silent as Woyzeck screams out his agony:

Woyzeck: Turn, turn. Go on turning, dancing! — Why don't you blow the sun out God? Let everything fall over itself in lewdness. Flesh, filth, man, woman, human, animal. — They all do it in the open day, do it on the back of a hand like flies. Slut!! — She's hot, hot!   (l.12)

Here again, the actor should concentrate on the visceral rage inherent in the language. The mood — realised through pace and volume — is more important than the content, which is bordering on the incoherent.

The almost savage rage with which these lines are spat out more than reflects Woyzeck's state of mind and exposes his psychological disposition to the audience. This should be a truly terrifying moment in the play. At this point, we know that something terrible and violent is going to happen.

Violence

The play, in places, makes use of strong violence. Following the dancing scene, Woyzeck seeks out the Drum Major. The Drum Major easily defeats him in the ensuing fight, which at one point contains the stage direction:

(Jumps on Woyzeck's back with his knees)   (l.15)

The brutality of this scene should be disturbing for an audience. It might be played surrealistically or even choreographed as a violent dance sequence. As we have seen, Artaud appreciated the disciplined physical work of the Balinese Theatre, and the director here may consider executing a more stylised than literal version of the fight. However, the impact of the violence should not be compromised, and an audience should be shocked and frightened by this moment of appalling savagery rather than admiring of its artistry. The injustices being heaped on Woyzeck and his developing madness as a consequence should be experienced by the audience rather than just passively accepted.

The most violent scene of the play is preceded by an atmosphere of eerie calm, as Woyzeck and Marie walk in the woods. Marie is unaware of what is to happen, and this makes the moment of the stabbing all the more terrible and frightening. The use of lighting and music could add to the dramatic climax, perhaps creating a cacophony of sound as well as highlighting the ferocity of the repeated stabbing.

The scream that Marie emits should be harsh, lengthy and filled with pain and perhaps echoed by other members of the ensemble.

Cleansing and closure

As the end of the play arrives, Woyzeck drowns himself in the river, taking the body of Marie with him. There is a ritual element about this self-sacrifice, as well as an image of cleansing. As we have already discussed, Artaud extolled the potential of theatre to offer spiritual cleansing.

It would be difficult to achieve a realistic setting for this challenging scene. A more surreal approach, such as immersing the actors in a blue light, might be a striking way of overcoming the problem.

The last two scenes of the play are additions by playwright John Mackendrick, Büchner's translator. As the play was unfinished at the time of Büchner's death, there are a number of options for how to end the play, and indeed several other versions exist. Mackendrick's version fits well with Artaud's vision, using red lighting and maintaining a mystical, almost ritualised conclusion.

Mackendrick's penultimate scene shows the Doctor carrying out autopsies on both corpses, showing that even in death Woyzeck cannot escape exploitation. The Doctor is confused that in piercing Woyzeck's body he cannot find any blood. In the final scene, the mysterious figure of the blind grandmother looks on, as Woyzeck's friend, Andres, picks sticks and discovers a patch of blood. The blood increases until it is revealed as 'Woyzeck's gore'. Andres rushes away in fear as red light fills the stage and the grandmother laughs.

Summary

Some directors might wish to take Artaud's concept of the theatre of cruelty further in this play. To some extent, at least, we are still subjugating all other theatrical elements to the text, since the script remains unchanged.

Some would argue that the text should be substantially reduced and a greater use of gesture, movement and dance be introduced. However, there is then a tension between delivering the author's text with integrity and delivering the vision of Artaud. A dramaturge would argue that the author's intentions should not be compromised and that the text should be as faithfully rendered as possible. This is a point for debate. Bearing in mind that much of Büchner's unfinished script was posthumously assembled and completed from notes, some compromise is inevitable. On this basis, it should be possible to retain the integrity of the text while still using principles of theatre presentation consistent with Artaud's vision.

Discussion questions

Make thorough notes on the points that arise from your consideration of the following questions, either from discussion or your own observations.

1 Reflecting on the plays you are studying, which of Artaud's ideas might prove useful for a director preparing a production?

2 What plays have you seen where you think the director or actors may have used some of Artaud's ideas in their preparation?

3 Are there any styles of play where the ideas of Artaud might not be useful? Explain your answer.

Essay questions

1 Plan a rehearsal of a play you are working on. Show how you might introduce some of Artaud's ideas on sound, light or design to your cast, either through text or off-text work.

2 Do you believe it is possible to incorporate the ideas of Brecht, Stanislavski and Artaud into one production? How would this work and with what play(s)?

Chapter 11

The work of modern directors and designers

It would be far too sweeping to suggest that all theatre directors over the last 100 years have been influenced by the theories of Stanislavski, Brecht and Artaud. While it is tempting to try to identify 'family trees' of influence from one leading theatrical exponent to another, it should be remembered that these three drama theorists were working in different social and cultural contexts. These contexts overlapped from time to time, when companies went on tour or when individuals visited and sampled other cultures.

The development of directorial practice has been a sophisticated process, yet these three practitioners in particular have helped to establish a discipline of directing and a theatrical world where the role of the director is pivotal.

Twentieth-century British theatre

Two great national theatre companies emerged in the UK during the twentieth century — the Royal Shakespeare Company (RSC) and the National Theatre (NT). Not only have they become associated with excellence in acting, they have also forged and nurtured talent in directing.

The National Theatre on the South Bank, London

James Ingle/Alamy

The Royal Shakespeare Theatre

The Royal Shakespeare Theatre is managed by the Royal Shakespeare Company (known to British theatregoers as the RSC) and is located beside the River Avon in Shakespeare's birthplace, Stratford-upon-Avon in Warwickshire. The original building, the Shakespeare Memorial Theatre, opened in 1879. This was destroyed by a fire in the 1920s and replaced in 1932 by a modern building designed by Elisabeth Scott. This building was named the Royal Shakespeare Theatre in 1961. The 1930s building is being redeveloped from 2007, with completion planned for 2010.

The National Theatre

The National Theatre's building on London's South Bank was designed by architect Sir Denys Lasdun, and its three theatres (the Olivier, the Littleton and the Cottesloe) opened individually between 1976 and 1977. During the previous 13 years, the National Theatre Company, as it was then called, had been based at the Old Vic Theatre in Waterloo.

The term 'Royal' was added to the National Theatre's name in 1988 to mark the twenty-fifth anniversary of the National Theatre Company's inauguration and the retirement of its board chairman Max Rayne. This change was opposed by the theatre's then director, Richard Eyre, as he feared that productions would be viewed as 'worthy' as a result. The addition was quietly dropped (but never rescinded) when Rayne retired.

Most British theatregoers refer to both the company and the venue as 'the National'.

British directors

Peter Brook and Peter Hall both enjoyed the early days of their careers with the RSC before developing their talent in other arenas. Brook has spent the second half of his career mostly working in France, while Hall became the director of the National in the early 1970s before becoming a freelance director in 1988.

Trevor Nunn, Richard Eyre and Nicholas Hytner have all been artistic directors of either the RSC or the National (in the case of Trevor Nunn, both) and now have enviable international reputations as gifted directors.

Other great directing figures include George Devine, the founding director of the Royal Court Theatre, probably the most important theatre in the country for the development of new writing talent. William Gaskill and Max Stafford-Clark were important successors to Devine at the Royal Court and are still active in the theatre.

Some — though not all — successful theatre directors develop their careers in the world of film, for example Stephen Daldry (*Billy Elliot*, 2000) and Sam Mendes (*American Beauty*, 1999 — for which he won an Oscar — and *Road to Perdition*, 2002).

Peter Brook (1925–)

The theatrical producer and director Peter Brook was born in Chiswick, west London. He was educated at Westminster School, Gresham's School, Holt, and Magdalen College, Oxford. An avant-garde, non-conformist and controversial figure, Brook engineers productions that utilise the whole stage, favouring bold, abstract and unembellished sets over realistic backdrops. His approach is notably physical, and he often requires actors to sing, play musical instruments and perform acrobatic feats.

Brook has been influenced by the pioneering theories of Bertolt Brecht, Russian director Vsevolod Meyerhold and Polish director Jerzy Grotowski, among others, in addition to the 'theatre of cruelty' of Antonin Artaud. In 1964, Peter Brook and Charles Marowitz undertook the 'Theatre of Cruelty' season at the Royal Shakespeare Company, exploring ways in which Artaud's ideas could be used to find new forms of expression and redefine performance methods.

Peter Hall (1930–)

Sir Peter Reginald Frederick Hall CBE is an English theatre and film director. He was born in Bury St Edmunds and attended the Perse School, Cambridge. He pursued his education at St Catharine's College, Cambridge, where he produced and acted in several productions. In 1953, the same year he graduated with his master's degree, he staged his first professional play at the Theatre Royal in Windsor.

Hall is best known for his work with the Royal Shakespeare Company, which he founded in 1960 at the age of 29. He served as artistic director there from that time until 1968. From 1973 to 1988 he was director of the National Theatre and was also a member of the Arts Council of Great Britain, ultimately resigning from both roles in protest over cuts in public funding. After leaving the National Theatre, he founded the Peter Hall Company. This new company worked around the world, appearing in more than 40 productions in London, New York, Europe and Australia. During this period, Hall also produced operas and directed films and television productions for the BBC.

TopFoto

Many directors are what may be termed 'jobbing directors', and just like most actors, their careers are unglamorous and poorly paid. A number of regional theatres have their own in-house theatre companies with their own artistic directors, for example Mark Babytch at the Octagon Theatre, Bolton or Ian Brown at the West Yorkshire Playhouse. Such individuals are not only responsible for the artistic repertoire of their companies but also — and often far more stressfully — their financial wellbeing.

Sir Peter Hall is best known for his work with the RSC, which he founded in 1960

George Devine (1910–66)

George Devine CBE was an eminent theatrical manager, director, teacher and actor in London. He also worked in the media of television and film.

While reading history at the University of Oxford, Devine developed a passion for theatre, and in 1932 he became president of the Oxford University Dramatic Society. After graduation, he moved to London and became an actor, appearing in a number of John Gielgud's productions. He co-founded the London Theatre Studio in 1936, and in 1939 he became a stage director with an adaptation of Charles Dickens' *Great Expectations* (1946).

During the Second World War, he was a member of the Royal Artillery, stationed in India and then Burma. Returning to London after the war, he was instrumental in setting up and running the Old Vic Theatre School and the Young Vic Company. However, severe disagreements with the Old Vic board of governors in 1948 led to his resignation.

By this time a renowned authority in stagecraft, Devine directed opera at Sadler's Wells Theatre and both directed and acted at the Royal Shakespeare Theatre in Stratford; he also directed at the Bristol Old Vic.

Tony Richardson shared Devine's ideas about transforming the English theatre. After Richardson cast Devine in a television adaptation of Anton Chekhov's *Curtain Down*, the two co-founded the English Stage Company.

Trevor Nunn (1940–)

Trevor Nunn was born in Ipswich, educated at Northgate Grammar School, Ipswich, and at Downing College, Cambridge. After graduation, he joined the Belgrade Theatre in Coventry as a trainee director, going on to become producer there. He has held the post of director at both the Royal Shakespeare Company and the National Theatre. At only 28 years of age, Nunn was the youngest ever director of the RSC. Nunn has directed acclaimed performances of almost all of the major plays of Shakespeare (and many of the minor ones), as well as classic texts by Ibsen, Shaw, Chekhov and Brecht. He has also worked with highly talented contemporary playwrights, including Robert Bolt and Tom Stoppard.

Richard Eyre (1943–)

Sir Richard Charles Hastings Eyre CBE is a renowned theatre, television and film director. He studied English at the University of Cambridge before becoming associate director, and then director of productions, at Edinburgh's Lyceum Theatre. He went on to serve as artistic director of the Nottingham Playhouse, and produced the BBC Television 'Play for Today' series.

Eyre's association with the National Theatre began in 1981, when he became an associate director. He subsequently became director, between 1987 and 1997.

Nicholas Hytner (1956–)

Nicholas Hytner is an award-winning producer and director. Born in Didsbury, Manchester, to a Jewish family, he attended Manchester Grammar School before reading English at Trinity Hall, Cambridge. While at university, he co-scripted and performed in a televised production of the 1977 Cambridge Footlights Revue and directed Brecht and Weill's *Rise and Fall of the City of Mahagonny.*

Following graduation, Hytner's first paid job was assisting productions at the English National Opera. He then worked as an associate director at Manchester's Royal Exchange Theatre between 1985 and 1989, and at the National Theatre in London between 1989 and 1997. He was appointed director of the National Theatre in 2003 and is renowned for choosing much more controversial pieces than his predecessors.

The directors and designers discussed on pages 159–84 come from diverse backgrounds and employ different methods of practice that have evolved over a period of time. Each has contributed significantly to the development and expansion of theatre, especially in terms of the audience it reaches and the imaginative techniques it employs.

It is not always appropriate to direct a play in the style of another director — certainly, this is impossible where directors devise their plays from scratch as well as directing them. However, it is useful to learn about existing directorial practices and philosophies, as their influence will always shape the work of young and up-and-coming directors.

Directorial constraints

The artistic aspirations of the vast majority of directors are subject to two controlling influences:

- financial constraints, in the context of a highly competitive profession
- audience trends (likes and dislikes)

For a regional theatre director to plan a programme of plays and events that does not pay due heed to audience tastes is to risk rapid financial ruin for the theatre company.

Steven Berkoff

Although Steven Berkoff's career began 50 years ago, he remains a potent and active force in British theatre. Now in his seventies, Berkoff continues to work in a physically disciplined and stylised way. While the length of his career means he is now part of the theatre establishment, much of his early work was regarded as controversial and groundbreaking.

Berkoff was born in 1937 in the East End of London. He was the grandson of Russian-Jewish immigrants named Berkovitch, although his father, a tailor, changed the family name to Berks in order to avoid possible aggravation. Berkoff's early life was unsettled as the family were constantly on the move. This, coupled with a stormy relationship with his father, led to Berkoff feeling isolated and something of a misfit. Although Berkoff was a bright student, his chaotic family life was detrimental to his education. In his late teens, he drifted in and out of a series of dead-end jobs and spent some time in a young offenders' institution for burglary. It was only in the late 1950s, as he approached his twenties, that Berkoff began to develop a mature appreciation of acting and enrolled in the Webber Douglas Academy of Dramatic Art.

Although Berkoff enjoyed the classes, he was frustrated at the lack of discipline in the school. He graduated from Webber Douglas in 1959 and worked steadily as an actor for a number of years, both in cinema and theatre. He received considerable critical acclaim in a 1965 production of Edward Albee's *Zoo Story* (1958). However, work did not follow this triumph and Berkoff turned once more to theatrical training to develop his skills. He went to the Ecole Internationale de Théâtre Jacques Lecoq in Paris (a school that teaches methods in physical theatre, movement and mime), and also attended classes with Jean Louis Barrault — the French actor, director and mime artist who was well known as a teacher and theorist. On the experience of learning mime from Barrault, Berkoff wrote:

TopFoto

Steven Berkoff

> His techniques gave me the opportunity to invent ways of presenting works whereby all elements of the human being are brought into motion. Some call it 'total theatre' and nowadays 'physical theatre'.
>
> (Berkoff, S. (1992) *The Theatre of Steven Berkoff*, Methuen Drama, p. 9)

Drawing on ancient myths

The extra training Berkoff undertook in Paris enabled him to develop his theatrical ideas into play-writing. Although the plays that emerged were hailed as new — indeed, almost revolutionary — Berkoff himself points towards a traditional source of inspiration:

> I attempted to write plays whose themes were non-representational images of human behaviour rather than simply 'life like' characters – *East* emerged in 1975 followed by *West* in 1977 followed by *Greek* in 1980, all of which could not have been written had I not been stimulated by the idea of a theatre drawing on its ancient myths.
>
> (Ibid, p. 10)

Berkoff's use of the words 'ancient myths' here refers to the world of Greek theatre, whose influence can be seen in much of his early work. He adapted Aeschylus's *Agamemnon* in 1977; *Greek* is an adaptation of the Oedipus legend, and more recently he made his own translation of *Oedipus Rex* (2000). There is a strong element of chorus work — important in Greek theatre — in some of his early work (e.g. *Agamemnon*) and also in his later plays. His adaptation of Franz Kafka's *Metamorphosis* (1969) makes use of a uniform, highly regimented response in some of the actions of the family and the chorus of lodgers.

Influence of Kafka

It is not hard to find links between the early lives of novelist Franz Kafka and Berkoff: they were both Jewish-born but of mixed-race parentage, and both had dysfunctional relationships with their fathers. They also experienced intense feelings of loneliness and inadequacy, with much of Kafka's work involving themes of isolation and alienation. For Berkoff, it was not just an understanding of Kafka's situation that drew him to the writer, but a realisation that the novelist's work provided specific challenges and opportunities suited to his own particular style of theatre.

Metamorphosis was the first of Berkoff's adaptations of Kafka's stories. The central character, Gregor Samsa, finds himself transformed into a gigantic beetle. This surreal story was meant to demonstrate how Gregor's existence as a travelling salesman had dehumanised him and turned him into a purely functional creature. Berkoff, with his long succession of dead-end jobs and unhappy youth, understood the theme of isolation in the piece and also felt excited about the challenge of performing the role, not least the daring required to convey the beetle-state of the character. In his introduction to the play he says:

> I, at one stage, had to climb out and hang from the ceiling like an insect — an interpolation of the story. So I practised in a gym and learnt how to climb and drop my body, hanging just by my

Gregor Samsa awakes one morning to find he has been transformed into a gigantic beetle legs and ankles, afraid nightly of being killed, but willing it, in my fanatic desire to outdo everyone else, my own self and my fears.

(Berkoff, S. (1988) *The Trial/Metamorphosis/In the Penal Colony: Three Theatre Adaptations from Franz Kafka*, Amber Lane Press, p. 72)

In Berkoff's play, the state of being a beetle was portrayed through the use of a skeletal steel scaffold and the actor's body. There was no attempt to use some kind of pantomime-like costume.

Precise staging directions

Berkoff's stage directions are demanding. However, his ideas are clearly and carefully articulated, as can be seen in this stage direction in Act I scene 4 of his Kafka adaptation *The Trial* (1971):

Traffic stops, screens re-shape into long office. CAST becomes the office of a busy bank, machinery, people walking robot like. Typists use their heads as typewriters. People move quickly, avoiding each other with clockwork precision.

The phrase 'with clockwork precision' gives an indication of the kind of rigorous preparation needed by an ensemble of actors involved in Berkoff's theatre.

Berkoff's stage directions are almost part of the script itself. They are precise, detailed and cannot be overlooked. Any director mounting Berkoff's work must pay close attention to the specifics of the author's stage directions.

Conflict between opposing forces

Apart from his own work, Berkoff has also directed a number of Shakespeare's plays, including several productions of *Coriolanus* (*c.* 1608). He directed this play in 1989 with Christopher Walken and later in the mid-1990s with himself in the title role. Of *Coriolanus* he says:

I liked the sinuous text and the conflict between opposing forces which occurs throughout the play: Plebeians versus Autocrat, State versus Individual, Aufidius versus Coriolanus, Mother versus Son.

(Berkoff, S. (1992) *The Theatre of Steven Berkoff*, Methuen Drama, p. 115)

With its emphasis on war and opportunities for staging fierce battles and moments of conflict, the play provided a particularly suitable vehicle for Berkoff's heavily physicalised style.

Summary of style of directing

- Physically demanding — based on actors creating complex physical imagery in a non-naturalistic style. The physical style of Berkoff's productions means that he demands a high level of physical fitness from his actors.
- Directs mainly his own work but has directed a number of other writers' work, mainly Shakespeare.
- He often identifies a chorus — in the ancient Greek theatre style of chorus — who provide images and synchronised responses. Examples of this include *Metamorphosis* and his own adaptation of *Agamemnon*.

John Godber

Like Berkoff, John Godber is renowned for productions of his own work. He is one of the country's most successful commercial playwrights, and his plays turned the fortunes of Hull Truck Theatre around when he became its artistic director in 1984. He mostly directs his own work but occasionally directs the work of other playwrights.

Godber, the son of a miner, was born in Upton near Wakefield in 1956. He was not particularly successful at school, but he went on to train as a drama teacher at Bretton Hall College in Wakefield. He rose to prominence through his work with Minsthorpe High School, where he was a drama teacher — his students regularly featured in the National Student Drama Festival. His play *Bouncers* — still one of the country's favourite and most frequently performed social comedies — was a hit at the Edinburgh Fringe in 1977. In addition to his work at the Hull Truck Theatre, Godber is Professor of Contemporary Theatre at Liverpool Hope University.

Role changing, pace and energy

Bouncers provides a good indication of both Godber's style as a director and his substance as a playwright. It tells the story of one night in a nightclub in a town in the north of England. The bouncers are doormen at the nightclub, but — without any change in costume or set — they become first a group of lads going for a night out and then a group of girls doing the same. The emphasis is on the actors' ability to transform quickly from one character to another. There is little subtlety and the characterisations are often almost cartoon-like stereotypes:

(In this section the Bouncers are all enacting the roles of boys going to the night-club)

Eric: Oooooh! Look at that. Somebody's spilt beer all over my suit.

Judd: Daft git

Eric: It's brand new

Les: It'll dry.

Judd: How many have we had?

Ralph: Ten.

Judd: Time for another.

Eric: I've only had nine.

Ralph: Are we off?

Eric: Do you think we'll get in?

Judd: Should do?

Les: Hope there's no trouble?

Eric: There's four of us.

All: Yeah.

Ralph: Come on. Let's get down there and pick something up.

All: Right.

Eric: Hang on.

Les: What?

Eric: Piss call.

All: Oh yeah.

(Godber, J. (1993) Bouncers 1990s Remix, Josef Weinberger Plays, p. 14)

The dialogue is short and the characterisation obvious and immediate. The pace is relentlessly quick and the energy required of the actors is considerable. Nevertheless, this is not just a fast-paced celebration of a night out. While the play is undoubtedly a comedy, it depicts violence and scrutinises human behaviour, particularly sexual behaviour, through its swift and sharp dialogue and several extended monologues from the most senior of the bouncers, 'Lucky Eric'.

Eric: […] Two drinks and they're going; legs opening to any particular denizen of the night with car keys and Aramis splashed face, maybe even old spice; drunken, free, giddy, silly girls wanting to be women, done too soon.

(Ibid, p. 28)

When Godber moved to Hull, he wrote his most successful play, *Up 'n' Under* (1984), which is set in the world of rugby league. The play is a comedy, and tells the story of a bet between two coaches that the team languishing at the bottom of the league cannot beat a top-flight team. The deal is struck and the central character, Arthur, sets about the seemingly impossible task of turning a completely hopeless team into a match-winning one.

The play is remarkable for its stage conventions, which are typical of Godber's work. Although the major characters are members of the 'hero' rugby team, at times they change roles to become players on the opposing team. This is done by the actors turning their backs on the audience and adopting a more aggressive posture and deeper, more resonant and menacing voices. Few props are used on the set, and the pace is swift. The play won the Laurence Olivier award for best comedy in 1985 and was made into a film in 1997.

Godber's work as a director is always economical, physical and energetic. The actors are frequently called upon to play more than one role (particularly in *Teechers*, 1987).

Characters fighting circumstances

Godber's characters are often representative of a particular type: people who are beaten down by their economic circumstances but who somehow manage to rise above them. For example, *April in Paris* (1992) is about a couple who argue constantly and are forced into a life of considerable hardship by the man's long-term unemployment. They win a trip to Paris and rediscover the romance in their relationship. The semi-autobiographical *Salt of the Earth*, written for the centenary of the City of Wakefield in 1988, tells the story of a mining family from the end of the Second World War to the culmination of the Miners' Strike in 1985.

While Godber's work often has a strong political imperative, he always shows compassion for his characters and optimism about their ability to fight against their circumstances.

Summary of style of directing

- Highly physicalised style — especially in his early plays, for example *Bouncers* and *Up 'n' Under*.
- Directs mainly small ensembles in his own work; occasionally directs work by other writers.
- Work has a small-scale 'chamber' feel to it. Hull Truck — where Godber has been artistic director since 1984 — has an audience capacity of 320. The new Hull Truck, due to open in the spring of 2009, will have an audience capacity of 450. Godber prefers the immediacy and intimacy of smaller venues and crafts his productions accordingly.
- While physically demanding, his productions are often simply set. Plays such as *Happy Jack*, *Teechers* and *Bouncers* take place across many different scenarios which are created through the actors' work rather than through complex scene changes.

Katie Mitchell

Katie Mitchell is an associate director of the National Theatre and one of the country's foremost female directors. She was born in 1964 and attended Oakham School (where she directed her first play at the age of 16) and Magdalen College, Oxford. After working in stage management at the Kings Head Theatre in north London, Mitchell undertook early directing work with Pains Plough and the RSC. In the 1990s she formed her own company called Classics on a Shoestring, and then became an associate director with both the National Theatre and the Royal Court.

It is impossible to describe Mitchell's work in quite the same way as that of directors like Berkoff or Godber. Unlike Berkoff and Godber, she is not a play-wright and she has directed very different plays in terms of both era and scale, for example Euripides' *Iphigenia in Aulis* at the National Theatre (2004) and Bach's *St Matthew Passion* at Glyndebourne (2007). She has often worked on classical texts, such as Chekhov's *Ivanov* for the National Theatre in 2002 and *The Seagull* (adapted by Martin Crimp) in 2006.

Influence of Stanislavski

In her youth, Mitchell visited eastern Europe and became familiar with the work of Russian and eastern European writers and artists. While she was influenced by a number of practitioners, she was particularly struck by the intense and rigorous working practices of Stanislavski. She approaches the rehearsal of a play by asking the actors to investigate the play's facts (which characters are married to whom, where the play is set etc). This establishes the unarguable details for the play — what Stanislavski might refer to as 'the given circumstances'. The process is described in an interview with Charlotte Higgins in the *Guardian* (24 November 2007). After the unarguable facts, the actors then have to address issues of character, which Mitchell descibes as 'all the grey areas you put down as a list of questions'. This analytical process enables actors to approach their characters without introducing too much subjectivity. The characters, then, are the result of a studious process rather than an impulsive series of ideas. In her production of *Women of Troy*, Mitchell employed the services of a psychiatrist to 'diagnose' the characters; consequently she presented Cassandra as manic depressive and Helen as bulimic.

Mitchell requires her actors to undertake extensive and thorough prepara-tion, and her rehearsal process is methodical and detailed. In researching the background to their characters, the actors use a degree of interpretation to create their 'back story'. Mitchell is drawn to the precise detail involved in applying Stanisalvski's discipline and she ensures that her actors are fully engaged in this fairly exhaustive process. Since this is unquestionably a complex and involved process, Mitchell likes to use the same actors in different productions. The results are often remarkably detailed and highly visual. However, her work cannot be described simply as 'naturalism'. Jane Edwardes, writing in *Timeout* (12 November 2007), claims that:

> [...] her productions have been distinguished by the intensity of the emotions, the realism of the acting, and the creation of a very distinctive world.

Mitchell also frequently combines the use of video with stage action — according to Edwardes, she is 'one of the few directors who understands how to use video in theatre'. Live video was used in her 2007 production of Martin Crimp's *Attempts on Her Life* (1997), and her adaptation of Virgina Woolf's novel *The Waves* in 2006 included film made by the actors themselves. This use of video indicates a realisation that theatre can, on occasion, engage with elements of multimedia to create more effective productions. This is a modern innovation also to be found in the work of Emma Rice and Kneehigh Theatre (*Brief Encounter* 2008).

A film of the actors is played behind the real actors in Katie Mitchell's adaptation of Virginia Woolf's *The Waves* (Cottesloe Theatre, London, 2006)

Critics' reactions

Critical responses to Mitchell's work are often polarised. In an article entitled 'From heroine to villainess', Dominic Cavendish records a discussion with Mitchell, who described the extreme reactions of members of the audience and critics to her production of *The Seagull*.

> A violent fury seized some people on watching *The Seagull* at the National Theatre this summer. On press night, I heard groans in the stalls within

minutes of the start, prompted by the sight of Konstantin scuttling about with a microphone — this was before anyone's eyes had time to adjust, through the gloom, to other flagrant anachronisms or widen in disbelief at strange outbreaks of tango dancing.

(*Daily Telegraph*, 30 October 2006)

Later in the article, Mitchell expresses regret that her production upset some people, explaining that she had deliberately used anachronisms in the production to remind audiences 'how radical *The Seagull* was' and how ahead of its time.

Mitchell's trademark is her bold manner of working, and much of her other work, especially Greek tragedies at The National (*Iphigenia at Aulis*, 2004, and *Women of Troy*, 2007), have been positively received.

Summary of style of directing

- ◆ Directs a vast range of material. Often associated with the work of playwright Martin Crimp but has also directed Greek tragedy, Chekhov and opera.
- ◆ Uses multimedia in her productions, particularly video.
- ◆ Has a highly disciplined, systematic approach to her work, influenced particularly by Stanislavski.

Max Stafford-Clark

Max Stafford-Clark (born 1941) is one of the most enduring and highly respected of all British directors. He was the longest serving director of the Royal Court Theatre, London (1979–93), and was responsible for the first productions of now famous plays, perhaps the most well-known being *Rita, Sue and Bob Too* (Andrea Dunbar, 1982) and *Our Country's Good* (Timberlake Wertenbaker, 1988).

Stafford-Clark has become synonymous not only with the creation of new work but also finding new writing talent, notably during his time at the Royal Court Theatre. However, he has also been responsible for new work through his other companies, Joint Stock Theatre Company, which he founded in 1974, and Out of Joint, which he founded in 1993 on retiring from the Royal Court.

Stafford-Clark's career — particularly at the Royal Court — reflects the ways in which economic circumstances can affect repertoire and practice. While the purpose of this chapter is to investigate the ways in which different directors approach their craft, it is important to note that economic realities also mark their work. Directorial decisions may well be influenced by economic constraints as well as artistic choice.

Most of Stafford-Clark's productions are of new plays, so it is difficult to identify his precise processes. These can vary, depending on the aims of the production or, indeed, the behaviours and practices of the playwright. For this reason, it is worth reflecting on the process involved in the two productions cited above, as well as his production of *Macbeth* in 2004.

Fostering new work

A Bradford-born playwright, Andrea Dunbar, came to the attention of Stafford-Clark in 1980 through the Royal Court's Young Writer's Festival. He recounts how he first encountered Dunbar's writing:

> …in 1980 there was one outstanding play: *The Arbor.* Written boldly in green biro on pages ripped from a school exercise book, it told the story of a Bradford schoolgirl who became pregnant on the night she lost her virginity. A family argument was depicted with brutal authenticity, and the final scene was heartbreakingly affecting and bleak.
>
> (Roberts, P. and Stafford-Clark, M. (2007) *Taking Stock: The Theatre of Max Stafford-Clark*, Nick Hern Books, p. 109)

When Stafford-Clark first contacted Dunbar about her work, she was staying in a refuge for battered women. His book describes how he worked with her on developing her script and its eventual progression into a full-length play. It was a frustrating process as Dunbar, who was only a teenager at the time, came from a background that was as troubled and deprived as that of the characters she portrayed. Describing the process of putting on the full-length version of *The Arbor* in 1980, Stafford-Clark says:

> Andrea's world had no agents, no telephones and no bank accounts. Occasionally a few pages would arrive, but the norms of communication with a writer couldn't be taken for granted… But Andrea was nobody's fool, and as she became more engaged in writing her standards became higher.
>
> (Ibid, p. 112)

Dunbar's was a new talent from an environment that did not necessarily recognise talent. The process Stafford-Clark went through was one of engaging the writer's interest and encouraging her craft. It was a painstaking, difficult, often frustrating, but ultimately important achievement.

The work on Dunbar's play *Rita, Sue and Bob Too* was also difficult. She had no inclination to move away from the Buttershaw estate in Bradford where she lived, and Stafford-Clark often found that he could not contact her or that she would be in the middle of a domestic crisis if he did.

These examples from Stafford-Clark's experience as a director remind us that if someone is promoting a theatre that not only puts on new work but also seeks to find writers who may not consider themselves to be writers, then it is difficult (or impossible) to establish norms in the director's approach.

Developing a new production

Stafford-Clark was staying in New York when his production of Caryl Churchill's *Serious Money* (1987) was given its premiere on Broadway. By chance, he came across a copy of Thomas Keneally's *The Playmaker* (1987) — a historical novel that charts the events surrounding a production of George Farquhar's play *The Recruiting Officer* (1706) in the convict colony in Sydney in the 1780s.

After reading Keneally's novel, Stafford-Clark decided to put on a production of *The Recruiting Officer* in tandem with an adaptation of *The Playmaker*. For the task of adaptation, he approached Timberlake Wertenbaker. In Wertenbaker's mind, the story displayed the redemptive power of theatre as the convicts' respect and affection for each other grow while they rehearse the play. The story also showed the harsh, sometimes bigoted, views of the officers towards the play: the character of Major Ross feels strongly that the play should not go ahead.

Stafford-Clark involved the actors in the process and development of this production: they did not simply wait until Wertenbaker's script arrived. He took them to see a production of Howard Barker's *Love of a Good Man* (1981) at Wormwood Scrubs prison, in which the prisoners played the major roles. Here, Stafford-Clark's actors had the opportunity of meeting and talking with prisoners who were also working as actors.

As the play, *Our Country's Good*, was rehearsed, so the script evolved. Rehearsals involved actors being asked for their views about scenes, and the director and playwright debating which ideas worked and which did not. Therefore, the writer and actors were a fundamental part of the rehearsal process, constantly contributing to and responding to ideas.

Confronting contemporary issues on stage

In seeking to promote new writers and new work, Stafford-Clark has often been at the forefront of creating plays that comment on contemporary issues. *Our Country's Good* — despite being set in the 1780s — clearly reflects an attitude of antipathy towards the arts that he and Wertenbaker felt was prevalent at the time in the UK, principally from the Thatcher government.

His production of *Macbeth* (2004) incorporated images from the Rwandan civil war and the uprising in Haiti. Interestingly, his stimulus was mostly visual imagery: photographs of recent conflicts. He says of this production:

My starting point is usually the story. Not so with *Macbeth*. The images and photographs helped create a very clear setting that provided a tangible and graspable alternative to Shakespeare's medieval Scotland.

(Ibid, p. 223)

Summary of style of directing

- ◆ Stafford-Clark has directed both new works and classics.
- ◆ He often has the inspiration for a new play and then hires a writer to help him realise it. Perhaps the best-known example of this is *Our Country's Good* by Timberlake Wertenbaker.
- ◆ The work he directs often has polemic (political) content, and he has worked with high-profile, successful political playwrights such as Caryl Churchill (*Cloud 9*, 1979; *Top Girls*, 1982; *Serious Money*, 1987) and David Hare (*Fanshen*, 1975).
- ◆ To date, Stafford-Clark is the longest serving artistic director of the Royal Court Theatre — dedicated to promoting new work. During his tenure, he frequently came into conflict with the Arts Council and his own board of directors because of his controversial and often anti-establishment productions.

Declan Donnellan

Declan Donnellan was born in 1953 and grew up in London. He read English and law at university and was called to the Bar in 1978. However, he then became involved in the world of theatre and in 1981 he co-founded the Cheek by Jowl Theatre Company with the designer Nick Ormerod.

An actor's theatre

Interestingly, for one of the country's most renowned directors, Donnellan believes strongly in an actor's theatre. In an interview in 2005 with Suzanne Worthington from the RSC, he said:

> I think that the theatre is the actor's art first and last, more than it's about directing or even writing. My sort of theatre is. What I do is to try to get actors to work together as well as possible. I'm a coach of actors more than a teacher.

This approach, with the actor at the centre of the process, is perhaps reminiscent of Stanislavski's quest to generate an atmosphere conducive to creating truthful acting.

Declan Donnellan (left) is often referred to as an 'actor's director'

An actor's director

Being described as an 'actor's director' testifies to Donnellan's fascination with the process of acting, as does his book *The Actor and the Target* (2002), in which he dissects and analyses performance techniques in minute detail. Through his work with Cheek by Jowl, as well as undertakings with the RSC, the National and the Maly Drama Theatre in St Petersburg, he has earned an international reputation as a director of classic texts, both plays and operas. Despite not having a dance background, his curiosity has led him into the world of ballet, and he directed the Bolshoi's production of *Romeo and Juliet* in 2004.

Improvisation and insight

What is distinctive about Donnellan's practice? Is he a natural successor to Stanislavski in his pursuit of truthful acting and his desire to create a theatre that is a vehicle for the 'actor's art'?

For someone interested in classic texts, there is little that can be said to be traditional about Donnellan's approach. He never starts with a read through, preferring initially to improvise around the main themes of the play, and claims always to be looking for fresh insights. Rather like Peter Brook, whom he cites as a major influence, Donnellan despises some of the conventional practices in British productions of Shakespeare.

Donnellan investigates classic texts in as thorough and rigorous a way as possible, using the ensemble of actors at the centre of the process. Indeed, his methods of casting are lengthy, often choosing to see actors three or four times before selecting them. He regards the function of a director as being 'someone who releases an actor's confidence in their ability to act'. Although highly disciplined as well as creative, Donnellan starts the rehearsal process with few preconceived ideas.

Matthew Macfadyen, one of the stars of the television series *Spooks*, has worked with Donnellan. He said in an interview for the *Daily Telegraph* (8 June 1998):

The most striking thing is that when you enter rehearsals there's seemingly no plan about how to proceed. Both of them [Donnellan and Ormerod] are hysterical when they're in a rehearsal room and you have tremendous fun. So many directors have a preconceived idea of what they want, but we played lots of games and the process was as organic as possible.

Design

Donnellan may be an actor's director, but undoubtedly design is a vital part of his theatre. Designer Nick Ormerod is present throughout the rehearsal process, and his creative ideas emerge as the rehearsals progress. In part, this is to ensure that the design is responsive to the work of the actors, rather than the actors fitting their performances into a pre-planned set.

Summary of style of directing

Donnellan usually directs classic texts and works from a completed script. His directorial style embraces the following ideas and beliefs:

- Actors must have learned their lines before rehearsals commence.
- Design is an important part of the theatrical process and the designer should attend all rehearsals.
- An actor's theatre is more important than a director's or a writer's theatre.
- There should be no preconceived ideas about a play before rehearsals commence.
- Painstaking care should be taken over casting, in order to create the right ensemble.
- A director to actors is like a coach to athletes.

Peter Cheeseman

Peter Cheeseman was born in 1932 and has earned a reputation as a director of theatre-in-the-round (where the audience is seated on all four sides around the auditorium). Cheeseman was artistic director of a regional theatre in Staffordshire for more than 30 years.

After working with theatrical pioneer Stephen Joseph in the 1950s, Cheeseman became artistic director of the Victoria Theatre (a theatre-in-the-round in Stoke-on-Trent) and later the New Victoria Theatre in Newcastle-under-Lyme. He retired from there in 1998 but carried on working as a freelance director.

Spatial relationships

Cheeseman refers to traditional proscenium-staged theatre as 'mono-directional'. Clearly, the influence of Stephen Joseph as a pioneer of theatre-in-the-round proved pivotal, not only to him but also to his colleague, the playwright Alan Ayckbourn, who stepped down as the artistic director of the Stephen Joseph Theatre in Scarborough in early 2008.

Not surprisingly, given his passion for theatre-in-the-round, Cheeseman is preoccupied with the spatial relationships in theatre, and during his early years he found the remoteness of the actor a continual source of frustration. As television began to gain a greater currency in the cultural life of Britain, much of the aloofness of acting and drama was overcome, as audiences could watch intimate drama in their living rooms.

Breaking down barriers

With the development of 'thrust' (or 'apron') stages, attempts were made to break down barriers with audiences. Cheeseman recalls the sense of freedom he felt when he first directed for theatre-in-the-round. In proscenium theatre, he saw the necessity to organise groups of actors and almost choreograph them. However, theatre-in-the-round affords all its audience members the same opportunities to view the play. It is likely that in an ensemble piece a member of the audience will have to watch an actor's back at some point; thus the old adage about never turning your back on an audience has to be broken. Cheeseman sees nothing definitively wrong with such a situation, since theatre-in-the-round is 'structured like life'.

Like Declan Donnellan, Cheeseman is concerned with integrity in theatre. He believes that theatre-in-the-round, in particular, exposes the actor to the audience's scrutiny and that therefore dishonest acting (or 'lying') will soon be discovered.

Documentary theatre

Although during his long career Cheeseman has directed many classic texts, including those by Shakespeare, Molière, Brecht and Ibsen, he has developed a reputation for creating original documentary theatre: dramatic productions based on real events.

Living and working in 'the Potteries' in Staffordshire (where most of the UK's china factories are found), he chose to create plays about his local community, using the reminiscences of members of that community as a basis for a script.

The process of preparation for such plays has developed over the years. He has used tape recordings of local residents or even involved the original people themselves in improvising in front of actors, for instance for *Nice Girls* (1993), which was based on the story of three women who occupied Trentham Colliery.

When Cheeseman creates a piece of documentary theatre, he is adamant that the actor who plays a role is an 'advocate for that person' and that there is no pretence at being the person. The actor is required to address the members of the audience directly and tell them that he or she represents the person he or she is playing but is not that person. One could argue that this distancing of the role from the actor is a Brechtian technique. Certainly, the ambience generated by the theatre-in-the-round is similar to the 'boxing ring' atmosphere advocated by Brecht.

Cheeseman's work in revealing stories from the community is motivated by social conscience and the need to communicate a political message. Thus we are presented with stories of workers from particular industries or wives of redundant miners. Perhaps this message is not underpinned by a revolutionary aspiration, like Brecht's, but there is clearly a strong desire to tell uncomfortable truths about social deprivation and injustice.

The audience's representative

It is almost as if Cheeseman feels that he needs to be the audience's representative. Although he is interested in acting, perhaps the main contrast with Donnellan is that he is more absorbed with the *experience* for the audience. By spending most of his working life in a particular geographical region, he has developed a loyalty to the interests of that area and a sense of responsibility as to how theatre should represent the region. Rather like John Godber in Hull, by focusing on the community as a source of inspiration for new pieces of theatre he has been successful in attracting local people to the theatre who perhaps would not ordinarily attend.

Summary of style of directing

Cheeseman's directorial style is outlined by the following observations:

- He is a strong advocate of theatre-in-the-round.
- He has a preoccupation with spatial relationships between actors, and between actors and the audience.
- He has directed classic texts, new writing and original documentary/community plays.

- He is motivated by social and political factors when creating documentary theatre.
- He believes that, as a director, he is the audience's representative.

Lloyd Newson

Lloyd Newson was born in Australia in 1957 and has worked in the UK since 1980. He trained in contemporary dance but also has qualifications in psychology. Since 1986 he has been the artistic director of the dance theatre group DV8 Physical Theatre.

Newson and his company have been responsible for some of the most innovative theatre pieces of the last 20 years. His interest in both dance and psychology has led him to develop a highly analytical approach to movement, which questions why we use certain movement patterns and how these patterns express relationships, cultures and traditions.

Physical theatre

Although Newson is credited with coining the term 'physical theatre' when he established DV8, it is a phrase he is now reluctant to use:

> When we formed the company in 1986 in Europe, nobody that I knew of called themselves a physical theatre company. Within 2 years there were schools in physical theatre in Britain. I thought, 'I have hit a term that is appropriate and a lot of people want to throw themselves into'. Then I got very upset seeing all these physical theatre companies emerging who for me weren't physically trained, and I thought that this has lowered the tone of this term, and I don't want to be associated with that term.

All of Newson's actors are rigorously dance trained and his work is unequivocally physically led.

Arguably, Newson's work allows for the use of a wider-ranging theatrical language than that found in traditional theatre. The frustration with a theatre subjugated to text, which led Artaud to develop his manifesto for new theatre practices, is echoed in the philosophy of Newson, who uses physical interpretation of ideas before the development of any text. However, Newson does not abandon the use of words, and where they are necessary he incorporates them. Much depends on the nature of the piece he is creating.

Improvisation

Although the storylines for his pieces are devised in advance, Newson uses improvisation extensively. The performers participate in the cultivation and development of story and style, and this gives them a greater ownership over the final result. Video cameras are constantly trained on the action during the rehearsals and there is a lengthy process of editing and selecting following the improvisations. A 3-hour rehearsal might only yield around 30 seconds of material that is retained and developed.

Controversial subject matter

Newson and DV8 are concerned with exploring prominent social issues and controversial subjects through their work; the results are often hard-hitting and with an unashamed edge. When *MSM* (1993) — a play about sexual encounters in male public toilets — reached London's West End, a lawyer was present at rehearsals to monitor levels of decency, following concern from the theatre management.

A performance of *Never Again* by DV8 in 1989

Is Newson's work designed to shock?

Newson's work with DV8 focuses on taboo subject matter to create engaging pieces of physical theatre. In his refusal to adapt his work to expectation, many of his pieces tend to shock. This is certainly the case at the beginning of *The Cost of Living* (2003), when a dancer, David Toole, emerges from a box on stage and we realise he has no legs. However, this shock is a response that reflects the audience's perception, rather than anything intrinsically shocking: after all, why should seeing a man with no legs come on stage be a shocking experience? What does the shock say about the audience's prejudices and preconceptions?

The shock that we experience as members of an audience derives from an uncompromising approach to the dynamics of theatre that reflects and explores society's and humanity's extremes.

Devised work

Newson always creates new work, so he is concerned with devising as well as directing. Although he has been invited to direct various pieces, he finds little in plays or books that reflects how he sees the world. He is responsible for innovating not only the technicalities of the physical production but also the intricacies of the script. As such, he is as much an author as a director.

His actors are a crucial part of the creation process, rather than performers who are presented with a completed script or a preconceived piece of choreography. Newson is clear that everything that occurs on stage is the result of his decisions. He described his role in an interview with Jo Butterworth in 1998 as 'stimulator, facilitator, editor and constructor'. It is an interesting relationship with performers since, on the one hand, there is no misunderstanding that all physical and vocal action has been subjected to approval and creative shaping. However, he strives to find innovative and individual performers, without whom he says 'nothing'.

Other elements of production

Newson is interested in the stage environment and the relationship between 'architecture and the body'. In a style of theatre that is led by imagery and visual stimulation, this is unsurprising. Music and lighting also play an important role in his work. Lighting designer Jack Thompson has worked on a number of DV8 productions, and over the last 20 years, the company's pieces have always been performed to commissioned new scores.

Summary of style of directing

Newson's directorial style is extremely dynamic:
* His work is movement led — but cannot be termed purely 'dance'.
* He is interested in the 'psychology of movement' and why people express themselves through the use of particular movement patterns.
* His work is often hard-hitting and controversial.
* Although there is a starting point and a theme, much of the work is created from improvisation.
* His work is always original.
* His work often contains text but is not text-led.
* Design and music are important features of his work.

Designers

The influence of a designer on a production can be considerable. Far from simply providing a backdrop or an environment, a designer contributes to the world of the play in a tangible and philosophical way. Design, therefore, is much more than an accompaniment to a production; it is part of the production itself.

Ralph Koltai

Ralph Koltai is one of the nation's most celebrated and high-profile designers. Born in Berlin to Hungarian parents in 1924, he worked with British intelligence at the end of the Second World War and then settled in England. Interestingly, he worked in the library for the Nuremberg Trials and, years later, would design the set for Rolf Hochhuth's *The Representative* (1963), a play about the Holocaust.

Themes and concepts

According to Tony Davis, Koltai is sometimes 'credited with introducing the idea of the theatrical "concept"' (*Stage Design*, p. 27). Koltai himself says:

> When in 1997 I put together my retrospective exhibition, I discovered to my astonishment that my concern with concept and with metaphor were there from the start, totally unconscious.
>
> (Ibid, p. 28)

Koltai, therefore, thinks in terms of the play's themes and concepts more than the storyline. He aims to get to the heart of the play's ideas rather than simply finding a suitable or realistic setting. For example, when designing the 1967 Young Vic production of *As You Like It* (*c.* 1600), he created an abstract Forest of Arden in order to establish the idea of the young lovers being involved in a kind of romantic and surreal dream.

In 1977 Koltai designed the set for a dance piece called *Cruel Garden* by Christopher Bruce. In this production, he watched rehearsals before arriving at the concept for the set. He commented: 'You can't design contemporary dance without observing the development of the choreography in rehearsals' (*Stage Design*, p. 35). This surreal piece is based on the life of Federico Garcia Lorca — a Spanish poet and playwright — so Koltai decided to set the dance in a bullring.

Koltai also designed the set for Sam West's 2006 revival of *The Romans in Britain* by Howard Brenton (1980). *Guardian* critic Michael Billington described his contribution thus:

Veteran designer Ralph Koltai has created a stunning image of a warped, gnarled, knotted tree-trunk above a standing pool and a rolling greensward.

(*Guardian*, 9 February 2006)

Another reviewer (John Highfield in *The Stage*, 10 February 2006) referred to this set as creating an almost alien landscape, entirely appropriate to the play's theme of the brutality of invasion.

Three-dimensional work and innovative materials

When creating a design, Koltai always works three dimensionally rather than through drawing. For example, when working on a production of the musical *Metropolis* (1989), he bought a gear box from a scrap yard. The casing fell away and the exposed cogs he saw formed the basis of the idea of a machine room that eventually formed the set.

Koltai's work is also innovative in its use of materials. When the Royal Opera House staged a ballet danced to Gustav Holst's *The Planets* in 1990, Koltai created the effect of ever-circling spheres using a series of mirrors and two-way mirrors made from polycarbonate. For the 'Jupiter' scene, a giant scenery flat depicting a huge apple was hung behind the mirror.

In summary

Koltai's idea of the play's 'concept' as a starting point is important. He works closely with directors but does not follow a text slavishly, and usually prefers to read it only once so that it does not block his intuitive ideas. He is a spontaneous designer.

Bill Dudley

Bill Dudley originally trained in fine art in London, but was drawn to the world of theatre design while working at the Tower Theatre in Islington. He has worked for major companies such as the National Theatre, the RSC and the Royal Court Theatre. However, he has also completed some landmark design work for the Scottish writer and director Bill Bryden.

Two-dimensional work

Unlike Koltai, Dudley uses drawings extensively because of his fine art background, but is clear that he regards them as being ciphers for the real thing (i.e. the constructed set). He embraces new technologies, and in an interview he described himself as being 'deeply affected' by changes that have occurred in graphic art, such as the ability to experiment with uses of light created by spray guns and airbrushes, and the use of computer graphics:

You could even print the thing out on the newly introduced cheap colour printers and you could distress the paper and then you could put the airbrush over that. Also it's sensationally good for creating the effect of light.

(Davis, T. (2001) *Stage Design*, Rotovision, p. 78)

Light effects

Creating eerie surreal light effects was a feature of Dudley's design for Roger Michell's 1997 production of *The Homecoming* (Harold Pinter, 1964). This was staged at the National Theatre and involved the construction of a large and foreboding set that suggested a Victorian Gothic terraced house. Tony Davis described the way in which Dudley managed to achieve a sense of the presence of a family who had occupied the house for several generations:

> Dudley used a series of dark gauzes upon which vertical lines were hand painted and computer-sprayed. One gauze showed the ghost of the set in 1964 and revealed behind it the décor of the 1930s when the parents were married. Dudley wanted the cut away set, made from aircraft flooring, to transmit light through its translucent surface.

Dudley himself added:

> When their marriage is over at the end, we lit up the back of the set, so the whole house looked like glass — a strangely unnerving effect.

(Ibid, p. 79)

Settings that are integral to the action

Undoubtedly, two of Dudley's most famous contributions were his sets for Bill Bryden in the Harland and Wolff shipyard for *The Ship* (1990) and for *The Big Picnic* (1994). In an interview for the *British Theatre Guide* (June 2003), Dudley is described as 'still a committed socialist'; in the same interview he portrays these two projects in particular as 'real people's theatre'.

The Ship was staged in the closed-down shipyards of Harland and Wolff, which had once employed a large number of men, and told the story of the shipbuilders' lives. Dudley's set — which also housed the 1,200-capacity audience — was a ship 67 feet wide. As he recalls, at the end of the play the audience would:

> ...launch the ship — the whole edifice slid 300 feet to the other end of the shed. The set wasn't this decorative, useless afterthought, it was integral; it both housed the play and it was the object of the play. It was one of the most emotional things I can ever remember.

(Ibid, p. 81)

In the sense that Artaud wanted elements of theatre to work together with equal status and not just be subjugated to the text, so Dudley's set for *The Ship* was no mere background. It was as essential to the world of the play as the text itself.

The same vast space was used for Bryden's First World War drama *The Big Picnic*, which tells the story of a number of men from Govan who join up. Dudley used his set to create a visceral sense of the horrors of war. The huge space enabled him to conjure up the bleakness and expanse of no man's land on the Western Front. Lasers were used to convey the impression of bullets flying overhead, and dry ice produced a sense of the mist and fog of the trenches.

In summary

Dudley's remark that his set for *The Ship* both 'housed the play and was the object of the play' is an important commentary on the job of the theatre designer. A set can be far more than a background or a backdrop for the actors to perform in or against.

Maria Bjornson

Maria Bjornson was the designer of the spectacular fall of the chandelier in Lloyd Webber's musical *The Phantom of the Opera* (see page 12). After studying at St Martin's School of Art and Design under, among others, Ralph Koltai, her early days as a theatre designer were spent in repertory at the Glasgow Citizens Theatre. There, she designed 16 shows in 18 months:

> …we would open a show on a Friday and have to have the next show designed by the Monday. It was very good training because there was no model — you just had to think in terms of ideas which was quite frightening. Rep teaches you throwaway, everything has to be done so fast — you just have to get on with it.
>
> (Ibid, p. 92)

This is an important consideration when you comment on the work of a theatre designer. Judgements about designers' concepts — as with judgements about directors' concepts — need to be seen within the context of economic reality. Irrespective of whether or not Bjornson wanted to create a model for her Citizens Theatre productions, there was simply no time to do so.

Designing for opera and musical

Bjornson has arguably had most of her success in the field of opera and musicals. In her most well-known design, for *The Phantom of the Opera*, Bjornson was inspired by the knowledge that there is a lake underneath the Paris Opera, where the play is set. Her use of candles was influenced by a picture of Venice she had seen that showed reflections in the water. Harold Prince, the director, told her that he wanted 'Turkish corners, drapes flooding very heavily onto the floor' (*Stage Design*, p. 101). From this vague starting directive, she was able to create the eerie hidden world of the Phantom — a twilight and mysterious place that is part fantasy, part nightmare.

Bjornson identifies an interesting distinction between designing for an opera as opposed to designing for a play:

> With an opera the performers have got a voice, you're putting a design over them. In a play you're underneath them, supporting them from the bottom up.'
>
> (*Stage Design*, p. 99)

Maria Bjornson's design for *The Phantom of the Opera* makes extensive use of candles

A play develops in rehearsal and the design elements can therefore develop with the process. During the preparations for a production of Chekhov's *The Cherry Orchard* (1904), which she designed for the National Theatre in 2000, Bjornson was able to create a series of storyboards with intricate textual detail on them. From here, she went on to create a set dominated by doors because she believed the play to be all about 'entrances and exits'. In an opera, however, a performer may only be in rehearsal for a few days. Much of the design work has to be done beforehand because, quite simply, many members of the company may not be there.

Bjornson's staging of Janáček's operas with the director David Pountney earned her considerable critical acclaim early in her career during the late 1970s and 1980s. In a production of Janáček's *The Cunning Little Vixen* (Welsh National Opera 1980), Bjornson created a set that showed the seasons and allowed actors to move freely:

> My response was to do a shorthand for nature, so what I ended up with was a slab like a sort of rolling hill where the action would take place.
>
> (Ibid, p. 92)

Bjornson goes on to describe how the actors initially refused to work on the set. However, when the children who were also taking part in the production arrived they 'played' with it, running around freely and using the trap doors. When the actors saw this, they began to realise the possibilities of the set and 'started tumbling about' as well.

This is an example of a set that was created with the actors' movements in mind. Its conception moved beyond what it looked like to an audience and even what themes from the opera it expressed. The set's focus was on how it would influence and enhance the actors' quality of movement.

In summary

Bjornson's designs show how a set can physically influence an actor's performance. Her sets are visual feasts, frequently characterised by colour and drama, and her costumes often suggest wonderful fabrics and jewels.

Discussion questions

Make thorough notes on the points that arise from your consideration of the following questions, either from discussion or your own observations.

1 What plays have you seen that you thought were either strongly or weakly directed? Identify what specific aspects of the productions led you to believe that the director was either a positive or negative influence.

2 Reflecting on the directors discussed in this chapter, consider (a) What must a director do? (b) What should a director do? (c) What could a director do?

3 Discuss the design of a play you have seen. Identify specific elements in the design that contributed to the play's impact on the audience, in terms of theme or visual effects or both.

Essay question

Focusing on a production you have seen, analyse and evaluate the director's concept of the production. Give clear examples of directorial influence on the production.

Hints

* Directorial influence can be subtle and more focused on acting style than complex design ideas.
* In interviews and programmes directors and designers may discuss their ideas for a production in some detail. However, it is for you as an informed member of the audience to decide whether they are successful or not.

Writing the supporting notes

The supporting notes for your devised piece allow you to explain and justify the process that led to its creation. These notes should be treated as an analysis of the process rather than a diary account. When creating your supporting notes, you should divide them into three major sections.

Section 1: Evidence of research and dramatic intention

If your devised piece has a particular style, you should provide evidence that you researched the style. It may be that the style developed as the piece was rehearsed, but you should still indicate that you undertook appropriate research. Research in this context is not necessarily confined to reading books or surfing the internet, but can also include viewing productions. Be aware, and acknowledge, that plays you have studied, read or seen may have influenced your choice of style.

You should discuss the reasons for choosing the style you have used, and justify its relevance to the subject matter. You also need to make clear what dramatic intentions you had and what impact you wanted your piece to make on an audience. Consider the structure as well as the content of your piece, and think about what you want the audience to take away from their viewing experience.

Remember to link the decisions you made regarding style to your dramatic intention. In describing and analysing this process, ensure that you use correct and technical terminology. Inappropriate or inaccurate vocabulary reveals a lack of understanding or specialist knowledge.

Section 2: Analysis of the process

In this section, you should analyse the process of putting your piece together, making clear how you developed your devising strategies and evaluating their success. Ensure that you describe the process of rehearsal and refinement accurately, and analyse how you have developed ideas for your own contribution. Remember to consider your individual work as well as the group task, and explain how your research and discoveries have contributed to the development of your piece.

Analyse the effectiveness of the rehearsals and the feedback you received (from other group members or your teacher), explaining how these helped to shape further rehearsals.

Section 3: Evaluation of effectiveness

In the final section, you should analyse the effectiveness of your group's piece as a whole. You must evaluate the style you chose, the potential effectiveness of this for an audience, and the merits of the work as a piece of live theatre.

You should also scrutinise your own practice carefully, commenting on how you met the challenges of your task and how successful you think you were in carrying it out. You should identify the particular contribution you made, and comment on how your own skills as a performer, devisor and/or designer developed through the process. You should show an awareness of the production needs of your piece and how your group tackled the challenges of putting on a live production — including considerations of health and safety.

Unit 3

A2: Written responses to drama

Introduction to Unit 3

There are two areas of focus in Unit 3 as follows:

* Section A: studying one pre-twentieth century text, focusing on interpreting it from a performance perspective.
* Section B: studying one twentieth-century or contemporary text to make written suggestions for a complete stage realisation of any extract presented in the examination.

To address fully the demands of both sections of Unit 3, you need to develop a more profound knowledge of the texts you are studying than was the case for Unit 1 at AS. You should develop a firm understanding of the play, its context and its genre, and be prepared to realise a creative overview of it. Therefore, you need to research your chosen plays thoroughly, including previous performances of it and the impact these performances had on audiences.

Section A

For this section, you should focus on the interpretation of your chosen play from a director, designer and actor's viewpoint. You will be expected to write about your own chosen sections of the play to illustrate your ideas.

This requires you to think about both performance and production elements of the play, and to demonstrate a complete creative overview of it. You will be asked to answer one question from a choice of two on your chosen text. You will be allowed access to your annotated text.

The six set texts are:

* *The Revenger's Tragedy* (c. 1606)   Middleton/Tourneur
* *Tartuffe* (1664)   Molière
* *The Recruiting Officer* (1706)   Farquhar

- *The Servant of two Masters* (153)   Goldoni
- *Lady Windermere's Fan* (1892)   Wilde
- *The Seagull* (1895)   Chekhov

Section B

In the examination, you must answer one compulsory question on your chosen play from Section B. You will be presented with a section of text from the play you have studied and be asked about how, as a director, you might stage that section. When responding to the question, you will need to take into account all the facets of production, including the style of your production and the kind of impact you want to make on your audience. To be able to do this, you must have considered the context of the production and the implications that this will have on your designer and director. While you will be asked to address the challenges and opportunities of a specific scene, you are expected to consider how that scene will work within the context of a full production.

Your suggestions must be made from the perspective of the director, working with designers and actors to communicate an interpretation to an audience.

The set texts are as follows:

- *Blood Wedding* (1932)   Lorca
- *The Good Person of Szechwan* (1943)   Brecht
- *A View from the Bridge* (1955)   Miller
- *The Trial* (1971)   Berkoff
- *Our Country's Good* (1988)   Wertenbaker
- *Coram Boy* (2005)   Edmundson

You can use any edition of these plays except for *Blood Wedding, The Good Person of Szechwan* and *Coram Boy*. Your teacher will advise you.

In order to assist in your preparations, there follows a discussion of two of the plays on the list for Unit 3: *The Revenger's Tragedy* (Section A) and *A View from the Bridge* (Section B). The ideas and information offered about each text give you examples of the kind of information you will need to gather for the texts you choose to study. There are a number of questions for you to attempt as part of your preparation.

Chapter 12

Section A: Pre-twentieth century play

The Revenger's Tragedy

by Cyril Tourneur/
Thomas Middleton

Guidelines on background research

Before reading this play (or your chosen text) you should research its social, cultural and historical context. The notes below should give you an idea of the kind of information you need. Most importantly, you should find out as much as you can about the playwright. In the case of *The Revenger's Tragedy* (*c.* 1606), the playwright is uncertain. It used to be believed that the play was written by Cyril Tourneur, but more recent scholarship tends to the opinion that it is by Thomas Middleton.

When you have read the play, you need to undertake further reading to gain more detailed knowledge of the social and cultural context and information about previous performances. For example, an interesting account of a production of *The Revenger's Tragedy* by the Royal Shakespeare Company in 1969 is given by Stanley Wells in '*The Revenger's Tragedy* revived', *The Elizabeth Theatre*, volume 6 (1975).

Other interesting background reading could include 'Reading the body: *The Revenger's Tragedy* and the Jacobean theatre of consumption' by Peter Stallybrass in *Renaissance Drama*, new series 18 (1987), which discusses the emphasis on the body and its functions — especially eating and drinking — in the play, and *The Subject of Tragedy* by Catherine Belsey (Methuen/Routledge, 1985).

These are simply suggestions as far as *The Revenger's Tragedy* is concerned, and you should read about your chosen play as widely as possible.

The playwrights: Tourneur and Middleton

Little is known about Cyril Tourneur beyond the fact that he was definitely the author of one play, *The Atheist's Tragedy*, which was published in 1611. He served as a soldier in the Netherlands, wrote satirical poetry, and was connected with the stage from 1611 onwards. The King's Men, a Jacobean theatre company (the new name for the Chamberlain's Men, for whom Shakespeare acted and wrote), acted a play presumed to be by him called *The Nobleman*, and he probably helped to write another, lost, play performed in 1613. He spent many of his last years abroad and died in Ireland in 1626.

The Revenger's Tragedy, curiously, was translated into Dutch in 1618. Given Tourneur's connections with the Netherlands, this fact suggests that he might have been its author. However, over the last few decades, academics have attempted to prove that the play's author was actually Thomas Middleton. It has been claimed that the play 'exhibits a distinctively Middletonian linguistic pattern found in no other dramatist of the period' (Jackson, M. P. (ed.) (1983) *The Revenger's Tragedy attributed to Thomas Middleton: A Facsimile of the 1607/8 Quarto*, Associated University Presses).

Thomas Middleton was born in 1580 and worked for the King's Men theatre company, both on his own and in collaboration with Michael Drayton, John Webster and Thomas Dekker. Middleton's early plays are sophisticated comedies designed to appeal to small audiences who paid to see plays in private theatres (which were performed by boys). However, from about 1613 he turned to tragi-comedy and then to tragedy, producing his best known plays *Women beware Women* (c. 1621) and, with William Rowley, *The Changeling* (1622). He died in 1627.

Thomas Middleton

Mary Evans Picture Library/Alamy

Cultural context: revenge tragedy

The 'revenge tragedy' genre first appeared in the 1580s, and is often referred to as 'the tragedy of blood'. The common ingredients of revenge tragedy include:
- a quest for vengeance (often at the prompting of the ghost of a loved one)
- scenes involving real or feigned madness
- scenes in graveyards
- scenes of carnage or mutilation

Vindice, the 'revenger' in *The Revenger's Tragedy* says 'When the bad bleeds, then is the tragedy good' (III.5.205). This expectation of revenge tragedy produced 'counter-attacks', where the heroes refuse, or hesitate, to follow the convention. This happens in the most famous example of a revenge tragedy, Shakespeare's *Hamlet* (*c.* 1600).

As a genre, revenge tragedy dominated much of late Elizabethan and Jacobean theatre. The earliest example of an English revenge tragedy is Thomas Kyd's *Spanish Tragedy* (*c.* 1580s) — one of the most popular plays of its era. Other such plays include *Titus Andronicus* (Shakespeare *c.* 1591), *The Duchess of Malfi* (John Webster 1614) and *The Changeling* (Thomas Middleton 1622).

Murderous central character

The world of the revenge tragedy is one where the central character tests an audience's sympathies to the limit. Although his cause may be an understandable one (Hamlet, for example, is avenging the murder of his father by his uncle), he often stoops to murderous behaviour himself. Hamlet's bullying of his mother and his rash and thoughtless action in killing Polonius force us to wonder if his cause is a truly righteous one — or at least whether his actions are just. Similarly, in the course of *The Revenger's Tragedy*, Vindice is shown taking increasing pleasure in torture and murder.

Corruption

Revenge tragedy often describes a world of pervasive corruption, where the rulers have abused their position and power. Claudius (the king in *Hamlet*) has not only murdered his brother, but has also married his brother's sister. In *The Duchess of Malfi*, two brothers wield enormous power — the Duke and the Cardinal — but both are deeply corrupt men. The Cardinal is a high-ranking churchman who has used his position to gain enormous wealth. Despite the strict edicts on moral and sexual behaviour issued by the church he represents, he lives openly with his mistress and later callously murders her. His brother, Duke Ferdinand, has developed a jealous obsessive love of his sister, the Duchess.

The revenger may start out as part of one faction but then become its bitter opponent. In *The Duchess of Malfi*, Bosola is employed by the brothers to spy on the Duchess and then to serve as their 'hit man'. However, his conscience finally causes him to seek revenge on the brothers, killing both them and himself in the process.

Rank and hierarchy threatened

The world of the revenge tragedy is always one of rank and hierarchy, but the highest-ranking characters are often the most corrupt. The avenger may have a low social status (Bosola and Vindice) or a high social status (Hamlet), but even in the case of the high-status avenger there is the sense that he is working against the system. We do not see Hamlet as an establishment figure, and some productions (e.g. with David Warner at Stratford in 1964 and Christopher Eccleston at Leeds in 2002) have deliberately portrayed him as a rebellious 'angry young man' figure.

Social context: a changing society

The Revenger's Tragedy was written around 1606–07, in the early years of the reign of James I. The era from the late Elizabethan age to the start of the civil war in England in 1642 saw great changes in English society.

During the sixteenth century, London grew enormously as a trading centre, and between 1520 and 1600 the population increased from 50,000 to 200,000. During the latter part of the Tudor dynasty, land rents increased and wages fell in real terms, polarising the lives of the rich and the poor. On the other hand, the rise of the 'merchant classes' meant that power and wealth were not always concentrated in the hands of the ruling classes as had been the case previously. In *The Revenger's Tragedy*, the central character, Vindice, used to be a man of wealth, and his social position has been destroyed by the actions of the Duke.

Revenge tragedy, therefore, was written and performed at a time when centuries-old power structures were being questioned, traditionally powerful people were no longer necessarily so, and the right of kings to rule outright was a subject of debate. King James I — Elizabeth I's successor, who ascended the throne of England in 1603 — believed in the Divine Right of Kings (that a king was chosen specifically by God to rule and could therefore do so without parliamentary advice if he chose). James was an extravagant monarch and he allowed or ignored increasing corruption; he sold knighthoods and made expensive social show at court a requirement for advancement. There was much material available for playwrights who were interested in exposing and satirising the weaknesses of rulers.

During the second half of the sixteenth century, translations of French and Italian tales and histories began to appear in London. Writers in England were inspired by images of Italian city states as luxurious places inhabited by people who were both cultured and murderous. For instance, a book called *The Palace of Pleasure* (1567) includes the tale of the Duke of Florence who asked for the help of the brother of a girl he wanted to seduce. The brother arranged for his sister to wait for the Duke in her bed, but when the Duke arrived the brother and a servant murdered him. This has echoes of Lussurioso's attempted seduction of Castiza in *The Revenger's Tragedy*, and has some historical basis as well in the murder of Alessandro de'Medici in 1537. Alessandro's distant cousin, Lorenzino, was intensely jealous of the powerful and successful Alessandro (who was also a violent womaniser) and plotted to kill him. He lured Alessandro into a trap by promising a meeting with a beautiful woman. Alessandro went to the woman's room but when she did not appear he got drunk, whereupon Lorenzino set upon him and stabbed him to death after an ugly fight. Events in *The Revenger's Tragedy*, which to us may seem somewhat implausible, could therefore have been inspired by true stories.

Outline of the plot

We meet the main character, Vindice, carrying a skull. The skull belongs to his beloved, Gloriana, who was poisoned because she resisted the Duke's advances 9 years previously. Now Vindice has come to plot revenge against the Duke, whom he sees as a lecherous monster. He meets his brother, Hippolito, who works for Lussurioso, the Duke's son and heir.

Vindice disguises himself as a servant and gains employment with the Duke's family, where he begins to plan. The Duke has a bastard son, Spurio, and the Duchess has three sons by a former marriage: Ambitioso, Supervacuo and the youngest, referred to as 'Junior Brother'. Junior Brother has raped the wife of a nobleman called Antonio, and the Duke sentences him to be held in prison while he decides whether or not to have him executed.

Lussurioso has designs on Vindice's sister, Castiza, who is a virgin at court. Vindice (in disguise) makes petition to her on behalf of Lussurioso, but is delighted when his sister is repulsed and rejects his proposal. Vindice — still masquerading as someone working on behalf of Lussurioso — then persuades his mother, Gratiana, to put pressure on her daughter to sleep with Lussurioso given the financial rewards that could come her way. To Vindice's disgust, his mother agrees to try, albeit unsuccessfully.

Kris Marshall as Vindice with the skull of Gloriana in *The Revenger's Tragedy*, Southwark Playhouse, 2006

The intrigue continues to develop with the revelation that the Duchess is having an affair with the Duke's bastard son, Spurio. Vindice informs Lussurioso about this and tells him that the Duchess and Spurio are in bed together. Lussurioso decides to kill his half-brother, and is about to stab him in bed with the Duchess when he sees that the man with the Duchess is actually the Duke. Enraged, the Duke orders Lussurioso to prison.

The two elder sons of the Duchess attempt to use this situation to their advantage and produce a sealed order to have their 'brother' executed. However, the guards assume this to mean Junior Brother and they kill him.

Vindice takes Gloriana's skull once more and rubs poison into its mouth. He dresses it and hides it. He tells the Duke that he has found a young girl for him, and persuades the Duke to kiss the skull and so consume the poison. As the Duke is dying, he is made to watch adultery taking place between the Duchess and his son, Spurio.

Lussurioso is now Duke. Vindice and Hippolito murder him during his celebration masque. The two younger brothers, Supervacuo and Ambitioso, argue over who will succeed him and kill each other.

In the end, it is left to Antonio — the character whose wife was raped at the outset of the play — to re-establish order. Thinking that Antonio will be pleased, Vindice confesses to him that he and Hippolito were responsible for all the murders. In fear, Antonio orders that the pair be taken away and executed immediately.

Considerations for the director

The Revenger's Tragedy has a convoluted plot in which events unravel rapidly. Vindice is consumed with a desire for revenge, and he exacts it gruesomely. His manipulation of the Duke and his family — as well as the family's own relationships and plots — ensures that the pace of the play is unrelenting. A director's first task, therefore, is to ensure that the plot is clear to the audience, while at the same time avoiding any loss of pace.

Interpreting the nature of the tragedy

The play is called a 'tragedy', but the director needs to examine this idea carefully because it is different from Shakespeare's tragedies, such as *Hamlet* and *King Lear*. With the exception of *Titus Andronicus*, Shakespeare's tragedies rely less on plot and more on a serious exploration of the world of the tragedy. Hamlet is clearly in abject distress at the death of his father, and his vengeance appears to be motivated by a sense of duty and love. His hesitation in carrying out revenge demonstrates his indecisive and conscience-stricken nature. He contemplates suicide and taunts himself for his lack of action. The play does not have a relentless plot; indeed, after the first act the plot appears to break down. The events of the play arise largely from Hamlet's moral uncertainties, which the audience is invited to share.

By contrast, *The Revenger's Tragedy* is not bound by such a strong philosophical or intellectual dynamic. From the outset, Vindice rushes to take revenge and does not reflect on humanity's weaknesses. His opinions on humanity are confined to his experiences of the Duke and his family and are almost simplistically angry. In addition, while he speaks of Gloriana's beauty, he expresses no great love for her and does not seem to be grief-stricken.

Therefore, this play is not a brooding tragedy; it is about horror and melodrama. The audience is invited to enjoy the dramatist's manipulation of his characters; the tragic fall of the protagonist does not involve the audience's sympathy for his state of mind.

Interpreting the violence

Given the almost simplistic nature of this tragedy, what directorial decisions could be made about the presentation of its violence? Could the murder of the Duke, for example, be portrayed as almost comic in its extreme nature? The moment when Lussurioso believes he is going to kill his step-brother and then nearly kills his father is also potentially comic. Is it appropriate for the director to interpret the nature of the tragedy in a comedic way?

To answer such questions, the director must ask him- or herself what impact the violence in *The Revenger's Tragedy* should have. Should the violence shock, disturb or amuse an audience (perhaps all three)? Is there any kind of precedent for taking a slightly irreverent approach to horrific events and violent death? In cinema, there are a number of films that combine horror and comedy, such as *An American Werewolf in London* (1981) and *Shaun of the Dead* (2004). However, these examples are 'send ups' of the horror genre, and such an approach may not be suitable for *The Revenger's Tragedy*.

Nevertheless, genuinely comic elements can be found in the play. In common with many comedies, the play makes use of names that are intended to describe their character's principal function, e.g. Vindice and Ambitioso. (Interestingly, the meanings of most of these names can be found in John Florio's contemporary Italian/English dictionary *A World of Words*, 1598.) Such stereotyping through naming suggests a style of theatre where the characters are supposed to be one-dimensional, with that one dimension acting as their ruling trait and dictating most of their behaviour. The play, therefore, is one in which the plot and its violent acts are intended to provide all the interest and focus for the audience.

Presenting an extreme world

The Duke and his family enjoy enormous wealth, power and privilege. Yet they do not use it wisely or for anything other than their own gratification. We are presented with a court that is consumed by extreme lust: Lussurioso's lust for Castiza; Spurio's and the Duchess's lust for each other; and Junior Brother's lust for Antonio's wife, which lead to his rape of her and her subsequent death.

The extreme nature of the play can also be seen in the hypocrisy of some of the characters. Early in the play, the Duke makes judgements on Junior Brother's behaviour. He declares:

His violent act has e'en drawn blood of honour,
And stained our honours;

(*The Revenger's Tragedy*, ed. R. A. Foakes, I.2.3)

Given that the audience knows about the Duke's murder of Gloriana, the presentation of this statement poses some directorial and acting challenges. How is the audience expected to interpret the Duke? Similarly, although Vindice's acts of violence (unlike the Duke's) are given some background explanation, he continues in his violence after the Duke is dead. How might a director develop this extreme world of intrigue and vengeance for an audience?

The play could be set within its own historical context (i.e. the early seventeenth century). This would help to communicate the issues of the play as the playwright would have experienced and understood them. However, it could also be set in a more modern context to emphasise the nature of corruption, crime and self-indulgence in a way that is more accessible to today's audience. The Duke and his family could be made to resemble characters from the Mafia, with costumes and props (such as guns) helping to communicate this choice of style. Alternatively, the Duke might be interpreted as a warlord in a lawless state — someone who is allowed to exercise power unchecked, in a place where no moral system survives.

The director's task

In summary, a director of *The Revenger's Tragedy* needs to address the following:
- How 'horrific' should the production be? Will emphasising the horror diminish the tragedy?
- How far should the characters be played as figures of melodrama or as stereotypes? What impact will this type of performance choice have on an audience?
- Does the horror have the potential for 'black' comedy? What are the potential opportunities or pitfalls associated with such an interpretation?

- Should the world of *The Revenger's Tragedy* be one that the audience could recognise? Are there social or historical contexts that might help to communicate the themes of the play to an audience?

Essay questions

1 Identify a principal theme from *The Revenger's Tragedy*. Explain how you would develop this theme so that it had a lasting impact on an audience.
2 How would you make a production of *The Revenger's Tragedy* meaningful for a modern audience? Answer with specific reference to particular characters and scenes.

Considerations for the designer

The director's conception will strongly influence the design of the play. There are many different design approaches that can be taken. The play does not have to be set within its own time frame, and it can contain visual references and images that audiences might recognise from other eras. Given the criminal and self-gratifying nature of the Duke's family, a 'Mafiosi' style interpretation might be credible, perhaps using the Italian setting of the play to deliver that style or, indeed, setting it within another context in which the Mafia was an influential force (e.g. 1920s Chicago or gangland London in the 1960s). Choosing a historical and social context as specific as this will have an impact on design choices and must be researched thoroughly.

However, there are design elements that do not have to be tied to a specific historical period:

- The play has an extreme, almost nightmarish, quality to it and could be interpreted in the style of Artaud, with an emphasis on colour and sensory experience rather than historical accuracy. (Refer to Chapters 9 and 10 to gain an insight into how the play could be realised in this way.) Interestingly, Artaud's adaptation of Byron's *The Cenci* has a central character — Count Cenci — who, in his debauched and amoral lifestyle, is reminiscent of the Duke.
- Opportunities for costume, lighting and set could be realised in such a way as to enhance the almost surreal nature of the play and turn it into a piece of 'theatre of cruelty' (see pages 141 and 149–50).

Setting the scene

The set must suitable for a large company of actors. The opening of the play, with its prologue from Vindice, is punctuated by a grand entrance from the

Duke and his entire family as they prepare for the trial of Junior Brother. This is an important moment in visually setting the style of the Duke's regime. The court may be a majestic affair, established with pomp, ceremony, music and a clear hierarchy of characters. Alternatively, it may be more reminiscent of a 'kangaroo' court in a gangland regime. The design of this scene, including decisions on the use of levels and proxemics between the characters, provides a vital indication of the nature of the Duke's court and the attitudes of the characters it contains.

Rich colours and materials can be used to indicate the wealth and power of the people in the Duke's court. Julie Legrand as the Duchess, Pit Theatre, Barbican Centre, 1988

Defining the characters

The design should help to identify the status and wealth of individual characters. Rich colours and materials can be used to indicate where power and wealth reside. Particular colours may distinguish characters from one another as well as emphasise their wealth and status in society. A simple black costume may help to highlight Vindice as a character who has lost his wealth and is consumed with anger. The Duke and Duchess could wear red to emphasise both their wealth and their lustful personalities, and Lussurioso could wear a rich, brilliant colour (purple or blue) to draw attention to his wealth, vanity and self-indulgent personality.

Emphasising power and wealth

There are a variety of moments that emphasise the power of wealth and, sometimes, wealth over virtue. For example, Vindice is disgusted when he manages to convince his mother Gratiana that she should persuade her daughter to give up her virtue to Lussurioso in exchange for money. Lussurioso also pays Vindice to procure Castiza for him, and Vindice subsequently passes on the money to Gratiana. A designer may wish to find appropriate images to emphasise the power of wealth through costume, props and set design.

Drawing attention to lies and disguises

The Revenger's Tragedy is a play that strongly features secrets, lies and disguises. A designer may want to think about how these can be expressed through design. Obviously, the disguises involve a change in costume. Vindice has to be unrecognisable to his mother and his sister, so in this case the designer may wish to make the disguise quite comprehensive.

Lighting

As the play develops, the design could emphasise the ways in which the characters plot against each other. Most of the action is set in and around the Duke's palace. The set might consist of the imposing walls of a palace with many entrances, thus providing the physical imagery of a place of secrets. Alternatively, lighting might be used to create shadows, or spotlight or highlight specific areas of the stage. Although the acting area may be large (to accommodate the larger-scale scenes), there is also the capacity to create small, almost claustrophobic, spaces.

Particular moments of revelation may also be emphasised with lighting; for example, a bright light could be used when the Duke realises that he has kissed the poisoned skull of one of his victims, or when Lussurioso discovers that it is the Duke, not Spurio, who is in bed with the Duchess.

The designer's task

In summary, the design aspects of this play need to be coordinated carefully in line with the director's overall vision. Depending on the approach taken, *The Revenger's Tragedy* can be horrific, satirical (if the images and design features are recognisable to a modern audience), topical, surreal, or even grimly comic. Whichever approach is taken, the design will be a vital component in determining how the audience will interpret the play.

Essay questions

1 As a designer, how might you use colour (either in terms of set or costume) to emphasise some of the themes of *The Revenger's Tragedy*?

2 How might design features be used in the staging of the Duke's death in Act III scene 5?

The actor's perspective
Interpreting Vindice

The interpretation of Vindice's character depends largely on the director's vision. For instance, if the play is directed as a piece of political theatre where Vindice is seen as a vigilante, the audience may be expected to applaud his one-man war against the state.

When the audience first meets Vindice he is brandishing the skull of his dead lover and making clear his intentions for revenge. The first words the audience hears are:

Duke; royal lecher; go, grey-haired adultery;
And thou his son, as impious steeped as he;
And thou his bastard, true-begot in evil;   (I.1.1–3)

Vindice's feelings towards the Duke and his family are therefore unequivocal. However, an actor has to decide about how to convey Vindice's emotions more widely. Holding the skull of his lover and speaking about her suggests that Vindice has a disturbed and obsessive nature, so the actor could shout his lines with undiluted anger, conveying a psychotic and irate nature. However, the difficulty with such an approach is that it leaves the actor with a limited range of responses as the play develops. How will the actor playing him allow his character to develop later in the play, when he has to reiterate his anger and revulsion at the antics of some of the other characters? Perhaps it could be argued that the character's anger has to be allowed to develop gradually as the play progresses. Furthermore, if an actor 'batters' an audience with a high-volume assault — and then continues to express himself in a similar vein — then his audience will probably become bored.

Vindice is not a subtle character. However, he does express a variety of moods. For most of the play, his plans work perfectly and so we often see him elated. In scenes with his brother, we see him conspiratorial and intense. At the end of the play, his triumph at killing the Duke and Lussurioso, and his happiness about the remaining siblings killing each other, leads him to boast to

Antonio that he and his brother masterminded the entire plot. These different views of Vindice will all influence the choices made by the actor playing him. In order to master these shifts in emphasis, the actor needs to develop and exercise a wide range of expressions. In moments of conspiracy, his voice should perhaps express his words with a quiet yet excited intensity. There are moments — for example Vindice's almost sadistic glee at the demise of the Duke — when the actor's vocal choices and physical actions might hint at madness and therefore take on a louder, more manic expression. Finally, his posture and vocal choices should exhibit the arrogance of his character, as he gives himself away to Antonio and seals his own fate.

Relationship with the audience

Vindice talks directly to the audience, so a relationship has to be established between the two parties. The actor must work towards gaining the audience's understanding, if not its sympathy, for Vindice's actions. Although Vindice's character is vengeful, he has good reason to be angry. The audience may be taken aback by his extreme response to his grievances, but there can be little doubt that a man who has lost his love through murder will appeal to our sympathies.

Relationship with other characters

There are few problems for the actor in determining Vindice's objective or his motivation towards other people, because he articulates these clearly at the outset of the play. However, the actor might consider the character's feelings for those closest to him. When Vindice addresses Gloriana's skull, there is an opportunity to show tenderness:

(to the skull)
Thou sallow picture of my poisoned love,
My study's ornament, thou shell of death,
Once the bright face of my betrothed lady,
When life and beauty naturally filled out
These ragged imperfections,   (I.1.14–18)

Although his love for her is expressed in terms of her physical features rather than her personality, there is a softer tone implied in this speech and a sense of regret and longing. The actor playing the role will need to reflect on an image of Gloriana and the character's feelings for her. In order to fuel Vindice's sense of indignation and anger, there needs to be an underpinning of affection for his lost love.

Vindice frequently tests the resolve of the female members of his family. While in disguise as Piato, he tries to persuade his sister, Castiza to sleep with Lussurioso. Castiza rejects this idea and boxes his ears. The actor playing Vindice should consider the devices he might use to disguise himself — including posture and voice — and how to portray the moment of release (of both his disguise and his elation) when Castiza exits:

It is the sweetest box that e'er my nose came nigh,
The finest drawn-work cuff that e'er was worn!
I'll love this blow for ever […]   (II.1.41–43)

Later in the act, Vindice's anger returns — this time directed towards his mother, Gratiana. He persuades her to put pressure on her daughter to accept Lussurioso's attentions, and even though her attempts fail, his disgust at his mother's frailty is explosive:

Why does not heaven turn black, or with a frown
Undo the world? — Why does not earth start up,
And strike the sins that tread upon't?' O,
were't not for gold and women, there would be no
damnation; hell would look like a lord's great kitchen
without fire in't.
But 'twas decreed before the world began,
that they should be the hooks to catch at man.   (II.2.254–61)

The actor needs to be able to convey these sudden switches of mood and project them effectively.

Photostage

Antony Sher
as Vindice, Pit
Theatre, Barbican
Centre, 1988

Using the verse

The irregular patterns of the verse in this section suggest a mind in turmoil. The use of questions and invoking heaven to turn black and the earth to 'strike the sins that tread upon't' suggest that Vindice's rage is growing and becoming more manic throughout the passage. However, this is in contrast to the chilling couplet at the end, which hints at a more controlled and calm delivery:

But 'twas decreed before the world began,
That they should be the hooks to catch at man.

This is a more ordered and measured expression, as both the rhyme and the iambic pentameter (i.e. 10 syllables per line) suggest. Vindice is, therefore, completely in control of his temper when he claims that women and gold were put upon the earth to catch men out. An audience might well wonder at Vindice's sanity or his wisdom as he utters this sentiment.

Using melodrama

The other characters in the play also lend themselves more to a melodramatic interpretation than to a naturalistic one. These characters are led by a specific characteristic or personality trait — often lust. Their motives are clear to an audience because they make little attempt to hide them. For example, at the end of the second act the Duke says:

Many a beauty have I turned to poison
In the denial, covetous of all.
Age hot is like a monster to be seen:
My hairs are white, and yet my sins are green.   (II.3.129–32)

We are left in no doubt that the Duke has killed people out of lust and has no intention of stopping such behaviour. He does not scrutinise his motive, and there is no crisis of conscience: he simply states that he is bad and has only just started.

This kind of guileless, blatant behaviour runs through many of the characterisations in the play. The actors therefore have to convey these aspects of character clearly. There may be instances when the characters are constrained by a kind of courtly formality, as in the trial scene at the start of the play. However, they always pursue their motives with little question or regard for the consequences. This makes the actor's preparation highly focused: the aim is to identify his or her character's motive and objective, and then to pursue them.

If the production is designed to be interpreted as a melodrama, this will inform performance choices — both physically and vocally. A director who wishes to pursue a melodramatic rendition of the play would need to work with the actors to see how their performances might be 'lifted' to fit with the heightened experience that melodrama often evokes; there should be a sense of exaggeration without lapsing into parody.

Discussion questions

Make thorough notes on the points that arise from your consideration of the following questions, either from discussion or your own observations.

1 Discuss how you would play the role of Vindice both in the opening scene and in Act 2, scene 1 in order to demonstrate to the audience the extreme nature of the role.

2 Discuss how you might interpret the role of Lussurioso in two separate scenes of the play. Discuss how far you think the role may be seen as a melodramatic character.

Exam-style questions

1 As a director, what suggestions would you make to an actor playing the role of Lussurioso in Act I scene 3 in order to convey the sense of villainy of the character?

2 How should the character of the Duchess be received by an audience? As an actor, justify some approaches to playing this character with reference to Act I scene 2.

Chapter 13

Section B: Twentieth century
or contemporary drama

A View from
the Bridge

by Arthur Miller

Although you will be asked to comment on a relatively short scene from the play you choose for Section B, it is essential that you have prepared the whole play for production. Whatever play you choose to write about, there are a number of fundamental decisions that you must make as a director:

+ What are the major themes of the play?
+ How can those themes be realised in production?
+ What are the major challenges for the actors?
+ What rehearsal techniques and practices can be used to help the actors develop their characters and understand the demands of the play?
+ How should the historical, social and cultural context influence the production of the play — in terms of design as well as performance?
+ What kind of acting space (e.g. 'in-the-round', 'thrust') will you use?

Any commentary you write must demonstrate your understanding of the play as a whole and where the scene fits into the context of an entire production.

The following material should give you some idea of the kind of background research you need to do on your play. As with your Unit 3 Section A text, you should do some initial research, then read the play and follow this up with detailed research to support your emerging ideas about the play's production.

Planning your production

There are many approaches to planning a production. Perhaps most importantly, it is necessary to have a concept or a ruling idea for the play. For example, with *A View from the Bridge* you may wish to explore the notion of cultural clashes and diversity. Rodolpho and Marco represent a different culture from Eddie, and you may feel that the conflict that arises between them might — in part — be due to Eddie's inability to accept Rodolpho's more romantic and playful disposition. On the other hand, you may feel that the ruling idea should be one of suppressed passion and forbidden love. The feelings that Eddie has for Catherine may seem innocent enough at the outset of the play, but it is clear — particularly at the moment when he kisses her — that his emotions have developed into a jealous rage. As a director, whatever concept you arrive at will inform the other choices you make. How you help an actor make decisions about the expression of a line or a move or his/her relationship with other characters will stem from the initial ruling idea.

Often, major theatre companies (the RSC and the National, for example) keep archives of the details of previous productions, and it would be possible for you to see photographs and read reviews of these. You should not attempt to copy details from previous productions, but sometimes it helps to see how directors and designers have tackled the challenges of a play.

Broadsheet newspapers (the *Telegraph*, *The Times* and the *Guardian*) have online archives from which you can access theatre reviews. Reviews should be approached with a degree of caution, since what you are reading is an opinion — albeit a professional and an informed one. Reviews can be useful in order to ascertain if a particular idea or an interpretation of the play — in terms of the directing or the acting — has been successful.

Background material

It is essential that you find out about the playwright and research the social and cultural background to the play. This knowledge can be fed into your ideas for a production of the play on stage.

You should look at:

- the playwright's biography and his other work for the stage
- the social and cultural context of the play
- other performances of the play, including how they were interpreted through set, costume, lighting, sound and acting, and how successful these were felt to be by audiences and critics

Playwright: Arthur Miller (1915–2005)

Arthur Miller, the pre-eminent American twentieth-century dramatist, was representative of his times in both his life and in his writings. He was the second son of an illiterate but highly successful clothing manufacturer, Isidore (a Polish-Jewish immigrant to New York) and Augusta (who was born in New York to German-Jewish immigrants).

TopFoto

Arthur Miller

The family initially enjoyed a thriving business but then suffered sudden bankruptcy as a result of the Wall Street Crash in 1929. This forced the Miller family to move from their fashionable Central Park apartment to a tiny house in Brooklyn, which they shared with a number of relatives. While living there, Arthur observed the lives, ideas and attitudes of other Brooklyn immigrant families.

Miller's career as a playwright, which spanned more than six decades, was notable for the early successes *All My Sons* (1947) and *Death of a Salesman* (1949). *The Crucible* (1953) used the real-life Salem witch-hunt trials (1692–93) as an allegory for the McCarthy trials in the USA, which were dedicated to routing out Communists from American society.

Perhaps equally famous for his brief but colourful marriage to Marilyn Monroe, Miller was popularly regarded as one of the finest playwrights of his generation. He won many awards, including the Pulitzer Prize for Drama.

Social context: longshoremen on the New York waterfront

A View from the Bridge was written in 1955. During the first half of the 1950s, Miller became aware of the links between organised crime and the unions in the waterfront parts of Brooklyn in New York, where longshoremen (or dockers) worked. Indeed, the same subject matter was used for the famous film *On the Waterfront* (1956), which was directed by Miller's long-time colleague and friend Elia Kazan and starred Marlon Brando.

In his autobiography *Timebends* (1987), Miller reflects on how he became interested in the world of the longshoremen when he noticed pieces of graffiti referring to 'Pete Panto' painted in various parts of the city:

Pete Panto was a young longshoreman who had attempted to lead a rank-and-file revolt against the leadership of President Joseph Ryan and his colleagues, many of them allegedly Mafiosi, who ran the International Longshoremen's Association. Panto, one evening during dinner, had been lured from his home by a phone call from an unknown caller and was never seen again. The movement he had led vanished from the scene.

(Miller, A. (1987) *Timebends: A Life*, p. 146)

As Miller tried to investigate the story, he came across many longshoremen who were illegal immigrants from Italy. They were reluctant to reveal any information since they were dependent entirely on their bosses for work and, therefore, food. Miller describes the waterfront thus:

It did not take me long to learn that the waterfront was the Wild West, a desert beyond the law. The exploitation of labor was probably a minor matter compared to the Mob's skimming of commerce moving through the world's greatest port, a form of taxation, in effect.

(Ibid, p. 150)

It is against this political, social and economic turmoil that *A View from the Bridge* is set.

The American Dream

Over the nineteenth and twentieth centuries a great many people, including most longshoremen, left their homeland to make a better life for themselves in a new country. In *A View from the Bridge*, Rodolpho and Marco have come to New York in search of a new life. Their initial optimism is summed up by Marco in his first reactions to Eddie's house:

Marco: [...] I want to tell you now Eddie — when you say go we will go.
Eddie: Oh no. *(takes Marco's bag)*
Marco: I see it's a small house, but soon, maybe, we can have our own house.

(Miller, A. (2000) *A View from the Bridge*, Penguin Classics, p. 27)

The American Dream

The 'American Dream' is the ideal that any American, no matter how humble his or her origins, can aspire, through hard work and dedication, to achieve any position in society that his or her abilities merit, even becoming president of the USA itself. A number of Americans have fulfilled the dream. Abraham Lincoln came from an impoverished family in Illinois and rose to be the sixteenth president of the USA in 1861. More recently, Bill Clinton, brought up in a one-parent family in Little Rock, Arkansas, managed the same feat, becoming forty-second president in 1993. Even Miller's father, Isidore Miller, a Polish immigrant, rose to a position of power and prominence in financial circles before the Wall Street Crash.

Mary Evans Picture Library/Alamy

Immigrants waiting for inspection before entering New York in 1911

However, hard work and dedication did not always reward these people, and the American Dream could prove a snare and a delusion. Miller explored this theme most obviously in *Death of a Salesman*, in which the efforts of the central character, Willy Loman, lead only to despair, conflict and tragedy.

Outline of the plot

Act 1

Eddie Carbone is a longshoreman in New York. He lives with his wife, Beatrice, and his orphan niece, Catherine. At the opening of the play, Alfieri, a lawyer, introduces the story and the main characters. Eddie arrives home to Catherine and Beatrice. The atmosphere is cordial, although it is clear that Eddie is extremely protective of Catherine. He is concerned that she is naïve and too trusting. She has been offered a job, but Eddie is reluctant to allow her to take it. However, after being persuaded by his wife he relents, and Catherine is clearly delighted.

Eddie announces that Beatrice's cousins will be arriving later that evening by boat. They are illegal immigrants from Italy and are coming to the USA for the chance to earn more money. The cousins, Rodolpho and Marco, duly arrive. Marco is around 32 and Rodolpho around 20 years old. They describe life in Italy and the poverty they have encountered. Rodolpho is an extrovert character and starts to entertain the company with a song. Eddie stops him for fear that he will draw unnecessary attention to the household and arouse suspicion from the authorities. It is clear that, while Catherine is quite entranced by Rodolpho, Eddie is uneasy about him.

In the next scene, Eddie is waiting anxiously for Catherine and Rodolpho to come home from the cinema. Beatrice chastises Eddie for being too protective of Catherine. He disapproves strongly of Rodolpho but has no specific grievance against him. He simply feels that Catherine can do better.

It is clear that there are problems in Eddie and Beatrice's marriage, as she hints broadly that their relationship has not been physical for some months. Eddie refuses to talk about it and says he has been anxious. When Rodolpho and Catherine return, Eddie is angry. Rodolpho exits to go for a walk along the river while Eddie upbraids Catherine because he believes that Rodolpho does not 'respect' her. Catherine rejects this idea and tells Eddie that Rodolpho loves her. Eddie is incensed and tells Catherine that Rodolpho only wants to marry her so he can gain legal status in the USA. Catherine is devastated by this suggestion.

Later, Eddie visits the lawyer, Alfieri. He is determined to find some complaint against Rodolpho. Alfieri assures him that there is no possible legal complaint that Eddie could have except one: that Rodolpho and Marco are illegal immigrants. However, Eddie will not hear of having them arrested on that charge.

Eddie tries to suggest that there is something wrong with Rodolpho because he sings, can make dresses and is 'platinum blonde'. Alfieri warns Eddie that he has to let Catherine lead her own life and that he, as her uncle, cannot marry her. Eddie is angered at the implication of this statement and storms off.

A few days later, the family are at home finishing dinner. Eddie again brings up the subject of Rodolpho taking Catherine out to the cinema, which angers Catherine. She dances with Rodolpho and Eddie seethes with resentment. Seemingly in jest, he offers to have a bout of play-boxing with Rodolpho. No one senses any danger, although Catherine is wary. While boxing, Eddie jabs Rodolpho fairly hard, and Rodolpho is taken aback. Eddie attempts to laugh off the moment and tells Rodolpho that he has some potential as a boxer. Marco watches these events with concern and challenges Eddie to lift a chair with one hand, placed just under one chair leg. Eddie tries but cannot do it. Marco does so and as he lifts the chair aloft looks triumphantly at Eddie.

Michael Gambon as Eddie and Susan Sylvester as Catherine in *A View from the Bridge*, Aldwych Theatre, 1987

Act II

It is a few days before Christmas, and 6 months since the two brothers moved into the apartment. Rodolpho and Catherine are alone and discussing the future. Catherine tries to persuade Rodolpho that they should settle in Italy, away from Eddie. Rodolpho rejects this idea because they can earn money in the USA. Eddie returns home drunk — a crate of whiskey has 'fallen' from a crane as it was being unloaded from a ship. Catherine sees Eddie's condition and tries to flee the apartment. Eddie roughly kisses Catherine on the lips and Rodolpho is furious. He flies at Eddie, but Eddie pins him against the wall and aggressively kisses Rodolpho. Catherine and Rodolpho leave together.

Eddie visits Alfieri again, determined to find some complaint against Rodolpho. He claims that the assault he made on Rodolpho was an attempt to show Catherine that 'he ain't right'. Once more, Alfieri tells him — this time more firmly — that he has no legal right to prevent Catherine from doing anything and that if he does not stop his current course of behaviour his friends will turn against him.

Eddie goes into a phone booth and calls the Immigration Bureau. He tells them, anonymously, that there are two illegal immigrants living in the house. Later, he returns home. Catherine is helping Rodolpho and Marco to leave, and Eddie learns of her intention to marry Rodolpho the following week, thus giving him legal status in the country. Eddie tries to persuade Catherine to see other people and acknowledges that he has been too protective of her. Catherine says that it is too late, she is going to marry Rodolpho and would like Eddie to be there.

It is revealed that two other illegal immigrants have moved into the apartment at the top of the building. Eddie tells Catherine that she has to move Rodolpho and Marco out of the top room immediately because the two new occupants will attract attention from the Immigration Bureau. He says that Rodolpho and Marco should find somewhere else to live, away from the house. His conscience has got the better of him — but too late. The officials arrive and arrest the occupants of the upper apartment. It is clear to everyone that Eddie has reported them. Marco spits at him as he is taken away, and his friends and neighbours shun him.

Alfieri persuades Marco to keep the peace and says that he will bail him. This means that, although Marco will be deported, he will at least be able to work and earn money until that happens, and Rodolpho and Catherine will still be able to get married. Beatrice plans to attend their wedding but Eddie forbids it. Marco calls Eddie into the street where they confront each other. In the fight that ensues, Eddie pulls a knife but Marco turns it on him and Eddie is stabbed. He dies in Beatrice's arms.

The play in production

Whatever section of the play you are asked to scrutinise in the examination, there are a number of fundamental features that need to be considered:

- ◆ The era of the play. The immigration laws and social conditions controlling the action cannot really be changed from the historical context in which the play was written, i.e. New York in the 1950s.
- ◆ The set. Although the play takes place in different locations, there is no expectation by the playwright that the set will change.
- ◆ The world of the play. The world of the longshoremen in 1950s Brooklyn is a long way from our own in terms of time, distance and culture.
- ◆ The consistent theme in Miller's work. Miller is interested in the importance of an individual taking responsibility for his or her own actions but demonstrating an understanding of how those actions can affect society as a whole.

Understanding and communicating the historical and social context is an essential requirement of all of the participants in a production of this play.

The relationship between set and theme

In *A View from the Bridge*, Eddie betrays the trust of his wife and her cousins by calling the Immigration Bureau and informing them about Marco and Rodolpho. His actions cause disruption not only to his own family but also to the community of longshoremen and their families. This is shown through the reaction of Eddie's friends as they shun him after the arrests of Marco, Rodolpho and the other two illegal immigrants.

How is it possible to show this theme of betraying one's community in a play that, on the face of it, deals with individual, private tensions? The director needs to remember that Miller uses the entire neighbourhood rather than setting the play solely in the Carbone apartment. By showing the world beyond the apartment, the audience can be alerted to the fact that the consequences of Eddie's actions reach beyond the confines of his home and his immediate family. This is important from the point of view of the set design.

Perhaps one of the most famous productions of the play — at least in the UK — was that directed by Alan Ayckbourn in February 1987 at the National Theatre. Originally staged in the smallest of the three National Theatre venues, the Cottesloe, the production marked an outstanding achievement both by the director and the leading actor, Michael Gambon. The chief advantage of staging the play in such an intimate venue was the ambiance of claustrophobia that emerged. There was a sense of a closed-in community, and — through skilful lighting — the character of Alfieri appeared and disappeared at relevant moments, rather than entering or exiting. When the violence broke out — first between Eddie and Roldolpho, and ultimately between Eddie and Marco — it was made more terrible because of its close proximity to the audience.

Set design

The design of the set will undoubtedly influence the relationships established between the actors and the audience. Many of the scenes are of a quite intimate nature with one or two characters involved in intense dialogue. Some theatres — because of their proscenium arched structure and orchestra pit — may prevent the audience from watching these scenes at particularly close proximity. A theatre space that allows the development of an intense atmosphere would therefore be more appropriate than a vast arena where the subtlety of acting might be lost.

Consider your venue, and apply the most suitable design idea to the stage area. Think about how your audience will see the performance, from all positions in the auditorium. Whichever section of the play you are presented with, you need to explain how you would ensure that the design of the set would contribute positively to the performance needs of the actors.

The use of sound

A piece of music can be evocative of a time, a place and a whole culture. For this play, a director may wish to consider a number of options. Jazz or blues music from the 1950s may help to reinforce the historical context of the production. However, the director also needs to consider at what point in the play a piece of music is played, at what volume and for how long. Does the music provide an interlude within the action or does it punctuate the action, providing background sounds? Given that the play has moments of revelation, tension and passion, how might music help to 'ignite' these moments?

Sound effects may also help to establish the world of the play, for example noise from the waterfront where the longshoremen work could be used to open a scene. Again, it is important for a director to think in terms of specifics rather than generalities. He or she has to consider the volume of these sounds, the precise moment they are heard, and what impact they are designed to have.

The use of light

Lighting also plays a crucial role in the production. Within the play, there are several acting areas that need to be distinguished from each other, and light can assist in this process. However, appropriate lighting can also help to create atmosphere.

For example, Alfieri could be shown 'emerging' at points during the play; the use of side lighting onto the face or back lighting would help to form shadows and silhouettes. This would enhance the impression of characters emerging rather than just appearing. Also, many of the play's scenes take place at night or during the winter, so creating a cold and gloomy atmosphere might be appropriate. In all cases, you need to think about how specific lighting effects can have an impact on the production.

Actors' performances

You must consider how you would develop the actors' performances in the section of your chosen play. Therefore, you should give some thought to rehearsal techniques you might employ.

For example, think about how you would work with the actors playing Rodolpho and Catherine in the opening scene of Act II, when they are discussing their future together. In considering this specific section, you cannot ignore earlier scenes in which the relationship between Rodolpho and Catherine is explored. Clearly — as the play takes place over a period of around 6 months — the relationship has had moments that the play does not show. It has become more serious by the beginning of Act II than it was during much of Act I — there is a recognition between them that they love each other and want to be together. A director may therefore wish to use improvisation to create additional moments in the characters' relationship to help them prepare for the first scene in Act II.

There are also important decisions to be made around proxemics — the space and distance that exists between the characters at particular moments in the scene — and how this communicates and creates their relationship both to one another and to the audience.

The importance of the 'narrator'

Alfieri is a crucial character in the play. It is quite unusual — though not unheard of — for Miller to have a character who is also a narrator of the action. (For example, in *After the Fall* (1964) the character of Quentin talks to his psychiatrist, an unseen figure who is in the position of the audience.) However, for the most part, characters do not narrate in Miller's plays. A director must therefore determine what he or she feels the effect of Alfieri narrating much of the action should be, and how the relationship between narrator and audience should be developed.

In some respects, Alfieri may be seen as a link between the world of the play and our world. He is associated with the world of the longshoremen but not a specific part of it. As a lawyer, he is a professional — a person who comments on the action with authority — and the audience may identify with him to a certain extent because of this. He evaluates the course that Eddie seems determined upon and articulates our possible reaction of horror to this. His attempts to intervene in Eddie's life are futile but they echo our own thoughts about Eddie's growing infatuation with his niece and his irrationality.

Although in many respects the play is a piece of naturalism (in that the characters are ones of depth and psychological reality), the very fact that one of the characters 'steps out' of the action and speaks to us directly highlights the play's unreality. The director needs to consider how Alfieri will be presented. Is he visible all the time as a permanent link between our world and the play's world? Does he stay permanently in part of the acting area that features as his office, or does he emerge from the audience as 'one of us'? Even if the section you are asked to comment on does not feature Alfieri, you will still need to decide how this character appears in your production. If he is to be omnipresent throughout, then his impact on the scene you are writing about will need to be thought through, even if he has no lines in that section.

Exam-style question

Taking any 70 or so lines from the play, explain how, as a director, you would realise them in production. In your answer you should consider the acting and design of the piece and how you would develop them. Any drawings and sketches you use should be appropriately labelled and referred to in the main body of your answer. Do not simply provide a sketch without annotation or explanation.

Unit 4

A2: Practical presentation of devised drama

Chapter 14

The process of devising

The etymology of 'playwright' comes from Old English, where 'wright' meant 'maker' or 'craftsman'. A playwright therefore 'makes' a play, rather than merely writing the script. The purpose of this chapter is to draw your attention to ways and means of devising pieces of theatre that do not necessarily involve sitting down and writing. There are also some suggestions for developing your own style of devising.

When you are devising a piece of theatre, it is important to be aware of some of the practices of professional devisors. Many theatre companies create their own work, as well as producing previously written compositions. Lloyd Newson and Peter Cheeseman (see Chapter 11) are preoccupied with innovating pieces to reflect their own theatrical ambitions, albeit using widely differing methods. They are not alone: Simon McBurney of Complicite, Mike Alfreds of Shared Experience and Emma Rice of Kneehigh Theatre Company often create work from scratch with their companies. Sometimes a writer is involved (for example, Polly Teale with Shared Experience) and sometimes the director is also the author. Although the majority of his work is in film, Mike Leigh is well known for his use of improvisation, constructing characters and providing dramatic contexts for them to meet and interact with each other.

The process of devising often takes more time than the rehearsal of scripted plays, since the devised play has to be created before it can be rehearsed. Furthermore, actors often create their own characters, which then have to be researched and developed.

There are no specific, proven methods of success, and devisors employ different approaches depending on their choice of subject matter. Whatever the method employed, however, the success of the devising process depends on thorough, detailed and organised work. It may or may not lead to a final script, and it may be created in such a way that it uses or explores a specific genre of theatre. The choices are vast — and that, of course, is one of the potential problems. Constraints often lead to innovation, whereas limitless freedom can produce something hackneyed, wandering and self-serving. Demonstrate this to yourself by sitting down with a group of people to devise a play. How easy was it to produce a compelling piece of theatre?

The 'ruling idea'

For the devising process to be effective, there has to be a firm foundation, a 'ruling idea' that will help to shape the piece and influence its final form. For example, in her book *Devising Theatre* (1994), Alison Oddey refers to the theatre company Age Exchange and its work in devising a piece of theatre to commemorate the fiftieth anniversary of the outbreak of the Second World War. The anniversary provided it with a clear ruling idea. Even though the company was not sure about the final form or indeed the content of the piece, it had a specific context which it wished to explore.

Stimulus

A specific historical event or context is often a useful stimulus for a piece of devised theatre. For example, a group of students chose to create a play about the Jarrow Hunger March — a march of unemployed men from Jarrow to London in 1936. Having made this decision early in the process, they never looked back. The group first explored the historical background to the march, and then investigated the most appropriate genres of theatre available to tell the story. The result was a moving, compelling and thorough piece of documentary theatre. Furthermore, it was a piece about which each person in the group cared deeply.

However, the stimulus does not have to be as specific as a historical event. Famous images (for instance paintings and photographs), popular quotations or well-known music may also be used to initiate the devising process.

Stimulus materials can be chosen almost at random and need not have an obvious connection to each other. When you sample the materials, you should not feel confined to choosing just one stimulus.

Responding to stimulus material

Watching or listening to stimulus material should evoke a sensory response as well as an intellectual response. If you find your material dull, you need to re-evaluate its suitability. Your teacher will, however, take care to present your stimulus material in an inspiring way. One helpful method is to create the atmosphere of an art gallery by placing the stimulus pictures around the available space using theatrical lighting; the materials are viewed in silence and notes taken. Alternatively, materials can be shown in a PowerPoint presentation. In either instance, music can be used to heighten the atmosphere.

Initially, it is important for you to experience and respond to the stimulus material as an individual. Much of the work of the subsequent task of devising will test your teamwork skills but you must also be able to contribute a strong personal response. You will always find this helpful, particularly if your group is dominated by a vocal or persuasive individual. Everyone's response to the stimulus material should be treated as equally important. This is the means by which each individual can connect with the material and begin to feel a sense of ownership of it.

Your final piece does not have to demonstrate a direct response to the stimulus. A stimulus should do precisely what the name implies: stimulate ideas that will help to create a piece of drama. A photograph of an emaciated man looking through the gaps in a barbed wire fence may provoke thoughts on physical entrapment and incarceration, which may in turn lead your group to reflect on entrapment in a relationship, a society or a religion. The group's final piece may not, therefore, show much that is traceable to the original stimulus. However, all the stages of your dramatic journey, from experiencing the initial stimulus to the completion of the final product, should form part of your analysis and evaluation of the work.

Theatre visits

Theatre visits are a vital stimulus for introducing you to various dramatic genres, so that you are able to make informed choices about the appropriate direction for your piece. It is crucial that you see as much high-quality theatre as possible before and during your devising process, in order to enrich your understanding of genre.

Developing work from the stimulus

Once all the members of the group have individually seen, heard and made notes about the stimulus, you are ready to interact with one another in order to share ideas. This interaction may be conducted in a variety of ways, depending on whether your teacher wants to form groups at this stage. You might be asked to compare notes and ideas as a whole class and to make a joint decision as to how best to create a devised piece from the stimulus.

Using an image or tableau

It is often useful to come up with an image or tableau that demonstrates or underpins some of the ideas the class or group has exchanged. There is no need to 'explain' your ideas in this context; rather the image should serve as an expression, release or even exploration of ideas. Remember that an image can only serve to express part of the idea or ideas discussed by your group. This is fine — there should be no pressure to produce something that somehow manages to encompass all the ideas expressed by group members. Such a feat would probably be impossible anyway. You are looking for a starting point, a simple physical statement. The image then forms the basis of the work, even if it is not retained later.

Developing the image into action

Much depends on the strengths and aspirations of your group as to whether you choose to develop work physically or vocally from the initial image. Either option is valid.

1 Using the image as a starting point, your group could create a piece of movement that continues to underpin the ideas you discussed. This process may help you to encompass a greater number of the ideas put forward by your group. If your group is anxious about movement or someone feels that he or she lacks the necessary skills, then you could create a series of images to connect with the first one and, by a process of rehearsal, find a way to link these images together seamlessly.

2 Each member of your group could create a monologue connecting him or her to the image. If the image is naturalistic, and composed of realistic characters, this is a reasonably simple exercise. Each participant or 'character' needs to create a short passage or speech (about 2 minutes) that comments on or makes an expression linked with the tableau he or she is a part of. For example, a group of students decided to create an image of a murderer in America (Timothy McVeigh — the Oklahoma bomber) eating his last meal on death row while his captors and family looked on. Each student chose a person present in the tableau and created a monologue expressing the feelings of his or her character at the time. Chillingly, the student who played McVeigh made an almost childlike speech about the relative merits of the brand of ice cream he was eating compared with other types.

Using the monologue approach described above is more problematic if your group creates a conceptual image and therefore offers no realistic characters (for example a surreal or supernatural image, or a machine). How can someone create a monologue for a dehumanised concept? Here you should remember that the notion of monologue can be interpreted freely. There is no

Mike Booth/Alamy

In order to develop the image into action, each member of your group could create a monologue

reason why your speech should not contain a more expressionistic (perhaps Artaudian?) approach to language. Language may repeat itself or have a poetic, non-realistic style. Indeed, if the image itself is surreal, it is probably more appropriate if the language which accompanies it is similarly oblique. You have complete freedom as to the content, style and subject matter of your monologue.

In this exercise, it is important that all monologues are heard by each member of your group. Even if the individual monologues produced by members of the group seem utterly disconnected, this is no barrier to all of them being presented.

This work should be carried out individually rather than the group taking responsibility for the creation of each speech. It is essential at the early stages of preparation that each group member learns the significance of making an individual contribution to the material, rather than relying on other group members to do the work.

Developing the work into action

The work now needs to be developed into action. This can happen in a variety of ways, and much depends on the nature of the ideas you have created. You may find that more material needs to be created before you can launch into your devised piece; to achieve this you can revisit the stimulus material.

At this point, you should either discuss the monologues created by your group earlier, or adlib new monologues. These speeches may well provide ways to develop dialogue for your piece. Alternatively, your group may choose to focus on one particular monologue — either because of the strength of its content or its style — and develop it dramatically.

You now have a number of options for taking your piece forward: theme-based work, plot-led work, character-led work and genre-led work.

Theme-based work

As a result of ideas discussed before the construction of your chosen image, or as a consequence of the monologues, your group may decide that your devised piece of drama is going to be thematically led.

Finding a suitable theme

A theme is not defined by one word, for instance 'war' is not a theme. However, 'the effects of war on the civilian population' is a theme suitable for dramatic development. Similarly, 'homelessness' is not a theme, but 'the impact of homelessness on the spirit of the individual' is. In other words, a theme gives direction and focus to a piece.

Try to avoid issues that have a 'soap opera' feel to them. One of the noticeable features of soap opera is that issues are often dealt with simplistically and in such a way as to imply that they may be overcome in a matter of weeks or even days. The friends and family of Vera Duckworth, for instance, appeared to recover quickly following her demise in *Coronation Street*. Do not be too influenced by the soap opera approach.

A theme-based devised piece need not depend on plot — indeed, such a piece may be relatively plotless. A successful piece called *This is how it ends* chose to focus on the idea of truth being the first casualty of war. War scenes from the First World War through to the war in Iraq and an imagined future nuclear conflagration were depicted. The through-line in this piece was the theme — not the storyline or its characters.

Should there be tragedy?

Despite the preconceptions of many students, theme-based material does not have to be 'heavy' or tragic. One A-level group devised a piece entitled *We stand for things*, which depicted the preoccupation of members of the public with trivia and showbiz gossip, even when their country was at war. Much of the group's work was comic — albeit in a satirical, bitter way.

Do not expect the audience for issue- or theme-based work to be moved when a character dies. By their nature, issue-based pieces are short, and the identification necessary to establish a naturalistic relationship between character and audience cannot take place.

Should there be shock?

Often, a group of students will say that they want to 'shock' their audience. Shocking an audience gratuitously is unnecessary and, more importantly, it is also dramatically pointless.

It is, of course, important that a group has a firm idea of how it wants its audience to react, but the desire to 'shock' does not go far enough. Does your group want to achieve the Brechtian aim of stirring the members of an audience into action or instilling in them a desire to change the society they are in? In other words, does the piece of theatre have a political or social aim?

Alternatively, the nature of the 'shock' your group may wish to instil might be more closely identified with the work of Artaud. Again, however, the aim of 'shocking' an audience needs further clarification. Artaud's aim was to deliver a sensory experience that would enliven an audience.

Our society regularly witnesses the ravages of war via television broadcasts and the internet. We are increasingly difficult to shock. Do not be tempted to assume that just because a character dies, your piece of drama is shocking or thought provoking. You need to make sure that your work is focused and specific, and that the issue is clear.

Plot-led work

Most A-level devised pieces are either plotless or the plot is not the dominant feature. However, there are a number of exceptions. A few years ago, one group of students took the children's book *The Three Little Wolves and the Big Bad Pig* by Eugene Trivizas (which was one of the elements of their stimulus material) and decided to perform a straight adaptation of it. The plot is familiar, albeit an inversion of the traditional tale, and although there are clearly some social issues implicit in the piece, it is essentially plot led. In this case, the group's work, aimed at a young audience of upper primary children, was successful.

However, problems can arise in plot-led pieces, when every dramatic feature becomes enslaved to the plot. If you find yourself working on a group piece where the discussions are dominated by the issue of 'what could happen next', it is possible that your piece has become too plot driven. One group of students performed a piece that gave an account of a family's struggle during the miners' strike of 1984–85. Although it was sensitively performed and demonstrated a reasonable knowledge and understanding of the issues involved, the piece became very much plot driven. As a result, it sacrificed some of its theatrical potential in favour of storyline.

There is nothing wrong with a strong plotline. Remember simply that your piece is, by its nature, quite short, and it is therefore not advisable for the plot to dominate.

Character-led work

Your group may choose to create a piece based around the exploration of a number of key characters. The film director Mike Leigh works in this manner, and the results can be fulfilling and exciting.

You should take care to avoid overambitious character exploration, since the piece will probably last no longer than around 20–30 minutes. 'Hot seating' is always a good technique to explore characters for devised work — particularly if it is important to create a 'back story' for them — but you should always keep the questions focused on your drama. Do not gather information for its own sake.

Character-led pieces work best in smaller groups, so there is an opportunity to develop characters fully and for audiences to develop relationships with them. One A-level group created an intense piece about three sisters whose abusive father had recently died. The plot was not particularly strong but it did not need to be. The interaction of the characters with each other, and with the audience through monologues, ensured a moving and compelling piece. A less successful example was when a larger group attempted a story set in a psychiatric ward. The individual characters were insufficiently developed because of lack of performance time and so tended to drift towards stereotype.

Where characters are the most significant dramatic feature, it is important that you render them as compellingly as possible. If your characters are unconvincing, your audience will not care about their fates. As noted before, it is not a given fact that an audience will break down in tears when the central character kills him/herself, and this is even more the case where the character is a faulty creation in the first instance. Indeed, this kind of 'shock' denouement often serves to disappoint, and it can be embarrassing to watch if overacted or if there is insufficient development. Remember that in a 20-minute piece you are unlikely to be able to develop an audience–character relationship strongly enough to move the audience if that character dies.

Genre-led work

Having studied a particular play or practitioner, you may feel inspired to create a piece which is in the style of the source of influence. This is an entirely legitimate choice and often leads to dramatically articulate responses. Many students draw on the work of Artaud and the 'theatre of cruelty', perhaps excited by the anarchic possibilities and visceral dimensions that this genre opens up. Similarly, students are often inspired by 'in yer face' theatre and, in particular, the works of Sarah Kane.

Take care, however, that you do not struggle to fit your work into a particular genre. Remember that genre 'labels' are often coined by literary critics, rather than by the writers themselves. For example, when asked to define the term 'Pinteresque', the playwright Harold Pinter refused to do so, on the grounds that he had not created it. It is perfectly possible for a piece to contain elements of different genres — you could combine both physical and documentary, for example.

Genre may provide you with your initial inspiration and give guidance to the realisation of your ideas, but it should not be slavishly adhered to.

Styles appropriate for devising

The AQA specification allows you to choose your own theatrical style when devising your piece of drama. In some instances, the style of performance will emerge through rehearsal and the devising process. In other instances, you may choose to present a piece of work in a specific style. You should be aware, however, that writers and directors often do not consciously choose a style or genre for their piece. Max Stafford-Clark reflected on the success of a play he directed, *Our Country's Good*, which his daughter had recently studied for A-level:

> She has to address all kinds of questions about whether it was influenced by Stanislavski or by Brecht, which concerned us not a whit when we were working on the play.
>
> (Roberts, P. and Stafford-Clark, M. (2007) *Taking Stock: The Theatre of Max Stafford-Clark*, Nick Hern Books, p. 149)

This is an important point if you wish to devise a piece of theatre without specifically placing it in one genre or another. You should not try to follow the ideas and methods of a practitioner just so you can say that it is, for example, a 'Brechtian' piece. However, you should also be aware that your decisions about characterisation, dialogue and structure will inevitably have been influenced by the work you have seen and your own involvement in drama. You need to be able to acknowledge those influences and analyse how they may have shaped your process.

Some groups, however, prefer to choose a particular style to work in and, if this is the case for your group, the next section will help you to decide which style might best serve your piece. If you decide to use a particular genre or style such as the ones described on the following pages, it is essential that you research that style by undertaking further reading and also by seeing examples of the genre performed professionally.

Naturalism

This style of theatre is covered in detail in Chapters 5 and 6. Many students choose to devise a piece of theatre in a naturalistic style. However, in many ways naturalism is the most difficult style to adopt and use effectively. This is partly because you have only a short space of time to present your work, and naturalism — with its emphasis on well-developed characters, realistic dialogue and recognisable situations — often needs time to draw in an audience and involve them in the plot. Naturalistic dramas (e.g. *An Inspector Calls* and *Journey's End*) work as well as they do because the audience have time to digest the information and become involved in the situations. Sometimes the well-intentioned devised piece falls flat because the audience have not had enough time to become involved with the characters and the piece cannot achieve the desired impact.

If your group chooses naturalism, the task of devising the piece must be approached rigorously and with an awareness that presenting a well-rounded character is a serious artistic undertaking involving more than just 'being realistic'. For this reason, avoid calling the characters by your own names. You must approach your character as being more than simply an extension of yourself; otherwise, you are simply using your own personality rather than creating a new one.

Achieving emotional intensity and a sense of truth is a difficult undertaking for any actor, and for the young or inexperienced actor it is particularly challenging. Therefore, naturalism should not be used in the belief that it is the most straightforward option when presenting a piece of theatre.

Comedy/farce

Comedy, like naturalism, is a genre that needs to be approached with caution. Comedy is extremely difficult to get right — as can be seen from the large number of television comedies that only run for one series before being scrapped.

Anyone wishing to use a comic or farcical approach for a piece of theatre should read or watch well-crafted stage comedy. It is difficult to create a piece of theatre that will make people laugh, and it is important to consider the target audience. You should appreciate that what makes your own generation laugh may not necessarily have the same effect on older people. Furthermore, if your comedy is influenced by television comedy, it may not translate well to the live stage.

If you decide to create your own comedy piece, you should explore the work of successful comedy playwrights. John Godber and Alan Ayckbourn are two of the country's most successful playwrights of comedy, although they have somewhat differing styles (with Ayckbourn tending to take a more naturalistic approach).

Comedy in theatre should not necessarily be seen as a light-hearted entertainment or as a shying away from serious issues. Consider Dario Fo's farce

Accidental Death of An Anarchist (1970), which was written in response to events unfolding in Italy in the late 1960s. The play looks at the issue of police corruption and suspicions regarding the government's collusion in this corruption. A maniac posing as a judge breaks into the police headquarters, where an anarchist supposedly 'fell' to his death from a fourth-floor window. The 'judge' holds an inquiry with the police officers involved and appears to be helping them to find ways to cover up the fact that they pushed the anarchist out of the window. The pace of the dialogue is fast and furious:

Inspector: Quit putting me on! I'm beginning to think you really do have a mania for playing roles, but you're even playing the role of a nut. In fact, I'll bet you're even saner than I am.

Suspect: I wouldn't know. Certainly, your occupation is one which leads to many psychic alterations…let me examine your eye.

[He pulls down the Inspector's lower eyelid with his thumbs.]

Inspector: Look — just shut up and sit down so that we can get on with the report.

Suspect: Oh, good, I'll do the typing. I'm certified at forty-five words a minute. Where do you keep the carbon?

Inspector: Keep still or I'll handcuff you!

Suspect: You can't! Either the straitjacket or nothing. I'm insane, and if you put handcuffs on me — article 122 of the criminal code: 'Anyone wearing the uniform of a public officer, who applies non-clinical or non-psychiatric instruments of restraint to a mentally disturbed individual, so as to cause an aggravation of said individual's condition, commits a crime punishable by five to fifteen years' imprisonment and the loss of his or her rank and pension'.

(l.1. 76–91)

Comedy can be used successfully to make the subject matter hard-hitting: in this scene, the suspect uses his superior intellect to subvert the status of the inspector who is supposed to be interrogating him. The farcical nature of the play does not diminish the significance of the crimes of the police or somehow make the police officers into 'nicer' characters. Indeed, the unsentimental nature of the comedy serves to highlight the stupidity and criminality of the police that Fo is satirising.

Scene from Dario Fo's play *Accidental Death of An Anarchist* (Donmar Warehouse, London, 2003)

Photostage

Commedia dell'arte

Commedia dell'arte is a form of Italian comedy that was popular from the early sixteenth to the eighteenth century. There is a useful link between some of the work of Dario Fo and *commedia dell'arte*. Fo uses a number of the principles and practices of *commedia*, particularly in his creation of grotesque or exaggerated characters.

In *commedia* productions, troupes of travelling actors would play out set story-lines but improvise elements of the dialogue, sometimes incorporating local gossip or events into the action.

According to Ronald Harwood:

> A *Commedia* actor had to combine the skills of dancer, singer, acrobat, low comedian, pantomimist, and might also sing, or play a musical instrument. Many of the male characters wore masks; the women who were played by women actors, did not.
>
> (*All the World's a Stage*, p. 103)

This style of comedy therefore lends itself well to an improvised approach and makes dynamic demands of the actors.

While a group may not wish to perform a full *commedia* production (although this is possible), elements of the *commedia* genre could be used. For example, the emphasis on acrobatic performance skills might help with the visual elements of production. If a group wishes to use masks, *commedia* has many ideas to offer — for example, using a mask to exaggerate or highlight a particular characteristic, or to create a sense of ensemble or uniformity among the performers.

Commedia techniques require disciplined and extensive rehearsal. The results can be impressive, polished and highly entertaining, but only as the end result of hard work. If corners are cut in rehearsal, the results will be not only disappointing but the process could also be dangerous from a health and safety point of view.

Melodrama

You may wish to set your devised piece in a different era from the present day. If so, it is a good idea to consider using genres that are specific to particular eras in dramatic history. One example is the melodrama of the Victorian era. Melodrama dominated nineteenth-century theatre, even up to the advent of plays emanating from the naturalistic movement of the late 1870s.

Melodrama typically features a limited number of stock characters with clear motives and obvious patterns of behaviour. As Phyllis Hartnoll puts it:

...the noble outlaw, the wronged maiden, the cold blooded villain, working out their destinies against a background of ruined castles, haunted houses and spectacular mountain scenery.

(*The Concise Oxford Companion to the Theatre*, 1972)

Features of melodrama can be found in many modern dramatic contexts, particularly in film and television. The conflicts and relationships between characters in television dramas are often of an exaggerated and obvious quality, and the characters' motives are quickly made clear to an audience. Could these obvious intentions and exaggerated characteristics be of use to a devising group? Much depends on the content of the piece, but the effects of melodrama — with its sentimentality and strenuous dramatic gestures and language — can often have quite a comic impact.

The language of melodrama, which is often elaborate but not necessarily sophisticated or complex, can provide an opportunity for characters to reveal information about themselves. Sometimes the language can help to emphasise the idea that the characters come from a different era. Consider this speech from one of the most famous melodramas of the day, *Maria Martin* (Act I scene 5, *c.* 1840):

How dreadful the suspense each moment brings! Would it were over. There's not a soul abroad — everything favours my design. This knocking at the heart doth augur fear. 'Tis a faint, foolish fear that must not be. Suspicious self will sleep, ay, sleep for ever. Yet, twixt thought and action, how harrowed is the brain with wild conjecture. The burning fever round my temples gives to this livid cheek a pallid hue.

(Kilgariff, M. (ed) *The Golden Age of Melodrama*)

As a devisor, you cannot use sections of dialogue from another play but it would be helpful to study passages like this if you want to tap into the mood or style of a particular era. In this case, you can create your own dialogue using expressive and elaborate vocabulary in order to capture the melodramatic spirit.

Adaptation of stories or poems

Many works for theatre have started out as novels, poems or short stories. One of the most famous examples is Susan Hill's novel *The Woman in Black* (1983), which became a well-known play adapted by Stephen Mallatratt. Another famous example is Victor Hugo's novel *Les Miserables* (1862), which became one of the most successful musicals of the late twentieth century.

You have only a short space of time for your performance, so if you plan to adapt a poem, short story or novel, you must ensure that this is done both economically and effectively. Short stories or children's stories may lend themselves particularly well to adaptation for a short devised piece. You should bear in mind a number of important features:

- A good story does not necessarily produce a good piece of drama. Identify specifically what features of the story will work dramatically.

- Work out how many actors will be needed for the story, remembering that certain styles of presentation will allow for one actor to play many parts.

- Consider any aspects of the story you wish to alter. There are many examples of the events of a story being changed for the theatre or film adaptation. Examples from the film world are the *Harry Potter* stories by J. K. Rowling. The later books in the series are more than 400 pages long, and inevitably some material has to be left out in films lasting only 2.5 hours.

- A story communicates information in a different way from a play. A story may be written in the third person or the first person. Your adaptation must use dialogue effectively and bring the characters to life through what they say and do. You may feel that one way of preserving the character of the book is to have a narrator. For example, in Christopher Sergal's 1990 adaptation of Harper Lee's novel *To Kill a Mocking Bird* (1960) the characters were allowed to narrate the story. This technique is particularly useful when the events of the story need to be described to move the action on, rather than acted out.

- The illustrations in children's stories are sometimes as important as the narrative in telling the story. If you are adapting a children's story, you may find the illustrations useful when you think about your piece visually as well as in terms of narrative.

Political theatre

If you want your piece of theatre to make a political point about contemporary issues, you should investigate the history of political theatre. The description 'political theatre' does not necessarily describe a play that is supportive of one political system or another; rather, it often refers to a piece of drama created around a political issue.

A good example of this is Timberlake Wertenbaker's *Our Country's Good* (see p. 170). This play, set in the late eighteenth century in a convict camp in Australia, makes the case for the redemptive power of the arts (especially theatre), as we see the prisoners begin to bond and find new respect for each other while rehearsing a production of *The Recruiting Officer* (1706) by George Farquhar. Wertenbaker's play was written and developed in 1988 at a time when education programmes for prisons were being cut back and the Royal Court

Theatre (where the play was originally produced) was facing an acute financial crisis after systematic cutbacks in funding from the Arts Council. Although the play is set in the eighteenth century, it comments on the prevailing attitudes of the time as exemplified by the approach of the Thatcher government towards the arts and education.

Caryl Churchill's play *Top Girls*, first presented by the Royal Court Theatre in 1982, could also be described as a political play. In 1982 the Conservative government under Margaret Thatcher was arguably at the height of its power. The play tells the story of Marlene, an ambitious businesswoman who runs a recruitment agency. She displays a number of ruthless attributes, abandoning her child to the care of her sister as she pursues wealth and a more glamorous lifestyle. The play reaches its climax as she and her sister, Joyce, have an argument, which culminates in Marlene declaring that if people are 'stupid, lazy and frightened' she will not stand up for them. In the play, Marlene praises Thatcher, to Joyce's obvious disgust. There is little doubt that *Top Girls* was intended to be a strong denunciation of Thatcher's policies; in many respects Marlene represents the kind of individual seen as representative of the Thatcher ideal — successful and ambitious, but inevitably ruthless.

A 1991 performance of Caryl Churchill's *Top Girls*, with Lesley Manville as Marlene and Deborah Findlay as Joyce (Royal Court Theatre, London)

You should not forget the work of Brecht and epic theatre when considering the role of political theatre. 'Political theatre' often refers to the content of a play rather than the style, so you should be aware that many styles can be used to present political theatre. You could refer to Chapters 7 and 8 on the work of Brecht and how his techniques can be used to express the strength of a political argument. Important features of Brecht's epic theatre are easily identifiable character types (e.g. politicians, strikers, journalists), short episodic scenes that do not follow a strictly narrative structure, and the use of direct address to the audience in the form of challenging questions as well as the communication of information.

Finally, bear in mind that comedy and farce can be a useful vehicle for political theatre. The example of Dario Fo's *Accidental Death of An Anarchist*, described on pp. 227–28, is a sharp piece of political satire. Similarly, a much earlier piece of work — the Greek comedy *Lysistrata* (411 BC) by Aristophanes — satirises the warlike tendencies of men. Lysistrata leads a revolt by women, who resolve to withdraw their sexual favours until their men stop fighting.

How to avoid common mistakes

In general, you should try to avoid clichés. This may involve approaching the following areas with great caution:

- Court cases. While often compelling in film or on television, they rarely work in devised pieces. The language used is often a hybrid between different cultures and courtroom practices. Consequently, it is possible to devise a piece that is a combination of *Judge Judy* and *LA Law*. The serious point here is that a piece requiring technical or specialist language has to be impeccably researched, otherwise the result is embarrassing. Court cases in live theatre are often fussy, limited and dull.

- Chat show, game show and — in particular — reality programmes used as metaphors. Occasionally, a group might be able to pull off something funny or convincing using these formats. All too often, however, the pieces emerge as contrived and missing their point. You have to be certain of why you are using these largely televisual formats and the dramatic impact you want them to create.

- Psychosis or mental illness. Again, these issues need to be researched carefully. Frequently, pieces concerning mental illness become 'mental home' dramas, involving deranged teenagers who have violently assaulted their families and hear voices in their heads. Such issues are potentially compelling, but the characters and situations are often reduced to stereotypes in practice. Without realising it, a group of dedicated and intelligent students might create a piece of drama which is offensive, because it focuses on the immediacy of dramatic effect at the expense of soundly researched facts. Drama can be, and at times should be, shocking and disturbing, but in creating the dramatic impact there should be no dilution of fact.

The importance of research

Research is essential in creating effective devised work and can take many forms. There are some basic rules of research that should be acknowledged and followed, and these are discussed below.

Using the internet

Entering a concept, practitioner, theme or genre into a search engine will not automatically provide you with the information you are seeking, nor is all the information on the internet correct. The online encyclopedia, Wikipedia, should be used only as the means by which more specialised research material can be found. Anyone can put anything on the internet, regardless of its accuracy, but a book has to be published and its contents have therefore been scrutinised.

In short, the internet is a useful tool to point you towards more detailed and scholarly research. Thereafter, it is advisable to refer to books, journals and other published materials.

Using interviews and observation

If you are researching a true event — perhaps an industrial dispute, an accident or series of important events — it may be possible to interview someone who was involved.

If your piece is about children, it is useful to talk to them, observe them and see them at play. The same principle is true if you are trying to portray older people. Often, our interpretations of older people owe more to comic, stereotyped creations from the television than to characterisations based on observations and understanding.

Dedicated playwrights often carry notebooks around with them in order to record snippets of conversation, which they might adapt and use later. Finding the voice of a character is often a difficult undertaking, and there is no substitute for listening to and observing real people.

Going to see innovative theatre

Watching and listening to high-quality theatre work is an invaluable part of understanding theatrical processes. You cannot create theatre if you have not seen it. Without attempting to apply some kind of hierarchy of productions, it is clear that some types of theatre will be of more use than others. Big West End musical productions may contain magnificent techniques, but the size, scale and spectacle of them will probably have little in common with the A-level devised piece. Try to see productions by companies that focus more on innovative styles of acting — there is really no substitute for watching the likes of Complicite, Kneehigh, Shared Experience, DV8, Cheek by Jowl and Out of Joint.

It can be argued that watching and, where possible, taking part in workshops with ground-breaking theatre companies is the most effective form of research. You will then be able to bring to your own devising work first-hand experience of their innovative approaches to theatre and their daring attitudes towards realisation.

Undertaking genre and practitioner research

Your research does not need to be confined to the subject matter of your piece. Researching a genre or an influential play or practitioner is equally valid. It may be that a workshop has had a particularly strong impact on you and your group, inspiring further research into the work of the practitioner and the creation of a piece in that specific style.

It is important to realise that for some styles and practitioners there is a great deal of material. Therefore, you should always keep a strong focus for your research. The subject of physical theatre, for instance, is enormous, but if you focus on French postwar physical theatre, or the work of a specific individual, the material you have to cover is more confined.

Research is not purely about finding something out. It is about finding something out that will benefit and inform the piece you are creating.

The role of technology

The increasing availability and accessibility of multimedia facilities (video, PowerPoint etc.) has had a huge impact on theatre production. Although it may not always be possible to build convoluted or detailed sets for devised pieces — particularly if there are many pieces being created and shown one after another — it should be possible to generate images relevant to the presentation, which might enhance it.

Use technology with discretion, however. Bear in mind that while the use of technology can enhance your piece, it should not overwhelm the drama. It is worth reflecting on the philosophies of Brecht and Artaud and their approaches to the use of scientific, theatrical elements. Many devised pieces are created using their ideas, even though theatre technology is now much more sophisticated than when they were working more than half a century ago.

Design

When devising a piece, the full theatrical impact needs to be taken into consideration, as well as the acting and the content of the script. Often, the devising process is an opportunity for group members who may not favour acting as a specialism to exercise their skills in design — be it set, costume, lighting or sound. Remember, however, that a deliberately economic approach to design is just as valid. Clearly there are situations where, because of time or resource constraints, technical elements have be kept to a minimum, but often a 'forced simplicity' inspires highly imaginative ideas about staging and interpretation. Necessity, at times, is the mother of invention.

Your group needs to discuss its approach to technical features and make decisions appropriate to the genre and purpose of your piece, as well as to considerations of time and budget.

The role of the script

It may be possible to improvise your piece and never arrive at a final script. This is particularly true for pieces that are more movement-orientated or even choreographed. If dance is a strength within the group, a piece of theatre that is predominantly led by the creation of physical images, shapes and movement patterns is entirely legitimate. However, if the piece is driven more by the spoken word, a final script is more desirable, particularly if the language used is stylised or poetic. For example, it is difficult to improvise in the dialogue of a different era. If your piece is set in the past, inappropriate modern expressions can jar with an audience and damage the integrity of the piece you are creating.

Scripts can also be used as stimulus material (a speech from a play, for example), or the monologues described on pp. 221–22 under 'Developing the image into action' may be used to move the piece along but not form part of the final production. In other words, your script can be as much a working tool as a part of the finished article.

It is important, however, that as the script develops, so too does the piece. All too often, groups work hard at creating excellent scripts, only to leave too little time to realise them effectively. The rehearsal process must be evenly balanced between the creation of material and its preparation for performance. It is essential that there is some kind of finished document if a technician is to provide effects on the right cue.

Summary

Devising can and should be an exciting area of practical theatre to explore, providing a vehicle for your most innovative and creative ideas. However, in order to achieve your potential as a devisor, you must ensure that the process is coherent and well organised.

Your group must work effectively as a team, allocating specific tasks to individuals and providing an opportunity for feedback. It is also important to respect the ideas of others, even if you do not agree with them.

Ensure your group does not allow discussions to take up too much rehearsal time. As you create your piece, you need to rehearse it simultaneously, otherwise there may be too little time at the end of the devising process. Rehearsing ideas is a practical method of discussion, and is often about learning through getting things wrong. To see if an idea works, get it on its feet. Try a number of different methods of exploring ideas practically before deciding whether they are going to work or not.

If you are undertaking work on a serious issue or theme, the research must be thorough and detailed. Devised pieces fail to make an impact if they seem stereotyped, vague or ill informed. Even if your piece is led more by style than content, research may still be necessary in order to determine the effectiveness and relevance of that style. It may be useful to examine the styles of well-known theatre practitioners.

Technology can enhance the quality of your work, through lighting, sound, multimedia etc. However, do not allow it to dominate the work. You are not making a film, even if film is used as a part of the overall practical presentation.

Creating your supporting notes for Unit 4

When creating your supporting notes, you should divide them into three major sections.

Section 1: Research

This section should give details of your research into your chosen practitioner with reference to the play you intend to present. Make sure that you give a focused response and do not simply regurgitate a large amount of information on the practitioner. Remember that your task is to justify the use of a particular style for a particular play.

For example, if your chosen practitioner is Brecht and you are performing a section of John Godber's *Bouncers*, do not provide pages of information on Brecht, Godber and *Bouncers*. Instead, you should demonstrate your understanding of why the production ideas of Brecht would enhance Godber's play. It is difficult to formulate how one practitioner's approach might affect the work of a playwright. In the case of *Bouncers*, it could be argued that the play's social values, comedic characters and direct address to the audience could be enhanced by the documentary and epic ideas of Brecht. However, it could also be argued that Godber — being a practitioner as well as a playwright — has already incorporated his own ideas for production within the text. Therefore, you need to be clear about how the themes of the play might lend themselves to a Brechtian interpretation.

You could approach this task from the point of view of a director or group of actors working on the play. Whichever angle you adopt, your approach should be scholarly and thorough — not just, for example, making suggestions about using narration or film sequences simply because Brecht did. In this case, you would need to offer a careful analysis of the use of entertainment in Brecht's theatre, the ways in which some of his techniques were used, and how these techniques might be deployed in the production of a play that was written 20 years after his death.

In researching your chosen play, it is important to show an awareness of its cultural and (if appropriate) political context. To continue with the example of *Bouncers*, the play was written in the late 1970s and, even though it is still performed today and was updated in the 1990s, it continues to reflect much of the life of a northern town of that era.

Overall, your notes should be an accurate account of all the necessary research undertaken into the play, playwright and chosen practitioner. They must include *specific* detail of how the practitioner might approach the play.

Hints for section 1

The easiest trap to fall into here would be to select a piece of naturalistic theatre and then choose Stanislavski as the practitioner. While there is nothing wrong with this, in practice, this is where the least focused research is likely to take place.

It is perfectly legitimate to choose a section of Ibsen's *A Doll's House*, Chekhov's *The Cherry Orchard*, or a more modern play such as Anthony Neilson's *Penetrator* (1993), and then identify, using detailed research and specific examples, how Stanislavski may have realised it. However, you should ensure that specific detailed research is offered into how some of Stanislavski's ideas could be used in a production of your chosen play. Avoid vague arguments about the realism of the play and Stanislavski's emotional memory. You must show a clear understanding of the specific ideas Stanislavski had about approaching a role and how these ideas are relevant to the play.

Avoid a superficial approach to the play or practitioner, and do not rely on stereotyped 'received wisdom'. If your understanding is vague and superficial, your production ideas will be vague and superficial as well.

Remember that some practitioners lack a specific style. Katie Mitchell and Max Stafford-Clark are two of the country's most successful directors, yet their bodies of work are highly varied. Therefore, it is difficult to look for features in their productions that are representative of their styles. However, you could research how they might approach a production and apply a discipline to the development of a character or realisation of a scene. Stafford-Clark rarely starts from a visual perspective, whereas Mitchell might do so. In your notes, you should explain the director's approach and why this is relevant to the script on which you are working.

Section 2: Dramatic intentions

In this section, you should focus on the dramatic intentions of the piece and how the practitioner you have chosen assists in the process of staging it. It is important that you are aware of the dramatic significance of the play as a whole and that you arrive at specific intentions for the section you are considering.

For example, you may decide that you are going to present the final scene of Shakespeare's *Romeo and Juliet* — the tragic finale in the crypt when Romeo returns to commit suicide, not realising that Juliet has only taken a strong sleeping potion. You could develop the idea that since this is the emotional heart of the play, and the actors are reaching the emotional peak of their performances, the scene may benefit from using some of Stanislavski's ideas and the actors could work on developing a sense of truth in performance.

Hints for section 2

In analysing the dramatic intentions of the piece and the ways in which your chosen practitioner's work can help you do this, it is essential that you use dramatic terminology and technical vocabulary accurately. Applying general terms or theatrical terminology without understanding suggests you have only a superficial knowledge of both the play and the practitioner.

Section 3: Effectiveness of the rehearsal process

This section requires you to evaluate the effectiveness of your chosen skill through the rehearsal process — be it acting, directing or designing.

You should show an awareness of the ways in which your chosen practitioner may have influenced your contribution. You should also ensure that you produce an analysis, not a diary account, of the rehearsal process. As such, you need to assess your own progress and identify the key moments of development along the way.

Hints for section 3

Evaluation of the effectiveness of your contribution requires honesty but also clarity of purpose and an understanding of the process you embarked upon.

You should also evaluate your work in the context of presenting a piece of practical theatre, not just a student presentation. This means that attention must be paid to areas of health and safety. This is particularly relevant if you attempt a physically daring or risk-taking interpretation of a play in the style of Steven Berkoff or Lloyd Newson.

In summary

- Both practitioner and text should be chosen carefully and on the basis of a sound understanding.
- The research you undertake should go beyond the director's CV or the text's performance history. 'Padding' the notes with background information will not communicate your understanding of how and why the particular practitioner might be helpful in realising your chosen text.
- No practitioner should be regarded as an embodiment of a rule-book. In researching the practitioner's work and applying it to a text, you will need to make some important judgements yourself. You are involved in an interpretation exercise, not the application of a set of rigid principles. This is particularly the case if your chosen practitioner is either Stanislavski or Brecht.
- Refer to productions you have attended that might be relevant to your understanding of the practitioner's work, especially if he or she works with a theatre company you have seen. Remember that research is not simply confined to reading books or surfing the internet. It can be an active process, for instance when you are watching something as a thoughtful member of an audience.

Bibliography and references

Artaud, A. (trans. Corti, V.) (1993) *The Theatre and Its Double*, Calder.

Benedetti, J. (1982) *Stanislavski: An Introduction*, Methuen.

Benedetti, J. (1988) *Stanislavski: A Biography*, Methuen.

Berkoff, S. (1992) *The Theatre of Steven Berkoff*, Methuen Drama.

Brecht, B. (1949). 'A Short Organum for the Theatre' in J. Willett (trans.) *Brecht on Theatre: The Development of an Aesthetic*, Methuen, 1964.

Brown, J. R. (ed.) (2001) *The Oxford Illustrated History of Theatre*, OUP.

Davis, T. (2001) *Stage Design*, Rotovision.

Donnellan, D. (2002) *The Actor and the Target*, Nick Hern Books.

Hartnoll, P. (ed.) (1972) *The Concise Oxford Companion to the Theatre*, OUP.

Harwood, R. (1984) *All The World's a Stage*, Martin Secker and Warburg Ltd.

Kilgarriff, M. (ed.) (1974) *The Golden Age of Melodrama*, Wolfe Publishing.

Knapp, B. L. (1969) *Antonin Artaud: Man of Vision*, Swallow Press.

Miller A. (ed. Clurman, H.) (1971) *The Portable Arthur Miller*, Viking Press.

Miller, A. (1987) *Timebends: A Life*, Methuen.

Oddey, A. (1994) *Devising Theatre: A Practical and Theoretical Handbook*, Routledge.

Roberts, P. and Stafford-Clark, M. (2007) *Taking Stock: The Theatre of Max Stafford-Clark*, Nick Hern Books.

Stanislavski, K. (ed. and trans. Hapgood, E.) (1963) *An Actor's Handbook*, Theatre Arts Books.

Stanislavski, K. (1980) *An Actor Prepares*, Methuen.

Stanislavski, K. (trans. Hapgood, E.) (1980) *My Life in Art*, Methuen.

Unwin, S. (2004) *So You Want to be a Theatre Director?* Nick Hern Books.

Walton, J. M. (1980) *Greek Theatre Practice*, Methuen.

Willett, J. (1977) *The Theatre of Bertolt Brecht*, Methuen.

Index

Bold page numbers indicate definitions of key terms

A

absurdity 151–52
Accidental Death of An Anarchist 72, 228, 233
acoustics 26
acting 10–11
  in *Antigone* 39–41
  Artaud's ideas 138–41, 144
    application of 146–54
  Brecht's ideas 110–17
    applied to *Oh! What a Lovely War* 118–24
    applied to Shakespeare's plays 127–32
  Donellan's approach 171–72
  in *Revenger's Tragedy* 201–05
  in *Shadow of a Gunman* 75–77
  Stanislavski's ideas 85–92, 93, 107
    application of 97–106, 166–67, 238
  in *Taming of the Shrew* 57–61
  in *View from the Bridge* 215–16
actors, *see also* acting
  Elizabethan 45
  in Greek theatre 26–27
  Newson's approach to 178
  relationship with audience 202
adaptations 230–31
Admiral's Men 44
Age Exchange 219
alienation effect 112–13, 116, 121–22, 130
Alleyn, Edward 45
'American Dream' 35, 209–10
amphitheatres 26
analysis 186
Anouilh, Jean 35
Antigone 42
  acting 39–41
  background 23–27
  design 36–39
  direction 34–36
  plot outline 27–34
April in Paris 165
apron staging 14, 174
Arbor, The 169
arena staging 6, 14, *see also* theatre-in-the-round

Aristotle **25**, 110, 117
Artaud, Antonin 134–37, **135**, 143
  failed experiments 141–43
  ideas of 138–41, 144
    application of 146–54, 198
atmosphere 20, 116–17, 122, 175
audience
  actor's relationship with 202
  and alienation effect 113, 116
  composition 21–22, 26, 44
  director as representative of 175
  role of 112, 140
  and staging 5–6, 16, 26, 44, 140, 174
  tastes of 159
audience reactions 122, 147, 167–68, 177, 223–24, 225, *see also* theatre of cruelty
auditorium 14

B

Balinese Theatre 137
Barrault, Jean Louis 160
Berkoff, Steven 144, 159–63
Berliner Ensemble 108–09
Big Picnic, The 182
Bjornson, Maria 182–84
Black and Tans **69**
Blasted 147
blindness **33**
Blue/Orange 15, 20
Bogdanov, Michael 48, **128**
Bouncers 163–64
'boxing ring' atmosphere 116, 122, 175
Brecht, Bertolt **108**, 124, 175
  and Berliner Ensemble 108–09
  compared with Stanislavski 92, 109, 112
  ideas of 110–17, 132, 175, 232–33, 238
    applied to *Oh! What a Lovely War* 118–24
    applied to Shakespeare's plays 127–32
  and Shakespeare 126–27
Brenton, Howard 179
Brook, Peter 146, **157**
Brown, Ian 128–29
Bruce, Christopher 179
Büchner, Georg **148**
Burial at Thebes, The 37
Burke, Kathy 15